annie stories

by doris brett

Foreword by Dr. Stella Chess
Professor of Psychiatry
New York University Medical Center

D1445946

workman publishing, new york

Dedication

For Rose and Amantha, my mother and my daughter, who with so much love, have taught me how to be a mother.

Acknowledgment

I would like to thank my husband, Martin, for his untiring efforts in the preparation of this manuscript. He spent hours in front of the word processor typing and untangling my scrawl, and as always, is a source of constant, loving support.

Copyright © 1986, 1988 by Doris Brett

All rights reserved. No portion of this book may be reproduced—mechanically, electronically, or by any other means, including photocopying—without written permission of the publisher. Published simultaneously in Canada by Saunders of Toronto, Ltd.

Library of Congress Cataloging-in-Publication Data

Brett, Doris.
  Annie stories.

  Includes index.
  Summary: Nine stories explore common childhood anxieties and fears about such subjects as nightmares, new babies, going to the hospital, starting school, sickness, divorce, and death.
  1. Children's stories, American. [1. Anxiety—Fiction. 2. Fear—Fiction. 3. Short stories]
I. Title.
PZ7.B7556An 1987   [E]   87-42744
ISBN 0-89480-528-2 (pbk.)
ISBN 0-89480-529-0 (10-copy counter display)

Cover and book design: Charles Kreloff
Cover photograph: Martin Imber
Book illustrations: Amantha Imber

ANNIE STORIES was originally published in 1986 in Australia by McPhee Gribble Publishers Pty. Ltd., 66 Cecil Street, Fitzroy, Victoria 3065, in association with Penguin Books, Australia.

Workman Publishing Company, Inc.
1 West 39th Street
New York, NY 10018

Manufactured in the United States of America

First printing March 1988
10 9 8 7 6 5 4 3 2 1

contents

foreword

everything that happens to infants, everything they do, is a first time for them. And as soon as these are old and familiar, along comes a new set of first-time events, for development continues as long as we live. As we look at these newborns, we—their parents, their teachers, their aunts, uncles, grandparents and friends—want to smooth the way. We know they cannot remain babies forever, nor would we really wish them to do so. Ideally we hope they will become, as adults, independent, cooperative, beautiful, obedient, flexibly minded, determined, polite, giving, capable of self-defense, sensitive, and tough. All these things and many more—but of course in proper proportion and, of course, expressed only at the right times and in the correct places.

Can we provide a prescription, a set of rules to be followed, that will move these newborns, now so helpless and needing of care, smoothly through the experiences that will enable them eventually to become competent grown-ups? The adults we know and admire and wish to be like are themselves different kinds of people. And indeed, the new babies who come into the world are also different individuals from the start. One could not possibly write a single prescription for guiding babies, children, and adolescents through the maze of developmental experiences. The prescription that is correct for one child is bound to be wrong for others.

Doris Brett, in her book ANNIE STORIES, has avoided the temptation to give parents a cookbook of recipes to apply mechanically in the same way to all children. But she has succeeded in capturing the developmental steps through which children grow, the worries that so many children have about new events that seem to keep coming, the new abilities that are expected to be theirs. As something new looms on the horizon, it cannot be expected that youngsters will spontaneously recall that an old, familiar, and now-delightful activity was once one of these new happenings of which the world seems to have an inexhaustable supply.

Ms. Brett has brought into focus the kinds of worries that face children at different stages as they grow older. She has offered parents an effective method to help their children to meet and to master what is ahead—be it nursery school, nightmares, fear of animals, or a host of other potential worries of children. And the medium of help she provides is that most natural of parent–child activities, storytelling.

In her book, Ms. Brett makes it clear that she is very aware that each child is an individual, that each has his or her own temperamental individuality, and that the meaning of the new event will be determined only in part by the nature of the event itself. An equal partner is the child's own temperamental style, which acts as a filter, giving the event the character of a glowing new adventure, a worrisome hazard, or a "wait and see" situation.

The book is called ANNIE STORIES because Annie is the child in each story. She worries to her parents about different impending events, exploring the details of possible difficulties and trying out solutions suggested by her parents. Each story is a prototype of a common event, but since any particular child's concerns depend upon the actual situation at hand and on the child's temperamental style, parents can alter the details to fit the real circumstances that worry their own child.

For parents, the amount of repetition demanded by a worried (or an unworried but interested) child may bring boredom. But a bit of imagination can go a long way. Perhaps the parents can contrive a story about a nursery school attended by a shy dump truck, or about a baby whale whose friends don't like her because she keeps forgetting the rules of the game.

foreword

In each chapter there are a number of footnotes, explaining the purpose of including certain facets in the story and giving thoughtful suggestions for varying details to suit the individual child. These are helpful so that, as parents modify the stories or make up entirely new ones, they can check off the issues mentioned, decide which apply to their child, and learn how to weave them into the tale.

Dr. Stella Chess
Professor of Child Psychiatry
New York University Medical Center

how the stories work

annie Stories were born about seven years ago. They arose, as have so many valuable things, from a time of crisis. In world terms, the crisis was not very significant but in our three-year-old daughter's eyes, it was earth-shattering—she was about to start nursery school.

It was a normal Sunday afternoon and we had just finished not doing all the things we'd meant to do that weekend, when my daughter slid into the room.

"Mommy...," she said, in a voice that was reminiscent of Garbo-doing-Camille.

I looked up. Just a moment ago she had been laughing and giggling with Daddy.

"There's a headache in my tummy," she went on.

I looked at her. She really was upset. It didn't take much to figure out that the headache-in-tummy had arrived at precisely the same moment that Daddy had announced, in his best "isn't-this-exciting" voice, that nursery school started next week.

Amantha at that time was a rather shy child (she's now a gregarious ten-year-old who would kill for an audience and will shamelessly buttonhole strangers in coffee shops). At that time, however, group situations used to leave her hovering around my knees, and, as with many shy children, starting nursery school seemed as enticing to her as a spell at the Gulag Archipelago.

Martin, my husband, the computer analyst and ever the rational one in our household, had dealt patiently with her fears—sitting her down regularly and explaining simply that there was nothing to be frightened of at nursery school. He told her that the teachers would take care of her, the children would play with her, she would have a great time, and so on and so forth. Amantha humored him by listening quietly and not interrupting, but it was obvious from the look in her eye that there was a credibility gap the size of the Grand Canyon. Daddy might know about computers and fixing toys, but evidently he was terribly, sadly ignorant of the terrors and perils that lay waiting to pounce upon shy little girls in their first days at nursery school.

It was then I told Amantha her first Annie Story.

Annie was a little girl who lived in a brown brick house with a mommy and a daddy and a big black dog, just like Amantha's. And also, just like Amantha, Annie had a problem. She was worried about starting nursery school. The story (which you can read in this book) followed Annie through her struggle with her fears and on to a successful conclusion.

Amantha was riveted. She asked for the story time and time again, and when the first day of nursery school at last rolled around, she coped with it very well, much as Annie had in fact.

This was not surprising because, while on the surface Amantha had simply been listening to an ordinary children's story, underneath that she had, in fact, been using it, and most effectively, as a way of working through and overcoming her fears.

The way in which she had been able to do this was through identifying with the heroine, Annie.

Put yourself in their place

Children often find it very difficult to talk about their problems. It may be that they find their fears and anxieties difficult to verbalize or even to identify to themselves. It may be that they are so anxious that putting their problems into words makes them even more anxious.

Similarly, an adult might be so concerned, for instance, that her husband is on the point of leaving her, that she cannot bear to discuss the subject and instead makes frantic efforts to pretend that all is normal. We've all had experiences like this— of knowing something with one part of our mind and not wanting to know it with another part because it's too painful to think about.

Imagine then this woman, who is living with an unspoken terror, who is bursting with unasked questions. Is it really going to happen? Why is it going to happen? When? What can she do? How will she cope? And so on. Imagine her one day picking up a magazine with a short story in it. This story is about a woman of her age in identical circumstances with identical fears and feelings. The story tells how this woman coped with her situation, what she felt and how she handled those feelings, and, most of all, how she was able to live through and resolve a difficult situation in a way that felt positive and strengthening.

It's likely that the story would be read avidly. That the reader might experience it as having an almost magnetic pull for her and a powerful impact.

This is a woman who is bottling up intense and pressurizing emotions. It is too painful for her to admit to the reality of her toppling marriage, so she is unable to sort out or work through any of the myriad of troubling feelings arising from her perceptions. While she cannot bear to think directly about herself in this painful situation, it is easier to think about someone else in the situation, for instance, through hearing of an acquaintance's experience or through reading an article or a story on the subject.

This sense of safety—it is not happening to us, it is happening to someone else—enables us actually to think about the feared situation, to get close to it and understand it and the emotions arising from it in a way that has not been possible before, when we had barred ourselves from deliberating on it.

This in itself can be a great release and relief. The feelings that have been building up like steam in a pressure cooker may now be able to come out through this safety vent. Once we are able to look at them instead of spending our energies denying them, we may be able to see ways of dealing, not just with them, but with the situation they arose from.

The experience of reading a story about someone just like us—a woman who suffers, hopes, fears, and reacts in the same way that we do—can also be a very comforting one. This is because it can give us the sense of being truly understood. Someone out there really knows what it feels like to be us. This sense of being understood can be a nourishing one.

In addition to this is the recognition that we are not alone.

We are not the only people feeling so frightened and inadequate. The awareness that other people too have felt like this can be tremendously helpful for those who feel themselves isolated with their problems and inferior to other "normal" people who, we imagine, cope with their problems far better than we ever could. Young mothers who are struggling with their feelings of anxiety and inadequacy can testify to the relief they experienced on finding out that many other young mothers had similar feelings and saw themselves in the same light.

Finally, reading a story which shows a woman dealing with a threat in her life positively and successfully may give us a very useful role model. We may be able to learn from her, ways in which we also might cope better and gain from the story some hope and the sense that we too may make it.

The comfort of an alter ego

In the examples given above, I've referred to adult problems— ones that many of us can identify with. Annie Stories work on the same principle but are geared for children. Whereas the adult in the example had to read about her counterpart in a magazine, the child is able to hear about her alter ego through the comforting means of a story told by Mommy or Daddy.

This in itself is a very therapeutic experience. Quite apart from the content of the story, it means that the child is getting a comforting dose of quiet, loving intimacy with one or the other parent. Thus, at the same time that the story is helping the child deal with her various troubling situations, it is also strengthening the bond between parent and child, which is in itself a tremendous source of security and comfort. Not just for the child, I should add, but for the parent as well.

The beneficial way in which Annie Stories work fits in with the basic formulations of most major forms of psychotherapy. Psychoanalytically-oriented therapists would say that the listening child is identifying with Annie and able to learn and feel strengthened through this identification. Behavior therapists would say that Annie Stories utilize the therapeutic qualities of social modeling techniques. Imagery therapists would talk about the healing effect of the positive visualizations contained within the Annie Stories, and so on. In addition to this, many of the stories incorporate specific psychological techniques, such as desensitization (see pages 34 and 59, and the Glossary), as a part of the natural storyline. The therapies and techniques which are relevant to the rationale of Annie Stories are discussed further in the next chapter, Understanding Your Child.

What I would like to emphasize here, though, is that these stories are intended for parents to use. They are written for ordinary mothers and fathers and not for psychotherapists.

You do not need to have studied child psychology or to have amassed a library of books on the subject to be a good parent or to deal with the many everyday problems of childhood. There is a tremendous reliance these days on the outside experts and their advice, which is often couched in messianic terms. It's easy to be intimidated by such remote gurus and to lose confidence in our own instincts and common sense. I hope that these stories may provide a way back into trusting our own imaginations and getting back in touch with our own intuitive knowledge of our children.

It's important, too, to recognize that we can't, and don't have to, be perfect parents. In the real world there is no such animal. Simply recognizing this can be immensely relieving and helpful to us.

We all make mistakes and will continue to make them. We have times when we are so frightened about doing the wrong thing that we become paralyzed—unable to do anything. We have times when we have no idea what is disturbing our children or what to do about it.

Equally, there are times when we know what is worrying them but feel helpless to do anything about it. We want to solve their problems for them and yet have no idea how to go about doing so.

In fact we can't solve our children's problems for them. They must, in the end, learn to solve them for themselves. What we can do is help them in this process by giving them strength, a belief in themselves, and the confidence and hope to seek a successful resolution of their own.

We can do this through listening to them and trying to understand their fears and their worries. We can communicate our love for them so that they can learn to love themselves. We can let them know that we believe in them, so they can come to believe in themselves. We can also talk to them, through stories and other means, of the ways of the world, of the fact that there are seasons of hope as well as of despair, of the knowledge that there are times when even the strongest feel weak and times when even the weakest can learn to feel strong.

In the past such common wisdom was communicated to us by fables and tales and fairy stories. There were moralists and minstrels, and endless relatives, friends and elders of the tribe, all of whom carried on this oral tradition of storytelling and teaching. Today we are bereft of much of this. Television and computer screens have taken over. Many young parents are unsure of how to tell stories or unaware of their value and impact on the children who hear them.

Easier than you think

For those who have forgotten how to tell stories to their children or who have never thought about it, or who have wished they could but have never tried it, there is a wonderful surprise in store for you when you begin to use Annie Stories. In fact there are several wonderful surprises in store.

One is that they work. They really do help children deal with the situations or emotions that are worrying them. They don't provide a magic wand to whisk away all the trouble and pain of the real world, but they do allow children to learn about themselves and their problems in a way which enables them to feel comforted, supported, strengthened, and understood.

Second is the surprise that these stories are usually easier to tell and make up than you think they will be. This is because, as a beginning storyteller, you have the advantage of not starting with a blank page. In fact the plot is already made up for you. So are the characters. They are simply parallels of what is actually happening in your child's life. All you really need to make up is the ending and the means by which the ending is achieved. It is important that the ending of these stories be positive. You need to give your child hope that she will be able to find a way out of her distress. A child who believes there is no hope has no motivation to continue the struggle. She will simply give up. I've talked some more about positive endings and the need for hope in the next chapter.

The way in which you achieve your positive ending will vary from story to story. It should be something which your child can adapt and use. It may come through a practical technique, such as the desensitization used in the fear of dogs story, or it may come through the knowledge that as time passes, an acutely felt sorrow can dim and become bearable.

The stories presented in this book will give you some idea of the variety of ways in which hope can triumph over sadness and fear. Your own life can give you some more. Think back to the occasions when you overcame distressing circumstances. We have all had times, of course, when such circumstances overcame us, but at other times we were able to feel healed after a wound or helped through a difficult experience. Sometimes, just the knowledge that we have been able to survive these experiences is a help in itself.

Another surprise will be to find out just how much your

children love these stories. They will ask for them over and over again, correct you when you get the details wrong, and often prompt you when you are unsure of the subject matter. When my daughter asks me to tell her an Annie Story, I'll often ask, "What would you like the Annie Story to be about?"

"Tell me about Annie going to the dentist," she may reply, and invariably whatever subject she has chosen will be the one she is currently concerned about.

After the first Annie Story on first days at nursery school had been told and the nursery issue resolved, my daughter spontaneously started asking me for an Annie Story whenever she was troubled by something. She is now ten. She understands the theory and structure of Annie Stories as well as a ten-year-old can, and yet the magic has not dimmed for her. When she is upset or struggling to come to grips with a diffficult situation, she is still tremendously comforted and helped by an Annie Story.

I have taught many parents about Annie Stories and the feedback has been the same. They really do work. The child feels helped, comforted, and strengthened by them. Importantly too, so do the parents. From a position of not knowing what to do or how to talk to their distressed child, they are able to do something which is simple, natural, comforting, and therapeutic.

Annie Stories, as I've mentioned, should be based on the child's real life situation. Your version of an Annie Story is your child's story thinly disguised as fiction. This "fictionalization" is what makes the story nonthreatening to your child.

Your little girl, for instance, may be in the throes of coping with a new baby brother. She may be furiously angry at him, and yet it may be too distressing for her to admit to this anger. It may make her feel too "bad," for example, or she may be concerned that you would reject her if you knew. Talking directly to her about her feelings might be threatening for her. Telling her a story about Annie, though, a little girl who does have these feelings, allows her to think about them without feeling too anxious. Thus she has the opportunity to learn that these feelings are normal and to find out how she can best deal with them.

When I was writing the relaxation story, I first wrote out a script for teaching relaxation which was not incorporated within the context of a story. I read it to my daughter, whose reaction to it varied from indifference to irritation. "It's boring!" she pronounced when I had finished.

I then rewrote the script, this time incorporating it into the Annie Story framework. My little daughter was fascinated from the start, trying out the techniques alongside Annie, and when I had finished she showered the story with her highest accolades.

For me, this provided a very vivid illustration of the helpfulness and effectiveness of the Annie Story technique.

With the first reading, which was not in story form, my daughter had experienced the relaxation techniques as being thrust upon her. She had not asked for them after all. She was simply getting ready to go to bed and was in a rather tired and cranky mood. She responded by turning off and being bored.

In the second version, however, she had been intrigued by the story line, and because it was all aimed at Annie rather than her, had felt free to listen, to think about it, to recognize how nice it could feel, and finally to join in of her own free will.

After a while, children get to realize consciously that the Annie Story parallels their real life. This doesn't seem to disturb or impair the effectiveness of the story for them. It still leaves them free to pretend it's just a story when they need to, or to relate it to their own situation when that is appropriate.

Personalizing the stories

I picked the name Annie because my daughter's name is Amantha. "Annie" is similar in sound but not identical. Annie lives in a house like ours, has a dog like ours, but with a different name, and has a life style similar to ours. In fact, to borrow a popular phrase, only the names have been changed. It's this name change that seems to provide the essential sense of safety. As long as the names are changed, the other details can often remain identical. In fact your child may indicate this to you. If you have Annie wearing a white T-shirt on a visit to the hospital, for instance, whereas your child was wearing a green one, she may say to you, "No, Annie wore a *green* T-shirt."

Choosing a name

When you make up your own Annie Stories, change Annie's name to one similar to your child's and change Annie's background and life style to one appropriate to yours. If your child is a boy, Annie could become Andrew. It's possible, as a variation, to have the Annie character become a little animal facing a dilemma similar to the one your child is facing.

While the material in this book applies equally to boys and girls, to avoid the clumsiness of having to say "he or she" all the time, I have stuck to the female pronoun throughout.

As you make up your story, your child will let you know how you're doing. If she's interested and responsive, it's hitting the spot. If she's bored, perhaps she can't cope with it right now, or else she no longer needs it. When children have worked through a problem, they will generally lose interest in that particular story. If you're unsure as to what you should be telling the story about, ask them. If you're uncertain as to what Annie was feeling at some point you can ask them, "And what do you think Annie felt like (or felt like doing) then?"

Children can also draw and act out stories, or they can tell or write their own. My little daughter suggested that I include an Annie Story on being scared of the dark—something that she used to be a bit concerned about. I explained to her that although it was a good idea, there wouldn't be room for it in this book. A week or two later, she presented me with an Annie Story that she herself had written, about how Annie overcame her fear of the dark.

Children can also use what they have learned from one story as a way of helping them with another difficulty in their lives. Some months ago, for example, my daughter had a friend over to sleep who wanted to hear the Annie Story about fear of dogs. In this story, which is presented later in the book, I described the therapeutic technique of thought switching.

At the end of the story, my daughter's friend said, "That was terrific. Now I'll be able to use it when I have bad dreams."

"How will you do that?" I asked.

"Well, when I wake up scared from a bad dream," she said, "I'll just switch thoughts."

I didn't have the chance to find out how the thought switching went because a few days later she found out that there was an Annie Story about nightmares, which is also in this book. At her request, I told it to her.

After the story was finished, she said, "Could I have a dream ring like Annie's?"

"Of course," I said to her, and made a great show of getting out an invisible magic dream ring, which I presented to her.

Six weeks later, I saw her again.

"You know what?" she said with great excitement. "I haven't had a single bad dream since I got that ring, and I used to have them all the time."

Annie Stories can also be used with groups of children, in the classroom, or in other situations. They can provide vehicles for discussion and a way of sorting out feelings. In any classroom there will be children who have personally experienced the various situations dealt with in the stories presented in this book. Not only these children but also their classmates can benefit from the chance to understand and come to grips with some of the feelings surrounding many of these issues.

When to seek outside help

If your child's problems seem particularly severe or, despite your best efforts, do not resolve with time, consultation with a psychotherapist might be advisable. Long periods of depression, withdrawal, or aggressive acting-out in your children may also be an indication that you should talk to a therapist. Therapists who are trained to work with children or the family are the most appropriate professionals to seek help from. It is also advisable to have your child checked out by a pediatrician or physician. Many of the symptoms of anxiety, such as dizziness, headaches, and stomachaches may also be the symptoms of a physical illness.

Parents are helped, too

One of the comments people have made about Annie Stories is that "You feel good when you tell them." This is particularly interesting in view of the fact that most of them deal with rather distressing topics.

Partly, this sense of feeling good comes from the positive resolution of sad and difficult feelings. Partly too, I think, it comes from the experience of Annie's parents.

As I wrote these stories, I began to realize that Annie's parents are ideal parents—they are warm and wise and strong and supportive. They are, in fact, our dream parents—the parents all of us wanted.

I think that in some way, being able to experience these parents, even if it is only for a brief time in our imagination, touches us all. I hope that in telling and reading these stories, Annie's parents will nourish not just the child we read to, but the child in each of us. Perhaps some of that nourishment can allow us too to feel strengthened and comforted so that we can learn, as Annie does, to be gentle with ourselves, to tolerate our inadequacies, to find our strengths and to share with our children the best and most human part of ourselves.

understanding
your child

Children look like little adults. They have all the requisite external equipment—arms, legs, noses, mouths. They speak the same languages we do. It's tempting then to suppose that they think as we do. They don't.

Most of us as parents find this out the hard way as we try patiently to "reason things out" with a three- or four-year-old. No matter how faultless our reasoning, we still can't convince our little four-year-old that there aren't packs of instantly expandable wild dogs lying squeezed under her bed at night, just waiting for the lights to go off....

We sit back and wonder why it is that our children can't grasp such seemingly self-evident facts. Perhaps the answer lies in a closer look at what the world seems like to a child.

How children learn—play and imagination

Many of us have lost the memories of childhood fears and fantasies. It's been so long since we learned the laws of logic and the mundane physics of our dealings with the everyday environment that we've forgotten what the world looked like without them. We stand puzzled before the two-year-old who has suddenly become terrified of bath time. What is she scared of, we wonder. Is it the fear of being scalded by the hot water tap? Of death by drowning? Of knocking her head on the hard enamel? All good adult fears. No, it turns out. What she's afraid of is slipping away down the drain with the emptying bath water. As it goes down, it makes such horrible gurgling sounds that *everyone* knows there must be monsters there just waiting to slurp their supper up. A two-year-old simply hasn't developed a solid sense of the relative size of things. That's why, even apart from the monster at the drain's end, it's difficult to convince her that her little body simply won't fit down the drain. It will take the two-year-old many, many hours of playing with objects of various sizes before this piece of understanding clicks into place. You can explain all you like, but it is her own research into the various qualities that objects possess which will finally convince her.

Right from their earliest childhood we can observe how intensely and with what determination children pursue this way of learning. The baby who endlessly drops her rattle over the side of her crib with the monotony of a stuck record is not plotting to send you around the bend. She is finding out about some of the natural laws of the universe. (You too are finding out about some of the natural laws of the universe, that is, that temper increases inversely with the number of minutes elapsed since the last dropped rattle.) Your baby, however, is focused on a more serious mode—she is following in the footsteps of Newton and Einstein and discovering the astonishment of physics and gravity. She is finding out, for instance, that dropped objects fall rather than stay still, and that often they make a noise at the end of their fall. We, of course, have known about this for so long that we are jaded beyond astonishment. But for your baby, the excitement is tremendous.

Adults are accustomed to think of play and storytelling as purely recreational activities—things that serve no "serious" purpose. For children, however, play and fantasy are a major means of learning about the world. Play for a child is serving just as serious a purpose as is a day in the library for a research student.

Play is not confined to the human species. Baby animals

also play and are generally very endearing to watch. Most of us have been enchanted by watching a kitten pouncing on a wayward ball of string or a pup growling and shaking its head from side to side as it "kills" the old slipper we've donated. What makes puppies and kittens so delightful to watch is their baby clumsiness as they pounce and stalk, and the inappropriateness of their prey—string and old slippers instead of mice and birds. These highlight the fact that what play is essentially about for these baby animals is practice. Practice at things that they will have to be perfect at as adults in order to survive in the wild. In the animal kingdom it seems to be a rule that the more complex and adaptable a species is, the more the young of that species will need a "childhood" in which play-learning is a major feature. For simpler animals, such as lizards, which are born with detailed instinctive patterns of behavior that are perfect at first trial, there is no need for a playful childhood. Baby lizards grow up knowing exactly what to do as adult lizards—existential anxiety is not big in the lizard world. A saurian Sartre would never have been published.

For higher animals, it's a very different story. Species such as dogs, cats, monkeys, and most of all, humans lead very complex and varied lives. This may be news to some of us who get stuck in the boring same-day blues. But then, imagine what life would be like as a lizard.

Live and learn

We have an immense variety of developmental tasks to learn before we can safely go out into the world. Just to mention a few—we have to learn to sit, stand, walk, talk, reason, communicate, cooperate, and so on. These tasks are so numerous and so varied that it would be impossible to program them all instinctively for a faultless performance. They need to be learned and practiced. And that's where play comes in.

Some theorists also see play as a chance to work off excess energy. Everyone who's been in contact with children recognizes that they are possessed of a superior, seemingly endless, source of energy. Play can act in the same way as the vents in a pressure cooker, allowing excess energy to be siphoned off. If only we could arrange for its fair and equal distribution among the tired grownups of the world.

Some of the built-up energy that play can let out is aggressive energy. Most of us have had some experiences with this. It can be very satisfying to have a vicious game of squash right after an unpleasant encounter with the boss. Although we can't belt the boss around, we can certainly enjoy allowing the squash ball to be his proxy, and we usually feel much better afterwards. Likewise, children who have gotten into trouble and then been told off can often be seen berating a motley collection of dolls for committing exactly the same crime.

This sort of play also allows the child to "project" her own feelings of guilt onto the assorted toys. Guilt makes us feel anxious and bad. Putting the badness onto someone else ("it was *her* fault") can be an effective way of relieving anxiety. Many of us have a tendency to use this common means of coping with a sense of guilt, failure, or inadequacy. The saying "a bad workman always blames his tools" was made for us.

In addition, the child telling off her toys is also practicing the role of the morally correct adult. This "adult" part of herself will become incorporated into what we think of as our conscience—that part of ourselves that taps us on the shoulder and says "*No*, that was a bad thing to do!"

She is also repeating a disturbing event. This is something that children will do with great consistency. If a house has caught fire, they will often be seen playing pretend house-fire games over and over again. This is a way of mastering and digesting an upsetting occurrence. Adults also do this. If we've been mugged, for instance, it's quite a common reaction to repeat the horrifying story to friend after friend. After a while we find we can tell the story without the accompanying anxiety that thinking about the event used to produce. It's as if the constant repetition has lessened the emotional impact.

The continual reenactment of an event which has been puzzling to the child can also help her gain an understanding of that event. An adult example is the person who reads a "Dear John" letter over and over again trying to puzzle out what it is that led to this rejection. Each reading of the letter may set off slightly different thoughts and perceptions as attention is caught first by one phrase and then by another which has not stood out so much in the first reading.

You will find that when you tell your child Annie Stories which are relevant to her current problems, she will want to hear these stories time and time again. Don't get impatient with this repetition. Children need it to absorb facts, come to terms with feelings, and master their anxieties.

Child see, child do

Play can also be a way of exploring different feelings about an event. Through play, a child can experience what it feels like to be the teacher as well as the student, the heroine as well as the terrified victim. This can add new dimensions to her understanding of the problem. It gives her a chance to experience herself as successful and competent in an area that has previously overpowered her. This can lead her to see her problem in a different perspective, that is, as one that can be overcome.

When we watch children play, it is noticeable that much of their activity involves imitation. Children are natural imitators, as are the young of many highly developed species. This drive to imitate elders is part of nature's plan for the survival of the species. If a particular activity is too complex to install as part of an instinctive reflex, then the next best thing to ensure that the activity will be carried out properly is to implant in the young of the species a strong desire to imitate the adult who is already competently carrying out the desired activity.

Psychologists with theoretical stances as far apart as psychoanalysis, in which inner processes are of great importance, and behavior therapy, which focuses on the external, accept the importance of learning through imitation. Psychoanalysts explain it through the concept of identification (the process which unconsciously causes a person to think, feel, and act as she imagines the person whom she has focused on does), while behavior threrapists talk about the rewards and reinforcements that successful imitation brings. Both agree that it's a powerful form of learning.

Many studies have been conducted on the process of learning through imitation. In some, children are shown two films— one in which the "hero" gets punished, and another in which a different "hero" meets with a positive outcome. They have found that the hero more likely to be imitated is the successful one. Interestingly, there was no difference in how much the children remembered from each film but only in their actual behavior. In other words, they seemed to pay as much attention to each of the two films, but only the one with the successful outcome tended to affect their behavior. The positive ending in Annie Stories encourages this modeling effect. The example above uses a filmed model, but books and stories can provide equally potent models. Annie Stories, of course, are a particularly effective and enjoyable way of utilizing this principle.

The magic of "Once Upon a Time..."

Storytelling is an art that has been with us since man first learned to talk. The sort of children's stories we are particularly familiar with are those which have been handed down through generations upon generations of storytellers—they are folk myths or fairy stories. For countless years children have been enthralled by these—wanting to hear them over and over again. What is the magic of fairy stories and why are they comforting and compelling for children all over the world?

Some well-known psychotherapists have focused on this question. Bruno Bettelheim has written a book called *The Uses of Enchantment: The Meaning & Importance of Fairy Tales*, in which he argues that fairy tales play an important role in helping children come to terms with the various anxieties and conflicts that beset them in the course of a normal childhood.

From the psychoanalytic point of view, feelings and thoughts that cause guilt and anxiety are often suppressed and go "underground" into the unconscious mind. If these forbidden thoughts and feelings continue to build up, they will eventually "overboil" and make themselves felt in some way. The pressure cooker analogy is a good one. This overflow of tension need not take the form of an outburst of rage or tears. It can also appear in the form of physical symptoms such as rashes or tummy aches.

So if the forbidden feelings can't be ventilated, they will build up ever more pressure until they come out in some way that's generally experienced negatively. If, however, these feelings are so painful that we can't bring ourselves to talk or think about them outwardly, then how can we ventilate or work through them? It seems like a Catch-22.

This, according to many psychotherapists, is where fairy tales come in. Dr. Bettelheim suggests that the themes of many fairy tales are the exact themes that are problematic for many children. "Cinderella" deals with the theme of sibling rivalry and the perception that the "others" are more favored than you. "Hansel and Gretel" deals with the perennial childhood fear of being abandoned or lost. "Tom Thumb" details the experience of being lost, little, and alone in an overpoweringly bigger world.

We all as parents would like to see our children leading lives of total security, free from the overpowering fears and anxieties that beset us at times. And some of us do look back at childhood through a rosy glow, remembering perhaps the sense of love, laughter, fun, and companionship. What we tend to forget are the times of fear, rage, and anxiety over a world we can't control and an environment that is bigger than us. There are the night terrors, the boogie men behind the bed, the times of separation from our parents, the battles of will as we struggle for independence, the rage as well as love that siblings can induce, the cruelty of other children, the complexity of the developmental tasks we must master. Watch any child learn to walk and you'll get some idea of the struggle and courage involved. Even the happiest, most secure child must go through times of intense anxiety, fear, anger, and a sense of isolation. For, after all, no one can accomplish her tasks for her. Mother can be around to help her walk but she can't walk for her, and certainly she can't fall over for her. In order to learn to walk, the child has to learn to fall and then to pick herself up and try all over again.

This theme is one that is mirrored in many fairy tales. The young hero sets out on his journey and encounters various obstacles through which he perseveres towards his final success. It's also worth noting that the hero is generally the *youngest* son—that is, he mirrors the child's own experience of smallness, youthfulness, and inexperience in the world. Eldest sons rarely get to be heroes in fairy tales.

So what happens when the child who is struggling, for instance, with her own feelings of jealousy and inferiority within the family is given a chance to listen to "Cinderella"? Invariably she latches on to the story as if it were lemonade on a hot day. Why does this happen?

Psychoanalysts believe that at an unconscious level the child is recognizing the elements in "Cinderella" that apply to her own perception of the situation she is in. Although her own feelings may be too painful for her to admit to, through listening to Cinderella's experience she has a chance to think through and feel some of these "taboo" feelings at a distance that makes them nonthreatening. They are nonthreatening because they are seen as belonging to Cinderella rather than her.

The story may also allow the child to vent some feelings through her reactions to the characters and their situations. This can relieve some of the pressure of her own pent-up feelings.

As well, the fairy tale gets across the message that although life can be a battle and the things that happen to us unjust and beyond our control, if we keep persevering we will eventually win through. This is a tremendously important lesson. The child who does not believe in the possibility of success and happy outcomes is the child who will give up the struggle and never succeed. Children, indeed people, need to have hope in this world.

This message of hope despite struggle and setbacks is absorbed by the child and applied to her own problems at a level below that of conscious awareness. It is not necessary to point out in detail the similarities between Cinderella and herself in order for the point to be made. In fact, explaining and interpreting at a conscious level often robs the fairy tale of its magic. It can also rob the child of the chance to make her conscious connections at her own pace, usually after she has heard the story many times and thought about it many times more.

Annie Stories are like personalized fairy stories except that they are set in the real world. All the elements of threat, despair, recovery, and hope that are integral to the classic fairy story are included and are presented so that your child can immediately identify with them. They offer a learning experience that your child can take at her own rate, a model for your child to identify with and emulate, a way of experiencing and coming to terms with painful feelings, and a journey towards hope and understanding.

Your child as an individual

All of us can look back and remember certain watersheds that we passed over in our adult life. They were times of great excitement or apprehension—usually a mixture of both. We can remember how keyed up we were, how all-absorbing the events were to us at the time, and how they signalled a significant change in our lives. The events we typically look back on as watersheds are usually events that are common to a huge percentage of the population—a first job, the first move away from home, marriage, children, divorce, the death of a loved one. Most of us have to go through these "normal crises" of adult life and yet each of us will cope with these universal events in her own unique way.

Children follow the same pattern. They too have a number of normal developmental stages to master. Many parents are aware of this—it's common now to hear talk about the "terrible two" stage and the various other stages children go through in their journey to adulthood. What is not so commonly talked about is the fact that each child's approach to these common developmental tasks will differ depending upon her own unique style. Your two-year-old is not just *a* two-year-old, she is *your* two-year-old with her individual personality and particular approach to life. Understanding your child's personal style will be of immense value in deciding how best to help her, and you, through the various stages of childhood.

For many centuries there has been controversy over whether children's personalities were inborn, so that they came pre-packaged at birth, or whether they were formed in the years after birth by their interaction with parents and the environment. Nowadays, the consensus seems to be that there

27

is a mixture of both factors operating.

A lot has been written about how we as parents can affect our children's personalities, but it is also helpful to look at the personality factors which seem to be present from birth.

Much of our information comes from a very influential study conducted by Drs. Chess, Thomas, and Birch, that began in the 1950s in New York. This study concluded that babies do indeed seem to come with several personality traits already present. What determined the growing child's personality and her adjustment to the world was not just her inborn character traits or simply and solely her relationship with her parents, but a combination of the two. Different children thrived on different approaches.

The study found nine personality traits which were present from birth and tended to remain the same through infancy, childhood, adolescence, and presumably adulthood.

One was the activity level of babies. They seemed to come with their own characteristic levels ranging from very active to very placid.

Another personality characteristic was regularity. You could set your clock by some babies. They had their bowel movements at the same time each day, they slept at the same time, they were predictable in their appetites, and so on. Others were totally irregular and unpredictable in their daily needs and patterns.

A third characteristic concerned the babies' response to new situations or events. Some babies responded to new tastes, new sights, new experiences, with great enthusiasm and curiosity. Others shrank back and showed caution or fear.

Adaptability to change was a further characteristic in which babies varied. Some babies could adapt easily to alterations in routine, while others were much more rigid and inflexible.

There were also differences in sensitivity to their environment. Some were very light sleepers, for example, waking at the slightest sounds. Or they might be extremely sensitive to what they wore next to their skin. Wool, for instance, might be too scratchy for them. On the other end of this scale were children who could sleep through a thunderstorm and didn't mind what material their clothes were made from.

Intensity of response also seemed to be a characteristic that was present at birth. Some babies were very intense in their responses. When they were displeased, for example, they yelled the house down, while others simply frowned or grumbled.

The researchers also noted that some babies tended to be more cheerful whatever the situation, while others had a more gloomy outlook on life.

Concentration was another factor which varied from baby to baby. Some babies had longer concentration spans than others. They would focus on the activity they were engaged in for longer periods than other babies. The intensity of concentration also varied. The researchers called this factor distractibility. Some babies would characteristically concentrate so fixedly on what they were doing that nothing would distract them. Others would set out to do something but be easily waylaid by even small distractions.

What these findings highlight is that all children are not alike, and I would like to emphasize the importance of understanding and accepting your child as an *individual*. Don't try to apply rules and prescriptions wholesale just because you've read them in books. Think about them first and see how they apply to your particular child. Trust your intuition—you are the one who knows your child best after all.

Equally, when you're making up Annie Stories, match the heroine's personality style to your child's. If your daughter is a naturally cautious soul, for example, a heroine who charges into new situations with gusto and abandon is going to be much more difficult for her to identify with.

The cautious child usually responds best to a non-pressurized encouragement which allows her to become familiar with situations in stages. She can still reach the same successful endpoint as her more enthusiastic sister, and gain a solid sense of self-confidence—it's just that she doesn't like to be rushed. An appropriate Annie Story would incorporate this style of progress.

Rather than trying to make your child over in your image—a generally fruitless task if her basic characterisitics are different from yours—it makes sense to stop and try to understand where she is coming from. What are her natural ways of coping with the world? Can you help her strengthen and improve on them in ways that feel right for her? This takes a lot less energy than the make-over approach. It's like judo—you're working with the force rather than against it.

The view from the other side

The experience of trying to understand the world from someone else's perspective is something we don't do enough of. Particularly with regard to our children, it can make an enormous difference to the way we see a situation.

To take an example, let's go right back to the beginning.

As new parents, you have just brought your baby home from

the hospital and are in the process of dealing with an unpleasant fact about babies—they cry. Quite loudly and usually quite regularly. Here is where you might face your first dilemma. On one side you have people telling you, "You can't spoil a baby by too much love and attention. Pick her up when she cries." And just as usually, on the other side you have people saying, "If you pick that baby up every time she cries, you'll simply teach her to cry more and spoil her." How do you decide which is right?

As an aid to your decision-making, it can be helpful to try the imaginative exercise of putting youself in the baby's place. Just pretend now that you are only a few days old. This is difficult, I know. Perhaps to start with you could imagine having just come off a roller coaster ride—without the benefit of sitting in one of the cars. Having been shaken around rather a lot, everything goes a bit fuzzy and then the next thing you know is that you're awakening in what seems to be a strange motel room. (This is, of course, assuming a level of sophistication that babies don't have.) You're desperately, urgently hungry—you feel as if you haven't eaten for days, so you think you'll get up and find some food. This is where you discover that you can't move. Not to any useful degree at any rate. You can't lift your head to look around, you can't roll over on your side to get a better view, you certainly can't sit up, and the idea of walking is a joke. Every now and then a fascinating object with five elongated points on it dances in front of your eyes, but you have no idea that it's your hand, or that it can be used to grasp and pick up things.

Okay, you think, you'll yell for help. This is where you discover you can't speak the language. Or, in fact, any language. All you can do is cry. Which you do, as loudly as you can, in order to attract help, if there's any there.

At this point I might stop and ask a question. How are you feeling? Invariable the answers come back—scared, helpless, frustrated, confused, insecure.

Right, let's go on with the exercise.

Let's suppose that you do cry with all your frantic might, and, lo and behold, help turns up in the form of a large comforting giantess who is obviously most concerned at your distress. She can't understand your language but she soothes you down, searches out the cause, feeds you a hearty meal, generally convinces you that she has your best interests at heart, and stays with you until you've settled down. Some time later you wake again, terribly upset because you're soaking wet. Again you cry. Again she turns up like magic and fixes things up. This is most comforting, but in your rather helpless situation it's still a worrying setup.

What are the arrangements in this strange place? Does the giantess take holidays and what would happen to you if she does? Is she into thirty-five hour weeks with no overtime? Is she hard of hearing? Does she really have your interests as a prime concern? Will she always be there when you need her?

During the next few weeks you begin to be aware that yes, the giantess does always come when you need her. Sometimes she can't quite understand what you're trying to say to her, but it's comforting to know that at least she's there and concerned for you. She works the sort of hours that no unionist would be seen dead with and is obviously quite dedicated to her job and to you.

How are you going to be feeling now? Still helpless and vulnerable but much more settled and secure. You don't know what this is about but at least you can be reassured that you are safe and that you're going to be taken care of.

Let's take the other scenario.

In this one you've woken up in your strange motel room with all your doubts and fears. This time you discover that sometimes when you cry the giantess turns up, but, and this is a "but" that echoes with all the awfulness of impending doom, sometimes she doesn't.

Knowing nothing about the care-taking arrangements of this mystifying place, how can you know that she is ever going to turn up again? What if she's taken long service leave or is off on her Christmas holidays, or has left, claiming low job satisfaction and overlong hours? What, even worse, if she doesn't care enough and just regards you as a nuisance who needs to be taught a lesson rather than a helpless frightened person who doesn't have even the smallest ability to take care of herself?

How are you going to be feeling now? Scared, frustrated, angry are some of the words that are likely to come to mind.

Now to ask a question that has a rather self-evident answer. What sort of baby cries more—a happy secure one, or a frustrated, scared, or angry one? Obviously, just as with adults, a scared, frustrated, angry baby cries more than a happy, secure one.

And indeed studies do show that babies who cry and fuss a lot tend to be the ones whose cries have *not* been consistently responded to. Babies with mothers who have been responsive to their cries and signals are often much happier, unfussy babies. Furthermore, babies who have been given a lot of attention in the early months are showing far more independence by the end of the first year. The babies who have not been given enough early attention tend to be the ones who are extra clingy and dependent at twelve months. They're still looking for the attention they should have gotten in the early months, while the babies who got what they needed back then are free to move on to a growing independence.

As the baby grows older, of course, she can be "spoiled" by having all of her needs constantly met. The child who has always had all of her needs met instantly and has always been the total center of everyone's attention is not likely to be a well-adjusted child. One of the big crunches is likely to come when she first starts nursery school or kindergarten and discovers to her horror and confusion that she is not the center of everyone's world, that real life does involve some frustrations and delays, and that sometimes one's needs have to give way to demands of the environment. If we are never thrown back on our own resources, we never get to develop them. If we have never experienced frustration in our lives we have no chance to learn how to deal with it. A cosseted over-protected child who has never had limits set on her behavior is very unlikely to become a happy independent one. So, some frustration is good for children—it can be like grit for the oyster, culminating in a pearl. However, it's important to keep the frustration to a manageable level—each child will have a differing ability to tolerate frustration, and this ability will generally increase as she gets older. Generally speaking, the more secure the baby has felt in those early months, the more able she will be to deal with frustrations as she matures. That's because she will experience these frustrations against the background of a safe trusted environment and from the viewpoint of a secure individual. All of which make frustrations easier to cope with.

Looking back then, you can see that when we were trying to decide the question of whether attention could spoil a baby, we were trying to settle it by seeing things only through our eyes. We know that people don't respond to *our* every demand and wish. We imagine, perhaps, that if they did, we would become cosseted, demanding tyrants. At the same time we might feel envious and resentful of someone who got this treatment and desirous of having it ourselves. So there are a lot of confusing perceptions and attitudes mixed up in this question. However, they are all attitudes which assume an adult knowledge and experience of the world. We can see how drastically the picture changes when we truly try to see things from the infant's point of view.

It is very important to keep this in mind when telling Annie Stories. An incident that might seem trivial to you can be experienced as devastating from your child's point of view. A behavior that might be seen as malicious defiance from an adult viewpoint may be experienced by the child as a crucial step in her struggle towards mature independence. Thus, both sides, through seeing only their own viewpoint, can feel mightily wronged and misunderstood. Perhaps a good rule of thumb when dealing with your child's anxieties and problems is to really listen first and try to understand what it feels like to her. Don't make dismissive judgments or jump to hasty conclusions —they can sabotage your attempts to help before you've begun.

The background of Annie Stories—imagery and imagination therapy

From the earliest times, imagination and imagery have been important sources of healing and wisdom for troubled individuals. The dreams and visions described in the Bible are examples of this. Primitive witch doctors used dreams and visions in the way that doctors now use their textbooks of diagnostic medicine—as a way of understanding the symptoms and prescribing the treatment. In many tribes the rites of passage into manhood involved fasting and isolation until the individual was given a vision of his place in the tribe. Cultures from every region of the world have used imaginative parables and folk tales as ways of teaching and transmitting the moral and other rules of the society.

In more recent times, witch doctors with entrails and oracles have been replaced by psychiatrists and psychologists. Stripped of the assets of goat's-hair medicine bags, reluctant to use the entrails method (a touch too messy), and unwilling to prescribe fasting and isolation, modern therapists have had to turn to other means. However, for most of them, these still entail using the age-old healing force that their forefathers found so powerful—the human imagination.

Human beings have a highly developed ability to visualize and imagine things—it's one of the characteristics that sets us apart from other species. Most of us take this ability so much for granted that we never stop to think about it. Or to wonder what the world would be like without imagination.

Imagination can be defined as the ability to think about and experience the world through our "mind's eye." It is not just confined to poets and painters. We use it constantly. In simple things like doing the weekly shopping we must project ourselves into the future and think about what items we are likely to need in the days ahead. Without imagination, we would be unable to do this. We would be rooted to the world as it is right now. We would also be unable to look back into the past. When we recall an amusing film, for instance, our "mind's eye" does a flash-back, playing back the funniest or most relevant scenes in our head. We may see the scenes, hear the lines, recall the stitch we developed from laughing, smell the fresh popcorn, and so on, all in our imagination.

So without imagination, we are stuck in one time zone—the immediate present. We are also imprisoned spatially. If we lived in America, for instance, we would be unable to imagine how we might feel if we visited Australia. We could only experience our current position. If we were sweating it out in a heat wave, we would be unable to visualize the joys of a long cool dip. We would obviously be tremendously limited in the things we could do, plan, or create.

What else can imagination do?

This is a question that has intrigued psychologists for many years. We, in fact, are really only just beginning to find out what an extraordinarily powerful tool the human imagination is.

In this discovery, of course, we are some way behind the medicine men of primitive tribes who used to dispose of ene-mies by "singing" them to death. Many modern day parents undoubtedly suspect their teenagers of similar intent as they plug their ears with cotton to drown out the ever present radio or record player. The medicine man's singing, however, was of a different sort. Like pointing the bone, it informed the victim that he was going to die. To the victim, the medicine man was all-powerful and inspired total belief. The victim imagined that he was certain to die, and so, obligingly, he did, condemned by the power of his own mind.

In laboratories, psychologists have shown that when we imagine ourselves running, for instance, the muscles in our legs twitch as though they are being activated, even though we may be sitting with our feet up in a chair. Studies have shown that imagining yourself practicing gymnastics can actually increase your gymnastic proficiency. At the Olympic Games, you may have noticed the high jump athletes, for instance, standing with their eyes closed before jumping, nodding their heads and making strange facial expressions. What they were actually doing was visualizing themselves running down the track and making a perfect jump.

The effect of our imagination on our physiological system may be even more easily demonstrated. If someone were to offer you one thousand dollars on the condition that you in-crease the amount of saliva in your mouth by simply sending verbal instructions to your brain, you might be at quite a loss. It is likely that telegraphing the word "salivate" to your brain cells would produce little effect. In fact, the opposite might occur. As you got more and more frustrated, you might become anxious seeing the thousand dollars trickling away, so to speak, before your eyes, and anxiety has a tendency to dry up saliva. So, what to do? It's quite simple really. To collect that thousand dollars, all you need to do is imagine eating a very large, very sour lemon, and, presto, you have an excess of saliva.

Imagination can produce emotional responses as well as physiological ones. Imagining that someone you love is very sick can make you feel sad. Imagining that you've won a state lottery can bring a feeling of excitement. Imagining yourself sitting by a quiet stream in the country can produce a feeling of peacefulness, and so on.

Almost all of the varied schools of psychotherapy use the power of imagination as an essential part of the therapy.

In psychoanalytically oriented therapy—the type that is based on the psychological exploration of past traumas—the patient relives in her imagination the emotional blocks that have been preventing her from growing. Through bringing these events and emotions to the surface the patient is able to work through them and overcome them. Psychoanalytically oriented therapists believe that symptoms are only the external part of the problem. In their view, the symptoms arise out of deep-seated psychological conflicts, usually rooted in childhood. Therapy is thus based on treating the root cause rather than the symptoms.

On the other end of the psychotherapeutic continuum are the behaviorists. They believe in treating only the symptoms—they don't look for underlying causes such as childhood trauma. Yet, even though they take such a diametrically opposed view to the psychoanalysts, they too depend on the power of the human imagination for much of their therapy.

Desensitization

Perhaps the most widely used form of behavior therapy is a treatment called systematic desensitization, which is used in the treatment of phobias. In non-technical language, phobias are compulsive, intense, and irrational fears which are focused on particular objects, people, or situations. Phobias usually have elegant Greek- or Latin-derived names but there is nothing elegant about the experience of being phobic. Faced with the feared situation, these people feel stupid, mortified, out-of-control, and deathly terrified all at the same time. Telling them to pull their socks up and stop being silly is about as helpful as telling a falling hippopotamus to twirl his tail and fly. With one part of their mind they know their fears are irrational and "silly" and yet they are totally unable to control them and are caught in the grip of panic, with physical symptoms such as racing hearts, shortness of breath, dizziness, and faintness, all of which often make them feel as if they are about to die.

Phobias should be distinguished from normal childhood fears. These childhood fears are common and tend to be passing concerns which the child grows out of. Certain fears seem to be most commonly associated with particular age groups.

The newborn baby generally fears loss of physical support, and sudden loud noises. At around eight months, the infant fears separation from mother. The two-year-old is often scared of the flushing toilet or the bath. At three, fears are often centered on fantasy figures such as ghosts and witches. The fear of large dogs also peaks at three and may last two or three years. At four, the fear of the dark reaches its height and tends to decline at around six.

All of these fears are "normal" in that they are shared by a huge percentage of children and disappear as the child gets older. Fears become problematic only when they are excessively intense or inappropriate for the child's age group. If a six-year-old child, for instance, was still terrified of the bath, it could be termed a phobia rather than the normal transient fear which affects two-year-olds when they suddenly decide that if the drain can suck the water down with such terrifying gusto, it could slurp them down too.

The desensitization technique involves learning to respond to the feared object, for example the bath, with relaxation instead of panic. This can be done either through real life experience or through imagining the bath experience.

Desensitization through imagination is a very popular and successful technique for overcoming phobias. It involves imagining a series of scenes connected with the feared object. The first scene would be fairly innocuous, not frightening at all. The last scene would be very anxiety-arousing. Because the scenes are graded and the person is taught to relax after each scene, she is not confronted with an overwhelming amount of anxiety. Each scene is repeated until the person can imagine it and still remain calm. The fact that desensitization works so well through the use of imagination alone is a great boon for therapists. It saves them from having to climb up to the heights of dizzying scaffolding or cavort with a roomful of snakes when dealing with patients who have a fear of heights or reptiles, for instance. It means too that some of these techniques can be utilized within the Annie Stories, because as the child listens, she will be automatically imagining the scenes you describe.

Modeling

Another behavioral technique for helping children overcome fears involves modeling. This is really learning by demonstration, and research has shown that children learn very readily this way. The model acts out a way of coping with the problem the child is currently experiencing, and the child learns by observing and, later in the appropriate situation, imitating the model's actions. The modeling can be a real life demonstration or it can be a scene which is imagined by the child. When the child imagines someone else carrying out the actions successfully, for example, getting into the bath and splashing around happily, it is called covert modeling. This is an extremely effective form of modeling. Research has shown that when using storytelling as a covert modeling technique, the more closely the story's setting and imagery coincides with the listener's real life situation, the more likely it is that the message of the story will be absorbed and acted upon. Also, if a heroine achieves success at the end of the story, the child is much more likely to emulate the heroine's actions in real life.

Annie Stories make good use of the therapeutic effects of covert modeling in a very natural and unforced setting.

Dr. Richard Gardener, a child psychiatrist, has developed a therapeutic technique in which the child tells a story and the therapist responds with a story of his own using the characters and plot of the first story but providing a more positive resolution. The idea is to use the child's stories, which are assumed to be metaphors for her problems, as a vehicle for learning and change. Annie Stories work on a similar principle except that the story is originated by the parent and based on her knowledge of her child's current conflict.

Many other recognized therapies use imagination, visualization, and fantasy as the principal tools of healing. Techniques from various branches of therapy will be incorporated into the Annie Stories presented in the following chapters.

I've also mentioned drawing and painting as therapeutic modes of expression. They are a wonderful way for children to express and work through things that are troubling them. Often, for instance, children will draw a picture of the "monster" who has been bothering them, and then with obvious glee, make a show of tearing up the picture. In doing this they are symbolically tearing up the monster and demonstrating their mastery over it. I've included some of my ten-year-old daughter's drawings, which she produced in response to the stories. They highlight some of the emotional issues dealt with and illustrate the richness of this nonverbal communication.

how to use the stories in this book

Some parents I've spoken to feel a bit daunted at first at the idea of making up a story. It's usually a lot easier than you think. If one of the stories in this book fits the problem you want to help your child with, read it to yourself first. Think about what details you'll need to change. Sometimes it helps to make notes to yourself.

If you're feeling very unsure about your skills as a storyteller, you could start by reading the appropriate story, almost as is, to your child. Change the names and settings to ones that are suitable to your child. Read slowly and leave lots of space for interjections by you and your child. Try to get into the spirit of the story by saying out loud, "Wow, that must have been scary..." or whatever is appropriate. After you've read the story on a couple of occasions, try telling it without the book. Soon you'll be feeling much more confident about storytelling and will be making up your own.

When you're making up your own story, use the notes and stories in this book as a guide. If your child's problem isn't covered by any of the stories, read the first two chapters to gain an idea of the techniques involved and a few of the stories to give you the feel of the practical application.

Think about the problem that has initiated the need for the story. Try to tune in to how your child is feeling as she struggles with this problem. What must it seem like from her point of view? Then think about the outline of your story beforehand if you can. What ideas do you want to get across to your child? What sort of solutions would you like your story to suggest?

Keep it simple

The more understanding you can put into your story, the more the story will reach out to your listener. You don't have to be a psychology professor to do this, nor do you have to have your child's feelings analyzed to the nth degree. For instance, it would sound pretty strange to say "Annie's self-esteem had plummeted, she was having trouble integrating her conflicting impulses, and her mood was one of increasing dysphoria." All you need to say is "Annie felt terrible. She felt as if she couldn't do anything right. Sometimes she felt like running away and hiding and sometimes she felt like yelling at someone. But mostly she felt very, very sad." Simple language and simple concepts work best. And if you're really puzzled as to what your child is feeling, but just know she has a problem, an "Annie felt awful..." or "Annie felt worried..." will suffice. Don't forget, at any point in your story you can always invite your child to fill in the gaps by saying "And what do you think Annie felt like then?"

Remember as you build your story that you are simply creating a plot line that mirrors your child's problems and a heroine who mirrors her feelings. The characters, events, and settings will parallel her real life, friends, activities, and home-life. After you have set the scene in this way, you can then have the heroine go on to master her problems or come to terms with what has been distressing her. The solutions that the heroine finds don't have to be very complex ones. They can be solutions based on some of the techniques taught in these stories or they may be solutions based on ones you have found in your own life. These solutions may involve learning new practical or social skills; finding comfort through friends and family; learning that the passage of time can be healing, and so on.

Always be open to your child as you tell the story. Notice when she seems riveted and when she seems impatient. You'll get clues as to where the story's hitting home from your child's expression. It will also help you as you weave your story—one child might be very interested in the details of Annie's clothes while another might be bored. With this instant feedback you'll find it easier and easier to tell the sort of stories that are tuned in to your child's interests and needs.

Some children will prefer to listen quietly to the stories. Others will make comments or ask questions. Don't brush these comments or questions aside; they are all part of the story-telling process and will often give you valuable insights into your child's thinking. If you have trouble answering the question, fall back on the psychiatrist's friend and say "What do you think?" If your child helpfully says "I don't know," and the question seems an important one, say something like "Why don't we guess what she was doing there..." (or whatever the question related to). Guessing is an excellent way of finding out about things.

Don't worry either about making mistakes. You and your story don't have to be perfect. Ignore your fumbles and if you become aware of any goofs (often from your child's expression), simply correct them with an "Oops, I almost forgot, she didn't go by herself, she went with a friend," or whatever the mistake relates to.

Often your child will correct you with a pitying glance that says, "Poor mom, can't even remember a story right." This doesn't seem to dim either her enjoyment or her use of the story and neither should it dim yours.

Applying the described techniques

Apart from the general storytelling technique, some of the more specific techniques described in the book have a very wide range of application. The desensitization technique, described in the story on fears, for instance, could also be used to help a child who gets panicked by water, instead of dogs. In dealing with this fear you could use, instead of a dog that gradually grows bigger, a puddle of water that the child is able to splash in and control the size of. In her imagination the child could make the puddle very slowly increase to swimming pool size, controlling and feeling comfortable with every small gradation along the scale. Alternatively, in imagination or real life, you could practice the slow approach described in Part II of the fear of dogs story. You could slowly walk towards the swimming pool, stopping to relax when necessary or practice thought switching. Then the child could dip a toe in the water, a foot, a leg and so on. You would always make sure that she is relaxed with each step before you move on to the next. You could make a chart of her progress that you fill in together with gold stars. This gives her a sense of competence and achievement—a very concrete statement of what she has been able to do.

The relaxation technique taught in the story on relaxation can also be useful in helping children with insomnia. In fact the relaxation technique is generally useful either by itself or in combination with some other form of help for almost any child who is anxious or tense.

If your child tries out a solution you may have suggested in an Annie Story and it doesn't work, don't panic. First, talk to her about it so that you can find out exactly what she did, how she did it, and what happened. This will give you clues on how to shape the follow-up Annie Story. For example, let's say your daughter was worried about making friends. You had told her a story about a little girl with a similar problem who had learned to go up to her classmates and say "Can I join in?" or "Would you like to play hopscotch with me?" Your daughter may have come home with a very long face, having tried this and failed.

What you may find, however, is that she tried it with only one classmate and then gave up. In that case the follow-up Annie Story could be about a little girl who tried this, got very disappointed, and then learned that if she didn't give up, and asked perhaps a few different classmates, she succeeded in getting a friend to play with her.

Or you might find that your daughter popped her question in a voice that was barely audible and a posture that invited defeat. In that case the Annie Story might focus on how Annie learned to approach her classmates in a confident, friendly fashion. This story could, for instance, have Annie and her mom acting out the roles of a confident child and a shy child and then switching parts so that Annie gets to practice being confident.

It may also be that you really haven't a clue as to why the technique used in the story failed. In that case an Annie Story where Annie is disappointed about her failure but nevertheless resolves to find a way out of her dilemma may be appropriate. You can also focus on the fact that Annie and her family felt very proud of her for trying, even though she had failed.

Remember too, you don't have to suddenly metamorphose into Charles Dickens. This is not a college exam; no one's going to be looking over your shoulder and saying "H'm...poor syntax..., interesting argument..., but somehow it just doesn't seem to coalesce into a really organic whole..."

Children are usually extremely enthusiastic audiences. They love stories and they love time with you. The combination of the two is like a double-dipped ice cream cone—unbeatable.

nightmares

dreams are the constant companions of our night-side lives. More often than not we deny their memory, believing that we have had a dreamless sleep. Research has shown, however, that all normal people dream regularly—usually four or five times a night. Dreams are a complex and enormously fascinating subject, one from which we can gain a wealth of knowledge and insight. After this Annie Story, I have allotted some space to the discussion of dreams and the ways in which we can understand and learn from them. But before beginning the story I would like to distinguish between nightmares, as typified in this Annie Story, and night terrors.

A nightmare is a distinct dream. A frightened child waking from a nightmare will be able to tell you, "...there was a big green giant chasing me and he was trying to squash me...," for instance.

Night terrors involve a more extreme sense of panic than is usually engendered by nightmares. The child wakes suddenly with a piercing scream, is incoherent, extremely agitated, and in a state of intense terror, typically with no memory of having dreamed. Night terrors are relatively common in children, tending to affect the younger child (about three to five years old). Current thinking suggests that they may be due to an immature nervous system. We do not yet know exactly why they occur, although we know that they tend to occur earlier rather than later in the night. They may be due to a difficult "gear change," as it were, between the different levels of sleep, so that instead of drifting smoothly through each level as we normally do, we are suddenly catapulted awake from the deepest level of sleep. They can be precipitated by emotional stress and fatigue.

Night terrors are indeed terrifying to behold and although the child does not usually remember the event in the morning, the shaken observer does.

The best you can do for sufferers is to reassure them, stroke them soothingly, and talk to them gently. Don't try to forcibly

wake them up, and unless it is necessary, don't try to restrain them—it can intensify the outburst. Let your child return to a peaceful sleep as soon as you can. These attacks may occur more frequently when your child is under stress, so it is always worthwhile looking at this aspect and seeing if there are ways of alleviating such stresses.

Nightmares, as noted, are quite distinct from night terrors, and are practically universal in their occurence, striking child and adult alike. They can be defined as intense, frightening dreams. Cultural influences change the context, characters, and props in nightmares, but some of the general themes are relatively stable. The theme illustrated by this story, that of being chased by a wild animal, is one of the most common nightmares of children all over the world. All children have occasional nightmares, however if your child has frequent or repeated nighmares, they may be an indication that she is under extra stress of some sort. Try to find out what this stress is and what can be done to alleviate it.

Very young children cannot yet distinguish between fantasy and reality. They believe that their dreams have a concrete reality. As they get older they develop the understanding that dreams take place only in the mind.

A young child can also misinterpret shapes in the dark—the coat hung on the door hook can seem like a headless boogie man, and so on. Be sure to switch the light on and carefully point out what these "monsters" really are.

Lights-out time can be quite scary for children. We can all remember how alone we've felt in the dark. A night light can be a great comfort here. Having a favorite toy to cuddle up to in bed can be very reassuring too. Blankets are often particularly important to children. They may give their favorite blankets names, like Pinky, and the security of snuggling up to their familiar texture gives a wonderfully soothing quality to the bedtime routine. Pillows are important too. We've all had the experience of struggling to sleep on a pillow that's too hard, too lumpy, or not right in some other way. If your child is feeling tense or over-excited around bedtime or has trouble getting to sleep, the Annie Story on Relaxation can be very helpful.

Make sure, too, that you monitor your children's television intake. Watching a violent or frightening film just before bedtime is not conducive to peaceful dreams.

Bedtime is traditionally a time of special intimacy for parent and child. It can be a time to talk and listen quietly, to share the day's happenings, and to give your child a sense of being cherished and loved. Going to sleep feeling loved is a wonderful experience for all of us.

anncie was a little girl who lived in a brown brick house with her mommy and daddy and a big black dog.[1]

There were eight different rooms in the house. There was a kitchen, a laundry, a family room, a bathroom, a work room, a study, a bedroom for Annie's mommy and daddy, and a bedroom for Annie. Annie liked her bedroom very much.[2] It was usually a bit messy, but Annie could find things in it because she knew what part of the mess they were in. Sometimes she had big cleanups and tidied things away but within a few days they all crept out and arranged themselves in a mess again.

One of the things Annie liked best about her room was her bed.[3] It was white and red, and underneath it were two big drawers that Annie kept her toys in. Her bed was right next to a wall, and when Annie went to sleep at night she would sometimes curl up against the wall because the wall was very cool and Annie liked the feel of it. She called it her cold wall and, particularly in summer, thought she was very lucky to have it. She also liked her pillow. It was nice and soft and just the right size for her. When some of Annie's toys shared her bed she would let them lie with their heads on the pillow, and she knew that they thought it was a wonderful pillow, too.

Underneath the pillow was a sheet. It was white and looked like a big tablecloth and covered the whole bed. Over the sheet was a big eiderdown quilt that had letters of the alphabet printed all over it in red and white. Annie loved to snuggle in between the sheet and the quilt. Sometimes her mom would say she looked as snug as a bug in a rug. Annie had never seen a bug in a rug but sometimes she imagined them all curled up in their snug rugs with tiny little quilts over them. She wondered if their mommies ever said to them, "You look as snug as an Annie in a bed."

---

1. Vary the details here to fit in with your child's environment.

2. It is important for a child to feel that her room is a pleasant and welcoming place. Children who are habitually sent to bed as punishment can come to associate their beds with deprivation. This can lead to a great deal of resistance at bedtime and is not conducive to relaxed and peaceful sleep.

3. If possible, allow your child to choose her bed or part of it—sheets or color schemes, for instance. This helps it become her special place.

Annie used to go to sleep at 7:30 every evening. She would brush her teeth, get into her nightie, and pick out her favorite stuffed animal to sleep with.[4] Then she would get into bed, and her mommy or daddy would come to tell her a story. After the story they would give her a kiss and say "sweet dreams," and Annie would go peacefully to sleep.[5]

When Annie slept, she used to have dreams. At first she thought that dreams were real and that the things you did in dreams really happened.[6] As she got older though, she learned that dreams really only happened inside your mind. Still, when you were dreaming them, they seemed very real.

Sometimes Annie had good dreams, and she would wake up feeling very happy. Once she dreamed that she had a magic pet hamster who could talk. In her dream she took it to school to show all her friends. Another time she dreamed it was her birthday and there was a whole heap of presents rising in a pile up to the ceiling, just waiting for her to open them. Annie liked that dream.

Sometimes, though, she had bad dreams and she would wake up feeling frightened. When that happened she would turn on the little light next to her bed and get out one of her books and look at pictures or read.[7] Sometimes she would just lie awake and rest, trying not to go back to sleep. She was scared that if she went back to sleep she might get into the bad dream again. Sometimes, if she was really scared, she would creep down the hallway to her parents' room. Annie's mom or dad would come back to Annie's room with her and settle her down so that she went to sleep without being scared again.

One night Annie had a very scary dream. She dreamed

---

4. A regular time for going to bed as well as a regular bedtime routine is very helpful in establishing good sleep habits and providing a soothing sense of security.

5. The traditional "sweet dreams" wish that we give to our children at night is another comforting part of the bedtime ritual. Each language has its own popular phrase to convey the same wishes.

6. When they are very young, children believe that dreams are real-life events. They cannot differentiate television from real life either. It is only as they grow older that they are able to distinguish fantasy from reality.

7. A night light or lamp next to the bed is very reassuring for children.

that she was being chased by wild animals. She ran and she ran but she could hear the animals thundering behind her. They were getting closer and closer. She could hear them panting and feel their hot breath through the back of her dress. All of a sudden, just as they were about to snap their big, nasty teeth down on her, she woke up.

She looked at the clock by her bed. It said 7:00, so Annie knew her mom would be up. She went to find her to tell her about her terrible dream.

"Well," said Annie's mom when Annie had finished telling her about the wild animals, "that does sound like a scary dream.[8] What did you do when you saw the wild animals coming?"

"I turned around and ran as fast as I could," said Annie. "I was afraid they'd catch me and eat me up."

"What was the scariest part?" asked Annie's mom.[9]

Annie thought. "It was right at the end when I thought they were going to catch me because I couldn't run fast enough."

"That is an awful feeling," Annie's mom said. She gave Annie a hug. "Did you know that a lot of children have dreams like that?"[10]

"Really?" said Annie, and brightened up a little bit. It was good to know that she wasn't the only one who got scared in dreams. "Why do people have bad dreams like that?"

"Well," said Annie's mom, "usually we have bad dreams if we're worried about something or if something upsetting has happened to us.[11] Listen," she said, as she picked up some paper and pencils, "I've got a good idea.

---

8. Let your child know that you understand and accept her feelings.

9. This is a very useful question to ask. Sometimes the part that you see as the scariest is not in fact what your child was most scared of. This lets you know what part to focus on as you help your child work through her nightmare.

10. It is reassuring for children to know that many children have this type of dream and are scared by it.

11. Psychological stress is a common cause of nightmares. They can also be brought about by such factors as fevers, sleep deprivation, indigestion, and a withdrawal from certain sleeping pills.

Why don't you do me a drawing of your dream?"[12]

Annie liked that idea. She sat down at her table and drew a picture of the wild animals chasing her. There were two of them. They were tigers and looked very hungry and mean—just the sort that liked to eat little girls for breakfast.

"Wow, they're fierce looking tigers," said Annie's mom. "Isn't it lucky that we don't have any tigers around here in the real world? The only tigers we would ever see would be in the zoo, and they're locked up so that they can't get out.[13] I can see, though, that to meet a tiger like that in a dream could be very frightening, so I'm going to give you something very, very special."

"What is it?" said Annie. She leaned forward. She was very, very interested.

"I'm going to give you a magic, invisible dream ring," said Annie's mom.[14]

"What's that?" asked Annie. It sounded good.

"It's a special ring that's full of a very powerful magic. You put it on your finger like this . . ." Annie held out her hand and her mom slid the ring onto the third finger of her left hand. "It's invisible," she explained, "so you can't see it, and it's made of a fairy substance like air, so you can't feel it either because your hand goes straight through it, but once you put it on it stays on because it knows that it belongs to you."

"Gosh," said Annie. She was very excited. She touched her finger. Her mom was right, it did feel like air. "I wish I could see it," she said.

"Well," said Annie's mom, "there is a way. Sometimes

---

12. Drawing and modeling the fearful situation helps to defuse the anxiety associated with it. This is discussed in more detail in the previous chapter. Sometimes a child will want to tear up her drawing of a dream monster. By doing this, she feels a sense of mastery—she is showing the monster who's boss and getting rid of it.

13. Here you can let your child know that she is not likely to encounter wild tigers in the real world. If, however, the nightmare contains a possible real-life situation, such as a fire, you can reassure her by describing exactly what she should do to ensure her safety if that ever happened to her.

14. This magical talisman allows the child to feel less helpless and vulnerable and therefore better able to confront the nightmare monster. The more resources a child has in a situation such as this, the stronger she will feel and the better she will cope.

if you close your eyes and think about your finger you can see your ring. Everyone's ring is a bit different because it's specially made for them."

Annie closed her eyes and thought about her finger. "I can see it!" she said. "It's the most beautiful ring I've ever seen."[15] And indeed it was. It was sparkly, like a diamond, but instead of being white, it was purple, like a violet with a light inside. "I love it!" said Annie.

"Now," said Annie's mom, "this ring has a very special magic. It's a dream ring and that means it protects you in dreams. When you have it on you can't be harmed. All sorts of things can happen to you but you can't be harmed. So, if something frightening is happening to you in a dream, you just need to remember that you have your dream ring on and that you are protected."

"Wow," said Annie. "That sounds terrific." She felt much better now. It was nice to know that the dream monsters couldn't really hurt her any more.

"And do you know something else about dreams?" continued Annie's mother. "You can make things happen in them. You can actually change things around in any way you like."[16]

"Really?" said Annie.

"Yes, it's true," her mom said. "Dreams are special like that. All you need to do is remember in your dream that you can change it, and then you can make whatever you like happen. You can be the boss of your dream."

"That sounds great," said Annie.

"I've got a good idea," said Annie's mom. "Why don't we look at your wild animal dream and think about how you might have changed it."[17]

"Okay," said Annie. She closed her eyes so that she

---

15. Children have wonderful imaginations. Most children will be able to shut their eyes and "see" the ring. For those who can't, and notice that Annie's mom only said, "*sometimes* you can see it ..." reassure them that it's an invisible, invisible ring!

16. The more the child takes positive action in her dreams, the more competent and resourceful she will feel. This attitude can translate to waking life as well so that she is less and less likely to adopt the role of passive victim of fate in any area.

17. This is fun for the child and also enables her to see just how many resources and options she really has.

could remember her dream better. "I was just playing by myself," she said, "when the wild animals came out of the bushes and started chasing me. They looked like very mean tigers—they were big and yellow with black stripes. I ran and ran as fast as I could."

"Well, now that you know you can make things happen in your dreams, what could you have done?"

Annie thought. "I could have made a big hole in the ground open up and have the tigers fall into it."

"That would have been good," agreed Annie's mom. "Tigers certainly can't do much chasing when they're trapped in a hole in the ground. What's another thing you could have done?"

"I could have given myself wings and then I would have been able to fly right over their heads and they wouldn't have been able to catch me. I would have flown right past their heads and said, 'Nyah, nyah, nyah nyah nyah,' and poked my tongue out at them. Or," and Annie got quite excited when she thought of this, "I could have conjured up a big, magic stick that fights off all my enemies. It would have beaten the tigers up until they ran away."

"I know something else I could have done," she went on, getting even more excited, "I could have gotten Superman or even the Fairy Godmother to come and help me. If it was the Fairy Godmother, she would have turned the tigers into pumpkins!"

"That certainly would have been funny to see," said Annie's mom. "Did you know that there's a marvelous magical beast called Baku who eats bad dreams? He comes from a faraway country called Japan and his name means 'one who eats very fast.' They call him that because when he sees bad dreams he likes to gobble them up straight away. In Japan, if a child has bad dreams, they call out, 'Devour O Baku,' and Baku comes instantly and gobbles the nightmare right up. All bad dreams are terrified of him because he eats them up even faster than the Cookie Monster eats cookies. Because he's a magical beast, he's a friend to children all over the world and any child anywhere can call on Baku and he'll come right away and gobble up their bad dream. So you could have called Baku too."

"Wow!" said Annie. "I like Baku."

"What are some of the other things you could have done?" asked Annie's mom.

"I could have squirted some Super Glue onto their paws," said Annie, "and they would have stuck to the ground. I could have built a fence of fire around them or tripped them up with a trip wire. I could have put up a magical invisible shield all around me and they would have bumped their heads against it. Or," and she got really excited at this, "I could have made an elephant do poop in their paths and they would have slipped all over it."

Annie's mother laughed. "I bet you'd like that one," she said.

"Yes," said Annie, "that's my favorite so far."

"Do you know something else you might have done?" said Annie's mother. "You could have asked them why they were chasing you.[18] Sometimes when you do that in dreams you can end up making friends with them."

"Really?" said Annie. She thought it would be rather nice to be friends with a tiger. Imagine if you took it to school with you.

"You could ask it what it wants," said Annie's mom. "Sometimes monsters chase you in dreams because they want to tell you something. Sometimes they're even lonely and they want to make friends. You could offer to teach it something and it could teach you something in return. Or you could give it a present and it could give you one too. Monsters sometimes give the most wonderful presents."

"Golly," said Annie. "I never knew there was so much I could do in dreams." She couldn't wait for the next dream she would have.

"I've got a good idea," said Annie's mom. "Why don't we sit down and do some drawings about your dream and what you might have done in it?"[19]

So Annie sat down with her pencils and paper. First

---

18. It is sometimes possible to invite the dream monster to work with you rather than against you. Dream monsters who are befriended in this way are very special friends indeed.

19. Your child's drawing can suggest solutions. In my daughter's illustration, the hole in the tree might offer a source of sanctuary.

she drew the tigers chasing her. Then she did a drawing of the Godmother turning the tigers into pumpkins.[20] Then she did a drawing of the tigers slipping and sliding in elephant's poop. Boy, did they look funny. Lastly she drew a picture of one of the tigers giving her a present. It was standing on its hind legs and handing her a beautifully wrapped box with a big ribbon on top of it. Annie was dying to know what was in the box.

"Do you think I'll be able to dream about the tigers again tonight?" she asked her mom. She was dying to try out all the things her mom had told her about.

"Well," said Annie's mom, "sometimes, if you tell yourself just before you fall asleep that you want to dream about something special, that dream will come along. So, if you wanted to, while you're lying in bed tonight with your eyes closed and almost asleep, you could tell yourself that you wanted to be back in your tiger dream."

Annie thought this sounded really interesting. "Does it always work?" she asked.

"Not always," her mommy said. "Sometimes a different dream just wants to pop up, or sometimes you might not remember what you dream, but you get better and better at it as you practice."

So that night, just before she fell asleep, Annie said over and over to herself, "I want to be back in my tiger dream . . ." and then she fell asleep and started dreaming.

Sure enough, there were the tigers again. They came out of the bushes just as they did last time and started to chase her. They looked so scary that Annie started to run. And then suddenly she remembered her ring and all the things her mommy had told her. She stopped and turned around to face the tigers. The tigers got such a shock, they almost skidded into each other. They stopped, sat down, and looked very puzzled.

"Why are you chasing me?" said Annie.

The tigers looked at each other.

"Er . . ." said one.

"Umm . . ." said the other.

Then they both looked at each other again, nodded

---

20. Drawing possible solutions as well as the actual dream reinforces the notion of a positive outcome.

their heads and chorused, "We were chasing you because you were running away from us."

"Well, I'm not running away now," said Annie.

"That's right," said one of the tigers.

"That's right," said the other tiger.

Then they looked at each other and looked at Annie.

"Well," they said together, "what will we do now?"

"Why don't we make friends?" said Annie. She was enjoying this. Up close, the tigers didn't look at all frightening. In fact they looked like huge, striped, not-very-bright pussy cats. "Look," she went on, remembering that she could make things happen in her dreams, "I've got a present for you." And she reached her hands up in the air and clapped them. Immediately a beautiful roll of silver ribbon fell to the ground.

"I'm going to make you some beautiful bows to tie around your necks," she said. And she did.

The tigers were so excited they could hardly sit still. When Annie had finished, they jumped and jiggled around trying to twist their heads so that they could see the bows on the backs of their necks. They did look funny. "Why don't you look at each other's bows," said Annie, "and then you'll know what they look like on you."

"What a good idea," they said.

Then one of the tigers whispered in the other one's ear. They both nodded.

"Now we've got a present for you," they said.

"Close your eyes," said one of them, "and hold out your hands."

Annie did. "Can I open them now?" she asked.

"Yes," said the tigers.

She opened her eyes and there, lying in her hands, was the very same box with a bow that she had drawn with her mother.

"Oh!" she said. She was so excited that her voice came out in a sort of a squeak. "Whatever can be in it?"

"It's just for you," said the tigers. They were standing very tall now and somehow they looked more majestic than they had before.

Annie opened the box. There inside, nestling in a cushion of purple velvet, was a necklace with a beautiful shiny red heart on it.

53

"It's the Heart of Courage," said one of the tigers, "and every time you think of it you'll remember how brave you've been, and each time you think of it you become even braver."[21]

"It builds up the store of courage inside you," said the other tiger. "Each time you think of it you get more and more courage and the courage starts to grow more and more of itself so that you get even more courage still."

"Once it's been given to you," said both the tigers together, "it's always yours and nothing or nobody can ever take it away."

"Oh," said Annie, "that's wonderful. Can every little boy or girl get one of these?"

"Yes," said the tigers. "There's one for everyone somewhere. They don't all look the same of course because everyone is different, but you have to search for them and usually the person or thing that's taking care of your particular gift for you is someone or something that you're scared of.[22] So you have to find them and ask them for it or make them give it to you."

"Gosh," said Annie. She was amazed. She thought that she must tell all her friends about it. She wondered if her mother knew.

"Now that you've found yours," said one of the tigers, "we can keep it for you here safe and sound so that you'll always know where it is."

"And remember," said the other tiger, "all you need to do is think of it for it to start working."

"Oh thank you," said Annie. "I'm so glad I met you."

"So are we," said the tigers, "and we hope you'll come back and visit us soon."

"Of course I will," said Annie, and she gave them both a great big hug.

"We'd better go now," said the tigers, "because it's almost time for you to wake. Remember now, come back and visit us."

21. The tiger's present has become a personal symbol or talisman that will always remind Annie of her strengths and resources.

22. This highlights the idea that each crisis we face usually also contains the gift of inner growth if we can but find it and use it. The Chinese express this beautifully. In their language, the word for "crisis" consists of two characters—one meaning "danger" and the other meaning "opportunity."

"I will," said Annie. And she waved.

"And remember," called back one of the tigers, "if you ever need us in another dream, all you have to do is yell and we'll come running."[23]

"Immediately," said the other tiger. "We'll take care of you."

"Oh, wow," said Annie. She was so excited that she woke up with a great big grin all over her face. She could hardly wait to tell her mom.

More notes on dreams

Dreams have always been a source of wonder and study for man. From the earliest times they have been seen as the containers of special wisdom—a sort of postal service from the gods. One famous example of this comes from the Old Testament where Joseph was able to unravel the beefy symbolism of Pharaoh's dream.

In modern times, it was Sigmund Freud who renewed the emphasis on dreams as messages. Rather than the gods as senders, however, he saw the unconscious as the originator of the message. He called dreams the "royal road to the unconscious," and saw them as resulting from the repressed urges and desires, usually sexual or aggressive, of the unconscious id. Because these would provoke anxiety if they were to be consciously recognized, he postulated that they surfaced in a disguised form in our dreams. That, he reasoned, was why dream messages were not usually immediately obvious to the conscious, logically functioning mind. He believed that the true message had to be teased out by interpreting the language and images of the dream and the associations it provoked.

Jung de-emphasized Freud's focus on the sexual and aggressive origins of dreams. He believed that all dream elements and characters were part of the dreamer's own personality and that each had something to say to the dreamer. A dream of a stern school teacher, for instance, might be an encounter with the perfectionist part of himself. He talked of the symbolism of dream characters and felt there were certain universally recognized characters or archetypes who appeared in dreams. One of the most important of these for this story is the "Shadow" or the "Dark Double." The Shadow often appears in our dreams as

---

23. From being feared monsters, the tigers have now become another resource that Annie can call on in other dreams.

a criminal, a monster or a wild beast. It represents that part of ourselves we are frightened of, ashamed of, or don't want to know about. It will keep hounding us until we turn and face it and, through encountering it, reclaim its strength for our own.

Jung also talked about "transforming symbols" in dreams. These could be dream people or objects which have a compressed and intense emotional meaning to the dreamer—they provide a way of transcending our normal emotional conflicts and fears. A flag functions in this way for men going into battle —it provides a symbol, standing for such things as honor, country, and home, which spurs men on to transcend their natural fear of death.

In Annie's dream, the Shadow is seen in the persona of the two tigers. Perhaps they represent some "bad" side of herself that she feels worried by.

Tigers, lions, and wild dogs are common "shadow" marauders in dreams, and of course, in waking life, when these animals shake their catch with their teeth, we say they are "worrying" their prey.

The Heart of Courage is a transcending symbol which can help Annie rise above her fears and face what needs to be faced. It reminds her that precious things can come out of fearful experiences and sometimes can come through no other way. We would never find our courage if we were never faced with anything frightening. It is axiomatic that there is no courage without fear.

Today, most people working in the area of dreams and therapy see them as providing highly significant and meaningful pathways for self-understanding and growth. For many people, however, a common reaction is to feel that it's all very well for dreams to provide the pathways—but why do the directions have to be written so mysteriously?

Dream language, it's true, is very different to our waking, logical forms of thought, but it's not gibberish. Although a cursory glance at a dream may pick up only what seems to be a meaningless jumble, a closer look can discern the deeper internal meaning which, when translated, makes absolute sense to the dreamer. "Translated" is the key word here because, as noted, dreams do have a language of their own. It is the language of the unconscious—a pictorial language which makes use of puns, metaphors, fusions, allusions, and all sorts of wordplay. It also tends to show a total disregard for the natural laws of physics or logic. It's a marvelously witty and inventive language that leaves me constantly in awe of its capacity for freshness, originality, and insight. It's not possible to do justice to the delights of dream language in this book, but perhaps an illustration from one of my own dreams will provide an example of dream language in action.

I had been invited to do a call-in radio show on dreams and was thinking to myself that I should really review my dream diary, in which I had been recording my dreams, to pick out an appropriate example to use on the show the next day. Obligingly, however, my unconscious provided a compact little dream that night which neatly illustrated all those points I had intended to talk about.

To set the scene: on the day of my dream I had just heard, to my delight, that my poetry book, *The Truth About Unicorns,* had won the Fellowship of Australian Writers' Anne Elder Award for the best first book of poetry for 1984. I had at the time been rather neglecting my poetry due to the time-consuming demands of the other work in which I was involved. I had to make a decision as to whether to take on more of such work, leaving me even less time for poetry.

It is important to set the scene like this because dreams generally contain what is called the "day residue." These are fragments of events or thoughts that have concerned you during that or the previous day. The dream is often worked around the day residue.

That night, as I said, I went to sleep and dreamed. In my dream I was sitting at a large banquet table. My fellow guest, who was sitting next to me, was Albert Einstein. The table was spread with dishes of food which were colored either green or white. With my natural enthusiasm for such experiences, I was about to try and load a sample from every dish onto my plate. Einstein reached out a hand and stopped me, indicating that I mustn't overload my plate, and also that I should stick to the white stuff and not the green.

A simple enough dream on the surface it would seem. A cursory glance would rate it as enjoyable but relatively meaningless.

But, as a closer look will show, this is far from the case. The dream does indeed have a very clear message for me.

When I woke from the dream, I immediately wrote down what details I could remember. This is very important as dreams tend to fade from memory rapidly.

I then began to note down my associations to the characters and events in the dream. I was intrigued by Albert Einstein. In my dream he was white-haired and wise. I saw him as "an elder of the tribe." As this phrase came to mind, I picked up with delight the pun on "an elder. . . ." The poetry prize I had won was called the Anne Elder Award. In other words the prize was telling me something. What was it telling me? It was telling me to "stick to the right course" and "not to put too much on my plate." This corresponded to my real life decision as to whether to take on extra work. What course should I stick to? Well the dream had an answer for that too. If you remember, Einstein was telling me to leave the green food and concentrate on the white. White, for me, is associated with poetry. Robert Graves in his book on poetry talked about the "White Goddess." My book was called *The Truth About Unicorns* and unicorns, of course, are white. Green for me, is associated with money— "green stuff, greenbacks," and indeed the other activities which I had been thinking of taking on were much more lucrative than poetry. So, again, the message seems clear—don't take on the extra, lucrative work. Leave space, instead, for poetry.

In the dream groups that I run, people often ask how they go about understanding their dreams. There is no universal "dictionary" for dreams. Although some themes and symbols are common to many people, it is important to recognize that each dream is unique to the person dreaming it. Don't, therefore, try to force interpretations onto people. An interpretation is usually helpful only if it "clicks" with the dreamer herself.

You don't need to act as your child's therapist and interpret her dream for her, but gaining an insight into her dreams can help you in your understanding of what is troubling her. Dreams can give you a wonderful glimpse into your child's inner world— one which may startle you, perhaps, with the different perspectives you see. The huge towering bear-like figure which menaced her in her dream last night may be a reflection of what it felt like to be yelled at by Daddy during dinner the previous evening. And also, it may be a projection of her own perceived "badness" or wildness—an image that tells you how frightened children can be by what they perceive as a "bad" inner self. Many adults too, of course, share this fear that there is something terrible hidden within themselves.

My daughter has always been curious about why people dream certain things. I explained to her, in very simple terms, about the way dreams have their own psychological meaning. I told her about a couple of mine to illustrate the symbolism of dreams. She was fascinated by this and every now and then, would spontaneously analyze one of her own dreams—tracing it back to a worrying incident at school, or some such thing. It's important not to push your child into doing this, though. If she is spontaneously interested in it, you can help her, but be careful not to force your interpretations on her. Let her come to her own interpretations in her own way and time. Mostly though, children aren't interested in interpreting dreams, just as they aren't interested in interpreting fairy tales. They get their learning from these rich sources in other ways.

For a more in-depth understanding of dreams, there are now a number of excellent books which should be freely available from libraries and bookstores. I've listed a couple in the Recommended Reading section at the end of this book.

fears

i n this chapter my story is based on a common childhood fear—that of dogs. The method I use to deal with this fear is called desensitization and it can be applied to many other fears and phobias as well.

Desensitization involves working out a "ladder" of fears relating to the object or situation your child is scared of. At the bottom rung of the ladder is a situation that your child can cope with comfortably, and at the top end is one that would have her very upset. With a fear of dogs, for instance, the bottom rung might consist of looking at a picture of a dog in a children's book, while the top rung might be the experience of having a dog jump into her lap. In between these two rungs are a graduated series of situations relating to dogs that range from mildly discomforting near the bottom to fear-provoking near the top.

In using densensitization to aid your child in losing her fear of dogs, you would guide her up this ladder one rung at a time, starting at the bottom. Every time she begins to get anxious, help her to relax, then allow her to try that rung again. After a few repetitions of rung-followed-by-relaxation, your child will be able to feel more and more comfortable while contemplating or experiencing that rung of the ladder. When she feels quite comfortable and relaxed with it, she can progress to the next rung.

It's important to prepare the steps of this properly. Start with something that she feels comfortable with and then move slowly up. This prevents her anxiety level from getting too high and overwhelming her. It is easier for her to learn to control anxiety by dealing with it a little at a time. As a beginner, after all, you wouldn't attempt horseback riding by starting out on a bucking bronco.

Praise your child with each successful step she takes. The more competent she feels, the more confidently will she be able to face her fears. It can be helpful to construct a chart of your child's progress. Each successful step can be noted by a gold star; a very concrete symbol to your child of her growing confidence and competence. Children often enjoy filling in the chart themselves.

When helping your child with her fears, it is important that you communicate to her both verbally and non-verbally that there is nothing intrinsically dangerous about dogs. Of course you shouldn't attempt to do this with your child if you are also scared of dogs! If, for instance, you tense up every time a dog approaches, your child may pick up the message that dogs are indeed to be feared.

Sometimes this tensing-up on your part stems not from your fear of dogs, but from your apprehension about how your child will react. This tension may still be picked up by your child and interpreted as a lack of confidence—either about dogs or about her ability to cope with them. It's important when working with children's fears to maintain an aura of calmness and confidence.

Sometimes too, children's fears can be perpetuated because they get rewarded for them. In other words, when they get upset they may get a lot of extra attention that they don't get when they're not being frightened.

It's important to notice these patterns of behavior in your household. Essentially, what you are trying to do is reward competent behavior with attention and praise so that your child feels motivated to continue striving for competence. We all respond better when complimented on a job well done. If we were only noticed when we did something wrong, our morale and interest in the job would be likely to plummet quite rapidly.

Rewarding competent or coping behavior does not mean that your child should be punished for crying when she sees a

"Dogs can't harm you," said the woman.

dog. Comfort her, but don't make a big deal out of it. Let her know that you understand her feelings, but also let her know that you are confident that with time she'll be able to feel more comfortable with dogs. Equally, don't laugh at her fears or dismiss them out of hand—they are real and serious to her. My daughter's drawing illustrates how unhelpful such an approach can be. The caption "Would you buy a used car from this woman?" would seem appropriate.

Sometimes when a child has been scared by something—a TV show, for instance—she will demand to watch that show again and again. For worried parents, this may seem like the worst possible thing to do. However, when a child requests this she is usually trying to administer her own brand of desensitization. By watching the scary show over and over, she feels more in control of it. There are no more surprises—the strange dreaded witch has become a familiar old hag, she knows when the excitement is going to build up, she can control how much she sees and when by shutting her eyes and opening them when she's ready. Often she will want to act out or draw the scary scenes or characters. This, too, is part of her way of mastering her fear. She may also "conquer" the witch by proxy, by destroying either the clay model or drawing she's made of her. These symbolic victories help her feel stronger in the face of the "real" witch.

Everyone experiences fear at one time or another—it can be essential to survival. If we were not afraid of poisonous snakes we might die; if we didn't feel distinctly shaky at the thought of playing chicken with an oncoming train we might suffer the same fate. Fear in these cases is a very beneficial emotion. Many fears, however, are neither rational nor beneficial. They can be extremely distressing to the sufferer and place enormous restrictions on her life style. When fears are intense, irrational, and focused, we call them phobias.

Many childhood fears seem irrational to adults but are quite rational to children. The bath tub is a good example. The average two-year-old hasn't yet realized that her body is too big to be sucked down the drain, and a fear of the bath is a very understandable reaction. Some children's fears are common to the great majority of children and peak and subside at different ages. Others are specific to the individual child. Some can be traced back to a specific incident, but others seem to arise out of the blue. There is a great range, too, in the intensity of these fears, going from mild unease to panic.

Given that it is normal for children to have various fears, if they are hampering your child's lifestyle or sense of confidence and well-being, it's worth doing something about them. Annie Stories are one way of helping children through fears. Such things as drawing fears, acting them out with toys, modeling them in clay, and offering child-geared explanations are also helpful.

I have divided this story into two parts because of its length. Each part incorporates different desensitization techniques and could be told on successive nights.

Part I

*a*nnie was a little girl who lived in a big house with her mommy and daddy.

She had a room of her own, which was painted red and white, and a big grown-up bed and a toy cupboard which had a round red handle on it so that it looked as if someone had planted a tomato right smack in the middle of the door.[1] Annie sometimes wished

---

1. Vary the details to match your child's room, and later her best friend and a dog that she knows.

it really was a tomato, because then she could play a big trick on people. She would ask them to get something out of the toy cupboard and then watch as their hands went squish when they tried to turn the tomato! She thought it would be very funny.

She liked to think about funny things because mostly she was a very happy little girl. But every now and then she got very unhappy. One of the things that made her very unhappy was DOGS. Annie was very scared of dogs. Her mommy said that one day when she was very little a big dog had jumped out at her and scared her, but Annie couldn't remember that. All she knew was that she hated being near dogs. As soon as a dog came near, Annie would get very scared and shaky and want to cry. She would try to run away very fast or climb up someone as if they were a big high tree where she could be safe.

Her mommy and daddy understood how scared she was of dogs, but a lot of people didn't understand. They called her silly and laughed at her.[2] Even worse, they sometimes tried to get her to make friends with dogs. They would push their huge slobbering dogs at her and say, "See, he's friendly." Annie would be terrified. She would squirm and squeak and try to run, and the dog would leap and lick and try to push her over.

The more frightened Annie got, the more excited the dog got. It was a real mess. Annie decided that the best thing to do was to stay away from dogs.

However she had one big problem. This problem belonged to Helen, her best friend. Helen didn't think it was a problem but Annie thought it was. The problem was the big brown dog that belonged to Helen and her family. It lived in the house with them and was a great, shaggy dog with fur that always stuck up and looked as if someone had dragged a broom backwards through it. Annie saw a cartoon once of someone who had been given an electric shock and his hair was standing up all on end. Sometimes she wondered whether Helen's family plugged their dog in at night to the electricity socket to make its hair go like

---

2. This sort of approach to fears leaves the child feeling ashamed, inadequate, and even more helpless, which produces greater fearfulness.

that.[3] She knew, of course, that they didn't because she knew that you mustn't meddle with electric sockets because they could kill you. She just enjoyed the funny picture it made in her mind.

Annie used to love visiting her friends and having them visit her. As Helen was her very, very best friend, she would come around to Annie's place to play a lot. And Helen was always asking Annie around to her place too. Now Annie really wanted to play at Helen's place. Helen had really great toys and a nice mommy who let you have ice cream if it was a hot day. But one thing stopped Annie from going to play at Helen's. You guessed it—it was the DOG.

One day Helen came around to Annie's in a very excited mood. "Guess what," she said, "Mommy said I can have a costume party for my birthday!"

"Wow," said Annie, "that'll be great."

"Everyone has to come as animals," said Helen. "I'm going to be a teddy bear. We're going to have a prize for the best costume."

After Helen had left, Annie rushed upstairs to find her mommy. She was so excited she was jumping up and down like a baby kangaroo. "Guess what! Guess what!" she said to her mom. "I've been invited to my first costume party."[4]

"That's terrific," said Annie's mom. "We'll have to make you a really great costume. Dress-up parties are lots of fun."

That night Annie was so excited she couldn't get to sleep. She kept thinking about how terrific a costume party would be. She wondered if they would have it indoors or out in Helen's big backyard. She was just thinking about that when all of a sudden her tummy went "glumph" as if it had suddenly fallen down a big steep hill. It had just remembered the problem that lived at

---

3. Humor is very therapeutic as well as enjoyable. Finding something funny about the thing you're afraid of reduces the fearfulness of that person or object.

4. Helen's party provides and incentive in this story for getting rid of Annie's fears because it means that she will have to go to Helen's house and face her dog. You should substitute an incentive that's appropriate for your child when you retell this story.

Helen's house—it had just remembered the DOG.

"Oh dear," said Annie to herself, feeling very miserable. "I wish someone would help me feel better about dogs." And she said it again and again to herself until the words got all jumbled up and as she fell asleep all she could hear was "feel better about dogs, feel better about dogs, feel better about dogs...."

When she woke, there was a funny blue light in the room, and the strangest person was standing there looking at her. She had a very kind face and she looked like the sort of person you knew even though you've never met her before.

"I've been waiting for you to wake up," she said, sitting down on the end of Annie's bed as if it were the most natural thing in the world for a funny lady with a blue light to appear suddenly in your room in the middle of the night.

Annie stared and stared.

The lady certainly did look very strange. She wore a comfy, white jogging suit with silver spangles sewn on it in a funny pattern. Her hair was curly and rather messy, as though she had just been out in a very strong wind. Annie thought it was white too, but it was difficult to tell because all around the lady was a shimmering blue light. It went all around her body and legs and arms as if it were a second skin or a suit of clothes she had stepped into. It moved when she moved. Annie's mouth dropped open as she stared.

The lady looked a bit puzzled. "What are you staring at?" she asked. "Is my light on crooked?" She made a few grabs at the light, twisting and turning it a bit. "It's so difficult adjusting it in the middle of the night without a mirror. I think they've given me the wrong size, too. They said it's my fault because I've put on weight, but I said, stuff and nonsense, it's them. They've been boiling it up in detergent again, and the water's too hot and it's shrunk. All they can think of up there is washing. 'Cleanliness is next to godliness,' they keep saying. Well, I say, just because I'm a Fairy Godmother doesn't mean you have to boil my light every time I turn around. I'm quite clean enough without that, thank you."

Annie gulped. "Are you my Fairy Godmother?" she

squeaked, hardly able to believe her eyes.

The lady stopped talking and suddenly looked sheepish. "Oh dear, did I forget to introduce myself? That was very silly of me. I shall have to start writing myself notes to remind myself. Goodness knows who you must have thought I was." She gave a little wriggle again and adjusted her light.

"What do you mean, they made it too small for you?" Annie asked. "Doesn't it, well, sort of grow on you?"

The lady gave a short laugh. "Goodness no, my dear, though Heaven knows I wish it did. It's part of the regulation Fairy Godmother outfit. See, I can step out of it." And she stepped sideways, leaving the blue light standing next to her, like the surprised outline of a standing-up shadow. She hooked a finger through it and slung it over her shoulder. "It's designed for easy traveling—it's dripdry and you can scrunch it up like this and it doesn't crease." She demonstrated. "It came in last year with the new uniforms. See," she pointed to her jogging suit, "we have the most modern designs. Those wings and flimsy white fairy dresses we used to wear just weren't doing the job. Today's Fairy Godmother does so much more traveling than in the past—there are so many more children in the world." She patted the pockets of her spangled jogging suit, "we have to keep up with the times. I was on the committee that designed this you know."

"It's very nice," said Annie politely. Privately, she thought to herself that she would have preferred the wings and fairy dress.

"Anyway, I'd better get this light back on. Strictly speaking we aren't supposed to take them off until we're off duty. Some of the younger ones complain a bit. They say they're too restricting and old fashioned. Well, I'm certainly not one for being old fashioned, but we've got to have a bit of dignity with the job. If the young ones have their way, next thing you know Fairy Godmothers will all be racing around in skintight jeans and punk hairdo's."

Annie giggled at the thought. The Fairy Godmother laughed too. "That's better," she said, giving the blue light a shake and stepping into it. It immediately surrounded her like a shiny, blue raincoat. "I gave some people a real shock tonight. I was in such a hurry to get here that I was zooming through the streets, and they couldn't make out what I was. Should have seen their faces when I passed them. Anyway, enough of that, let's get down to business." She sat up straight and gave herself a little shake.

"Business?" said Annie.

"Yes, of course. That's why you asked me here, isn't it? You want some help with dogs."

"Oh," said Annie remembering, "oh yes, I'd love some help with dogs."

"Right," said the lady, taking out a funny old stick, "let's get started."

"Ooh," said Annie, "is that a magic wand? Are you going to make a dog appear?"

"No," said the Godmother, "that's just a funny old stick. Would you believe it, my wand's at the cleaners? I just feel a bit lost without something to hold. Anyway, I don't need to make anything appear. I'm going to teach you how to help yourself by using your imagination.[5] That's just as powerful as a magic wand, you know."

"Really?" said Annie, impressed. "How do I use it?"

"That's what I'm going to show you. Now just sit down."

"But I am," said Annie, because, of course, she was still in bed.

"Of course you are," said her Godmother. "Silly me. Sometimes I think they've been washing my brain at night and that's shrunk too." She tapped her forehead. "Okay, sharpen up in there," she said, "we've got work to do."

She turned back to Annie. "Now you just settle back and close your eyes," she said.[6]

Annie did. She felt very excited to think that soon she wouldn't be scared of dogs anymore.

"You know your stuffed toy, Bozo?" the Godmother asked.[7]

"Yes," said Annie. Bozo was one of her favorite

---

5. Try to give your child a belief in her own abilities. Recognizing that she has inner resources that can be just as powerful as the fears that beset her is very important.

6. Your child may voluntarily close her eyes at this point. That's fine—it doesn't mean she's stopped listening; she's just acting along with the story.

7. If your child hasn't got a toy puppy, you could use an appealing little dog from a picture book.

stuffed toys. He often slept with her in bed at night. He was a white puppy with a black patch over one eye.

"Think of him now," said the Godmother, "so that you can see him very clearly in your mind."

"Yes," said Annie. "I'm doing that now. I can see him sitting on my bed where he usually sleeps."

"Good," said the Godmother. "Now just to yourself, I want you to say the words, '*Gabbla-ka-galler, now become smaller,*' and you'll see that Bozo is shrinking. Just let him shrink until he's the size of your hand."

"He looks sort of cute," said Annie. She thought she might like to make him even smaller, so she said the words again, and, sure enough, Bozo shrank even more.[8]

"Now I'll show you how to do something really funny. Say to yourself, '*Gabbla-ka-giving, now become living,*' and touch his tail. It will turn into a real, live puppy dog tail."

"Gosh," said Annie, and she did what the Godmother had told her to.[9] Sure enough, as soon as she had said the words and touched Bozo's tail, it began to wag furiously, as though he was very pleased to see her. It looked very funny.

"What part would you like to make come alive next?" asked the Godmother.

Annie thought about it. "I think I might like to make his head come alive because then I could pat him on the head and say 'good dog,' and he would be able to feel it."

Bozo's tail wagged even faster as Annie said this, as though he thought it was a good idea too.

"*Gabbla-ka-giving, now become living,*" said Annie solemnly as she touched Bozo's head. At once it became very soft and warm. Bozo turned his head and gave Annie an adoring look. He couldn't move his legs, of course, because Annie hadn't made that part come alive yet, but he looked as if he would like to cuddle up in her arms, the way he did when they went to sleep. Annie wondered what it would be like. He did look very cute, and he was

---

8. With desensitization it is traditional to start with something that produces no fear and slowly work up to the more frightening objects or situations.

9. This allows the child to be in control of the situation. The more in control the child feels, the less fearful she will be.

so small and sweet. She patted his head again. Bozo gave her a big lick. His tongue was very warm, and his nose was very cold.[10] It felt funny but very nice. "Why is Bozo's nose so cold?" she asked the Fairy Godmother.

"That's because he's healthy. All healthy dogs have cold noses.[11] Look, he wants to lick you again. When dogs wag their tail and lick you, it's their way of saying they like you. When they put their ears back and growl, it's their way of saying that they're angry and you'd better keep away."[12]

Annie put out her hand and Bozo licked it. His tongue was long and pink and wet, like a smooth wiggly washcloth. When he licked Annie's fingers, it felt a bit ticklish.[13] Annie giggled. "That feels funny," she said. "I like it."

"I think I'll make his front paws come alive next," said Annie. So she said the magic words. Bozo instantly lifted his paw and put it on Annie's lap. Annie took his paw and thought to herself—"I wonder if I could teach him to shake paws as proper gentlemen do?"[14]

"Yes, you can," said the Godmother.

Annie looked up startled. "But I didn't say anything— I just thought it."

"Well, Godmothers can read thoughts, of course," said the Godmother a bit impatiently. "Superman has his X-ray vision, and we have sort of X-ray hearing. We have to hear thoughts from a long way off too, you know, otherwise we'd be in a real jam—people would be wanting us and we wouldn't be able to hear them. Mind you, there

---

10. Make your descriptions as vivid as possible. You really want your child to feel as if she is in the story. Use as many senses—touch, smell, sight—as you can in your descriptions.

11. Put in some facts that will intrigue your child. Curiosity and knowledge are opponents of fear.

12. It is helpful to educate children as to what these canine signals mean. They are less likely then to approach a dog who is giving off warning signals and may be likely to bite.

13. Describing licks as ticklish rather than intrusively frightening allows your child to think about them in a different way.

14. The idea of being able to train a dog not only stimulates a child's curiosity but allows her to experience herself as a master rather than as a frightened victim.

are times when I think I'd rather not be able to read thoughts. Some of the things people think these days . . . it's enough to turn your ears red."

Privately, Annie thought she wouldn't like to be around the Godmother when her ears turned red. She looked as if she could give someone a lot of trouble. Annie was glad she was on her side.

Bozo was looking a bit helpless now.[15] He was straining at his back legs, which were still made out of stuffed toy, and he obviously wanted to jump into Annie's lap and cuddle his mistress. Annie felt a bit sorry for him. Besides, she wanted to cuddle him too.

"*Gabbla-ka-giving, now become living,*" she said, and touched his legs and body. At once, Bozo jumped into her lap.

"Isn't he cute?" said Annie. He felt all squirmy and furry. As she bent down to pat him, he licked her nose. "Ooh," she said, a bit startled, but deciding that she liked it. "This is fun."

The Godmother looked on approvingly. "Now I'm going to teach you another spell. I'm going to teach you how to make him bigger."

"How much bigger?" said Annie, instantly. She was a bit worried by this.

"Not much bigger. Only as much as you want to."

"Oh, that's okay then," said Annie, relieved. "How do I do it?"

"Just say, '*Gabbla-ka-gibber, now become bigger.*'[16] Bozo will start to grow bigger and when he's big enough, you just say the word 'stop.' "

"That sounds easy," said Annie, and she repeated the magic words to herself.

At once Bozo's tail started to wag. He seemed to like this. Annie watched him carefully. She could see he was growing, but it was happening so slowly that you had to look hard to see it.

---

15. Bozo is helpless here, not Annie. This change of roles boosts a child's confidence and helps her make the decision to go another step forward.

16. It is important to do this slowly so that the child is not overwhelmed with anxiety but can take things a step at a time. Because the child is controlling the size of the dog, she can move at her own pace.

"Stop," she said, finally. Bozo had grown to about twice his stuffed toy size. Annie thought he looked very nice. Now that he was bigger, she could see what lovely eyes he had. They were the brown of chocolates and mud pies. Annie liked brown.

"If you could look even closer, you can see that they're blue-black in the center with a black ring around the outside," said the Godmother with her unexpected habit of reading minds.[17]

"Really?" said Annie. She looked closer. It was true. "I never knew that dogs had such nice eyes."

She patted Bozo. He wagged his tail very fast and gave her hand a lick. He was nice bigger, there was more of him to pat and his fur was so soft and warm. Annie was really beginning to like patting him.

"Now that you're used to him, would you like to make him a little bigger?" the Godmother asked. "If you get nervous, I'll tell you what to do."

"What do I do if I get nervous?" asked Annie, because she really wanted to know. It would be a big help if she knew what to do when she got nervous.[18]

"Well," said the Godmother, "when you get nervous, it's because of thoughts or pictures in your mind. When your mind makes scary pictures or thoughts, you feel nervous.[19] So, all you have to do is change the pictures or thoughts in your mind to nice ones and you'll feel better."

"That sounds easy," said Annie.

"Now what could be a happy picture that you could think of?" asked the Godmother.

"I could think about my birthday and how much fun it will be." Annie's birthday was still a few months away, but she was already planning what games she wanted to play and what sort of cake she would ask her mommy to make.

"That's a good thought," said the Godmother. "Now you're sitting here thinking about Bozo. Just imagine that you've thought Bozo into being quite big and you get a

---

17. This may intrigue the child, and perhaps she will want to see for herself.

18. Knowing how to control anxiety is a tremendous relief in itself. A good part of the horror of anxiety attacks is the sense of being powerless to stop feeling this way.

19. This is an explanation of anxiety in terms that a child can understand.

little scared by it. All you have to do is switch thoughts—like a TV channel—just start thinking about your party instead and presto—you're feeling better again. Simple, isn't it?"

"It certainly sounds easy," said Annie. "Will it really work?"

"You try it and see," said the Godmother. "Why don't you start making Bozo bigger."

So Annie said the magic words and started making Bozo grow larger and larger. When he was about half the size of a normal dog, she started to feel a little worried.

"I feel a bit worried," she said to the Godmother.

"That's okay," said the Godmother. "Now, all you have to do is put Bozo out of your mind and think about your party." Annie did.

There was a silence. The Godmother gave a little cough. "Well?" she said.

"It works!" said Annie. She had been enjoying thinking about her party so much that she had almost forgotten that the Godmother was still in the room.

"Now," said the Godmother, "I'm going to tell you another little trick. If you feel scared, just keep switching thoughts.[20] Think about Bozo, then, if you feel scared, think about the party till you feel better, then think about Bozo again, then about the party. After a while you'll find that you don't feel scared anymore when you're thinking about Bozo."

"Golly," said Annie, "will that really work?"

The Godmother drew herself up to her full height. "Did I say it would work?" she said.

"Yes," said Annie, her voice coming out in a bit of a squeak.

"Then it will work."

"Okay," said Annie, "I'll try it."

So Annie imagined Bozo. Just as before, she got a little bit scared, but she knew what to do now. She quickly switched thoughts to her birthday party. When she was feeling good again she went back to thinking about Bozo. Then she thought about the party. And, do you know, a

---

20. This explains the basic principle of desensitization, again in terms a child can understand. See Understanding Your Child, page 19, for more detail.

funny thing happened. As she kept doing it, she got less and less scared when she thought about Bozo. Finally—

"I can do it!" said Annie. "I'm thinking about Bozo and not feeling scared at all. It really works!"

"Of course," said the Godmother. She smiled kindly. "Godmothers are always right."

"What will I do now?" asked Annie.

"Go on making Bozo a bit bigger till you feel nervous again. Then you can do your trick of switching thoughts."

So Annie did. And just as it had last time, it worked beautifully.

"This is great!" said Annie, getting excited. "Can I do it again? Please. Can I make him bigger still?"

"Of course," said the Godmother. "You can do it whenever you like. Why don't you go on until Bozo is as big as Helen's dog, Buster?"

"Right," said Annie. She was enjoying this. It wasn't so bad to feel scared when you knew how to stop yourself feeling scared. She kept on doing her trick until she was imagining that Bozo was as big as Buster and standing right next to her. Annie was patting him and playing with him and she wasn't scared at all.

"That's very good," said the Godmother. "You've done that very well." She suddenly looked at her watch. "Whoops!" she said, "look at the time. It's ten past twelve. I'd better dash—I have to rescue Cinderella. That silly girl will insist on staying out too late at parties, and it's so awkward having to drag pumpkins around the street at night. I'll be back tomorrow to teach you some more things."

And she zoomed out of the window.

A minute later she was back. "I almost forgot," she said, "to tell you how to turn Bozo back into a toy."

"Gosh," said Annie. She had forgotten about that too.

"Remember, all you do," said the Godmother, "to make him smaller is to say, 'Gabbla-ka-galler now become smaller' and then, when he's the right size you say, 'Gabbla-ka-goy now become a toy' and he'll be a toy dog again."

"That sounds easy," said Annie.

And it was.

"Bye-bye," she called, as the Godmother zoomed out

of the window for the second time. "I'll see you tomorrow night!"

And the next thing she knew, it was morning.[21]

Part II

In Part II of this story, Annie is taken out to Helen's street by the Godmother. She and the Godmother slowly approach Helen's dog, Buster.

At first there is a fence between Annie and Buster. Then the fence is done away with although Buster is still restrained by a leash. Finally the leash is removed and there is free contact between the child and the dog.

The emphasis here is on the graduated approach to the final unrestrained meeting. This is something you can practice in real life after reading the Annie Story. It is important to take things step by step at a pace the child feels comfortable with. If your child starts to feel anxious during the approach you should stop and practice thought switching or any other form of comforting until she is calm again. Then you may again go forward a short distance, stopping once more if your child becomes anxious.

Be prepared to go slowly. With a really fearful child, each advance may be only a couple of footsteps closer, but that's okay. If you keep persevering in this fashion you will get there. You might pick landmarks to reach—for example, a lamppost or a tree—as goals along the way. It can be helpful to create a progress chart and give your child a gold star or some other reward as each goal is reached and mastered. Thus the task is broken up into manageable portions, and your child gets to experience success, which will bolster her confidence in her ability to make it to the final goal. Don't feel that you have to do it all in one session. Some children might respond quickly, but others may need many sessions.

Other helpful activities include drawing, painting, and making clay models of dogs, as well as looking at them in picture books and talking about them. As I mentioned in the introduction to the fear story, your child may want to draw pictures of fierce dogs and tear them up, or model a dog in clay and squash it. For her this is a symbolic way of mastering her fears and

---

21. This positive ending leaves Annie feeling excited, confident, and looking forward to more adventures with dogs.

saying to the dreaded dog, "Look, I can squash you! I'm going to be the boss over you!"

The "knee-up" technique described in the Part II story is a useful one to practice. You could play at being a dog—leaping up so that your child can practice blocking you with her knee. You could then reverse roles. As well as being fun for her, this will also give your child confidence and some very useful practice for the real thing.

Instructing your child in what various dog postures mean is worthwhile, too. For example, she should know that flattened ears and low growls mean "Don't come near me or I'll bite you."

nnie was really looking forward to bedtime that night. All day she had been thinking about what the Fairy Godmother had taught her. Sometimes she found a quiet spot and sat down and practiced imagining dogs and switching thoughts so that she felt good even when she was imagining dogs. She was very pleased to think that her imagination was such a magical, powerful thing. And besides, it was fun!

Finally bedtime came. Annie's mom tucked her in and gave her a goodnight kiss. Annie lay in bed wondering when the Godmother would arrive. She could hear all the usual sounds that she heard each evening—her mom and dad talking in the other room, a phone ringing, the rustle of the trees outside, but no Godmother. She strained her eyes, looking around the room and out of her window to see if there was any trace of blue light, but everything looked very ordinary. Finally, she fell asleep.

She woke with the blue light shining right in her eyes. The Godmother was sitting on her bed. She had a little cloth in her hand and was rubbing away at her light. She looked up as Annie woke.

"I'm just giving it a little polish," she said. "Some parts are very difficult to reach, and it's always a bit ticklish when I try to polish under the armpits. Not that anyone ever looks there anyway."

"Hello," said Annie. She wondered if all Godmothers were as funny as hers.

"I've got a great night planned for tonight," said the Godmother. "Are you ready?"

fears

"I certainly am," said Annie. "Are we going to use imagination again?"

"That's right," said the Godmother.

"Oh good!" Annie was excited. She thought she was getting very good at imagination.

"Now," said the Godmother, settling down on Annie's bed.

"Ouch!" said Annie. The Godmother had settled down on her toe.

"I'm very sorry, dear," said the Godmother, rubbing Annie's toe to make it better. "These modern beds are so narrow. In my day they used to have four posters and curtains and were so big you could have a dinner party on them. Not that we used to have dinner parties on them. Though occasionally a pea would get under the mattress, but that's another story. Now," and she settled herself back down, patting the bed first to make sure she wasn't on Annie's toe.

"This time," she said, "we're going to imagine ourselves outside the house."

"Can we fly?" asked Annie bouncing up and down. She had always wanted to fly.

"All right," said the Godmother. She held out her hand. "Hold my hand and we'll imagine that we're flying out of the window."

Annie took her hand. It was dry and smooth and warm. The sort of hand that's just right to hold.

"Here, wait," said the Godmother. "We'd better sprinkle some fairy dust on first."

Annie nodded. She had read in *Peter Pan* that children couldn't fly unless they had had fairy dust sprinkled on them first.[1]

"Hold tight, here we go!" said the Godmother as they soared out of the window and into the street.

"Oh wow..." said Annie. "This is...oh wow!"

"Oh, you get used to it," said the Godmother airily. "Here, watch this," and she tucked her legs under her and did a double backwards flip in the air.

---

1. This is a precaution that J.M. Barrie had to put in to prevent hordes of children launching themselves out of windows in attempts to fly like Peter and Wendy.

"Oh my goodness," said Annie, "I wish I could do that."

"It's a lot easier in the air than it is on the ground. There's nothing to bump your head on for one thing. Why don't you try it?"

So Annie did. It felt terrific. It was like swimming, except better because you didn't get wet and you didn't have to worry about getting water up your nose.

"Hey, I can see Helen's street." Annie pointed downwards. All the streets were laid out so that they looked like little Lego streets. The buildings had different colored roofs as if they had all put on hats and were going to a party. "Things look different from up here," said Annie.

"That's right," said the Godmother. "Sometimes when you look at something from a different angle it looks completely different. All sorts of things that really seemed big to you can seem quite small when you look at them in a different way."

Annie thought that sounded very interesting. She wondered if problems worked that way too.

"Yes they do," said the Godmother, reading her thoughts as usual. Annie could never get over her surprise at this. She was glad her mom couldn't read her thoughts —it could really get you into trouble.

"We're going down for a landing now," said the Godmother. "Hold tight," and she held out her hand.

"We're right in Helen's street," said Annie looking around her.

"That's right," said the Godmother. "Let's just walk along until we catch sight of her house."

"There it is," said Annie. It was a dark brown brick house with a green wire fence all around it. She could see a brown shape lying like a big mop just inside the fence. That was Buster.[2]

"What are we going to do?" asked Annie.

"We could practice some more thought switching if you want to."

---

2. This is the beginning of a slow approach to Buster. It uses the same desensitizing techniques used in Part I—that is, start with something comfortable and work your way closer and closer.

"Oh goodie," said Annie. She liked doing this. It was fun.

"Now," said the Godmother, "we'll just walk along here on the footpath to Helen's house. If you think you're getting too close to Buster, just say 'stop.'"

"Okay," said Annie.

They walked along. Buster was fast asleep behind the high fence. Annie didn't feel at all scared. She was very excited.

Just before the fence they stopped. Annie looked at Buster. His paws were twitching as he slept as if his toes were doing a little dance in the air.

"Why is he doing that ?" Annie asked.[3]

"He's doing that because he's dreaming," said the Godmother. "He's probably dreaming that he's chasing cats."

"He looks funny with his paws doing that," said Annie, "as if he's doing a little dance on his back."

"I wonder what he'd look like in a ballerina dress," said the Godmother, and she made a picture in Annie's mind.[4] It was a picture of Buster tip-toeing around on his hind legs in a fairy dress, trying to be a ballerina.

Annie laughed. "He really looks funny." Buster's feet twitched even more, as if he were imagining it too.

"Now," said the Godmother, "I'm going to cast a spell. He's not much good to us asleep," she explained, "and this is a spell to wake him up. Would you like to cast it?"[5]

"Oh," said Annie, "I've never cast a spell before. How do I do it?"

"Well," said the Godmother, "this is a spell-spell. It means that before you cast it, you have to spell it. Here it is." And she handed Annie a funny brown thing like an old, wrinkled walnut. Along its side, in gold, shiny letters, was written 'WAKE-UP SPELL.'

---

3. The more intrigued children are by canine characteristics, the more interested they will be in seeing for themselves.

4. Here, humor is used again to bring Buster down to less frightening proportions.

5. This puts Annie in control of waking Buster up. The more in control a child feels, the more confident she will be.

"Now I'll say the letters," said the Godmother, "and you can repeat them after me."

"All right," said Annie, and she repeated the letters. She was enjoying holding the spell. It jumped about in her hand as if it was full of bouncy magic.

"Why is it like that?" she asked. The spell had nearly bounced out of her hand.

"Because it's a wake-up spell, of course," said the Godmother. "You wouldn't expect a wake-up spell just to lie around doing nothing."

That made sense, thought Annie.

"Now that we've spelled the letters out," said the Godmother, "all you have to do is cast it."

"How do you do that?" asked Annie.

"Just throw it up in the air," said the Godmother. "You've thrown things before, haven't you?"

"Oh," said Annie, "I didn't know you meant like that."

"Go on, it's easy," said the Godmother.

Annie threw the spell. Actually she hardly needed to throw it at all because it practically sprang out of her hand. It flew up in the air above Buster's head and then came down very gently just behind his right ear. There was a sudden flash, as if someone had switched a flash-light on and off, and then Buster started to stir and open his eyes. He lifted his hind foot to behind his right ear and began to scratch with a puzzled look on his face.

Then he saw Annie. He started to wag his tail madly and bark and press his nose to the fence. He obviously wanted to greet Annie but, of course, he couldn't get past the gate.

Annie felt good.[6] It was interesting to watch Buster without being frightened of him. She liked it.

"I'm not frightened," she said to the Godmother, "so I don't even have to switch thoughts this time."

"That's very good," said the Godmother. "Look, I've got another spell that you might enjoy."

"Oh good," said Annie. These spells were fun.

"This is a listening spell," said the Godmother, and she

---

6. This is providing a good model for your child—someone like her who now finds she can enjoy being near a dog.

flicked her fingers and produced a pair of earphones.

"What do they do?" said Annie. "What do I listen to?"

"These are very special. When you put them on, you can hear animals' thoughts."

"Wow!" said Annie. "Can I try them?"

"Here," said the Godmother, "but first you have to say the magic words:

Buster, Buster
I'm not flustered
By your paws or jumps or snorts.
Here I am as keen as mustard.
Give me pause now for your thoughts.

All at once the earphones started crackling, and a deep, purry-growly voice came through them.

Annie jumped—she was so startled. Then she realized she was hearing Buster's thoughts.

"She's such a nice little girl," the voice was saying. "I like Annie a lot. I wish she'd play with me now."[7] Then the voice sounded sad. "But she never plays with me. I think she doesn't like me." Then the voice brightened up. "Maybe if I jump up and down a lot and bark so that she notices me, she'll play with me. Oh I hope she does. It's horrible to have no one to play with."

"Gosh," said Annie. "Do you mean that Buster's really thinking that?"

"If that's what the earphones are saying, then that's what he's thinking," said the Godmother.

"I never knew he felt so sad when I didn't play with him," said Annie.

"Well, he was talking to you in dog language, and you couldn't understand him."

"Poor Buster," said Annie. "It's awful when people won't play with you." She knew because sometimes at school, kids left her out of their games.[8]

She leaned forward to the gate and put her hand there. Buster poked his tongue through and gave it a lick.

---

7. This gives your child a different perspective on Buster's behavior. What she has always interpreted as aggression, she can now reinterpret as a wish to be played with.

"That feels nice," said Annie, "just as it did when Bozo licked me."

"Why don't we go inside?" said the Godmother. "I'll just fly over the fence and put Buster's leash on so that he doesn't get into the street when you open the gate."

"All right," said Annie. She could hear Buster's voice in the earphones. It was saying, "Oh, goodie, Annie's coming inside. Oh, I do hope she'll play with me. I feel so miserable when she won't play with me. Nobody plays with me. And I try my best to be playful. I don't think they like me. Boo, hoo, hoo."

"Poor Buster," said Annie. "I never knew he felt like that."

"You can come inside now," said the Godmother. She was inside the garden holding Buster on a bright red leash.[9]

Annie opened the gate and walked towards Buster. He was very excited to see her. He strained his head towards her to give her a lick, jumping up and down in his excitement. Annie reached out and gave his head a pat. "Good dog, Buster," she said, "good dog."

"Oh," said the voice in the earphones, "I'm so excited! Annie's playing with me. This is the best day of my whole doggie life!" And Buster jumped up so that his paws touched Annie's shoulders. In the past Annie would have been frightened by this, but now she knew that this was only Buster's way of trying to give her a doggie hug, so she wasn't scared at all.

"If you don't want him to jump at you," said the Godmother, "I can tell you what to do."

"Oooh," said Annie, "is it another spell?"

"Well, sort of," said the Godmother. "It's not a fairy type spell though. It's the sort of spell an ordinary human, even children, can do. I call it the knee-up spell."

"Well, how do you do it?" asked Annie. She was very curious.

"It's easy," said the Godmother. "If you want to stop a dog jumping up at you, all you have to do is put one knee

---

8. Annie is now able to empathize with Buster instead of fearing him.

9. Still going along with the desensitization, this is closer than having the fence between them but is not as frightening as encountering a dog without a leash.

up in the air as if you are just about to take a big, high step.[10] When the dog jumps up at you to give you a hug, your knee gets in the way and gives him a knock on his tummy. Your knee is much harder that his soft tummy, you know, so he'll soon stop jumping up if you keep putting your knee up."

"Well, that's handy to know," said Annie. "Maybe the next time he jumps up at me, I'll try it. Actually," she went on because she just had an idea, "why don't you take the leash off so that I can try it right now?"

And she did.

And it worked!

"This is great!" said Annie. She wanted to stay and play with Buster. "What a wonderful night it's been."[11] And then suddenly she gave a great big yawn.

"I can see that you're a bit sleepy," said the God-mother. "We'd better get you back to bed." She held out her hand. "Off we go," she said. "We can come back another time, or better still, you could get your mom to take you tomorrow."

"What a good idea," said Annie, and they whizzed off home to bed.

The next morning Annie woke up feeling terrific. She had learned so much and felt so much better about dogs. She would always remember it. Suddenly she had a great idea.

"I know what I want to wear to Helen's fancy dress party," she announced to her mother.

"What?" said Annie's mom.

"I'm going to go as a dog," said Annie.

And she did.

Can you guess who won first prize for the best fancy dress costume?

Yes, it was Annie in her dog outfit, barking happily and leaping at everyone in sight![12] "I'm glad the God-

---

10. This is an effective practical method for coping with bouncy dogs!

11. This is the positive ending with Annie providing a very good, successful model for your child to follow.

12. Pretending to be a dog can also help children work out their fears through the natural mechanisms of play. See Understanding Your Child, page 19, for more detail.

mother didn't teach Mom about the knee-up spell," she thought as she leaped up at her mother and gave her a great big hug.

One mother's success

Some time ago, I received the following letter from a mother who had read an article I wrote on Annie Stories. In it she describes how she used a variation on the fear of dogs story.

I have used an Annie Story to help my son Steven overcome his fear of dogs. For what seemed like an eternity, I tried all kinds of reasoning why he shouldn't be afraid of dogs, but nothing worked faster than putting it into story form. One night as I tucked him into bed I asked him if he would like to hear the story about Sam and his dog Ben's secret, which began:

"Once upon a time, there was a boy called Sam who had big dog called Ben. In fact Ben was the BIGGEST dog in the whole neighborhood. When Sam took Ben for walks down the street, people would take one look at Ben and cross over the road just so they wouldn't have to walk past him.

"Ben had big, long, sharp teeth, long pointy ears, and a big loud bark that used to make cats run up trees.

"Other dogs would never bark at Ben because they were afraid of such a big dog, and they would always let Sam and Ben walk past without even a whimper.

"But they didn't know Sam and Ben's secret. One day, a little dog, who wasn't afraid of anybody, rushed towards Ben barking furiously. Well, Ben took one look at him and ran for his life in the other direction! Yes, Ben, the BIGGEST dog in the neighborhood, with big, long, sharp teeth, long, pointy ears, AND a big loud bark that made cats run up trees, was really afraid of other dogs!"

Well, Steven was amazed that a big dog could be afraid, and I could actually see his body relaxing the more he thought about it. I went on to explain that he should always ask the dog's owner first before he patted a strange dog and how he should always be gentle. He was happy with that, and the difference in him has been incredible.

a new baby in the family

for most children, the arrival of a baby brother or sister carries the same sort of overtones that the arrival of the ice age did for the dinosaurs. It heralds the dawning of a new age and, certainly for the dinosaurs, not a good new age. It signals the end of their reign as the master race. Just as these lords of the landscape were forced to give way to the newer and smaller species, so, often, does the child feel that she is being squeezed out in order to accommodate the newest and smallest member of the family.

Very often, when parents are asked why they had another child, they will reply, "So that little Johnny, or Janet, can have a brother or sister. . . ." In their heads are the visions of a loving, caring, protective twosome who amuse each other, share unhesitatingly, and spend their days in a haze of love and harmony. This description, of course, is going a little over the top. But then so do many parents in their expectation of what a normal sibling relationship should be like.

It's true that many siblings share deep bonds of love and

caring. That as they grow older, they are remarkably supportive and nourishing of each other. That these are bonds which will never be broken.

However, many siblings grow up in an atmosphere where each is seen as the natural enemy, where competition is akin to survival, and where liking and trust are foreign notions.

Why is this so? Well, just for a moment, put yourself in the child's shoes.

You and your spouse have a wonderful marriage. You only have eyes for each other. You are the sun in each other's skies. You have been blissfully and solely immersed in each other for some years now and in your mind will continue to be so until the end of your days.

Suddenly, one evening, your husband comes home. "Darling!" he shouts, "I have wonderful news!"

"Yes?" you respond eagerly. Has he bought tickets to Acapulco? A honeymoon hideaway on Hawaii? A romantic rendezvous in Paris? You wait eagerly for his reply. You know it must be something very special because he is so excited. You haven't seen him so excited since the day you got married. What ever can it be?

"Yes darling," he says, "wonderful news! I've brought home a new wife!"

As you attempt to regain consciousness, your husband continues.

"Because she's new, she'll need a lot of special attention, so I'll be moving her into our own bedroom, and you can sleep out in the study. I'm dying for you to see her. She's so young and sweet and helpless—you'll just adore her. Because she doesn't know much yet, she's going to need a lot of my time, but I know you won't mind that—you're such a mature, competent person, you don't really need me all that much. And I know you're going to love taking care of her and sharing your clothes and friends and make-up with her. You're just going to adore her! Aren't you excited, darling! Darling? Darl . . . ? Aaargh!"

Enough said?

Sibling rivalry is normal and natural. Each child experiences her own particular stress in relation to her position in the family. The eldest child has to deal with the sudden dethronement she experiences at the birth of a sibling. The younger siblings have to cope with feelings of envy and inferiority as they see the eldest display the skills and privileges which are denied to them because of the insurmountable obstacle of their age and status.

Siblings are often in competition for space, possessions, achievements, individual identities, and parental love and attention. They may be totally different in personality—not the sort each would ever choose as a friend—and yet be forced to live together in a relationship far closer than friendship. Try as they may, there is no escape from this relationship.

Perhaps the astonishing thing about sibling relationships is not that they contain so much negativity, but that so many siblings are able to touch their relationships with the Philosopher's Stone—that magic transformer which alchemists believed was able to turn base metal into gold. Out of the darker emotions of jealousy, greed, fear, and anger, they can bring forth altruism, generosity, supportiveness, and love.

Such a transformation does not happen magically, of course. It requires time and effort on the part of the siblings—support and understanding on the part of the parents.

Lay the foundations for a good relationship by carefully preparing your child for the birth of a sibling. Don't paint an erroneous picture of an instant playmate, for instance, and don't expect that your child's reaction to the new baby will necessarily be the same as yours. It is common for children to show signs of stress at this time. They may regress to more babyish ways or become extra demanding or naughty.

Allow your child to show her feelings about the new situation. Play and artwork offer means of expression for children who are not very verbal.

Don't insist that your child express only positive feelings for the baby. This may be inducing the child to simply disguise her negative feelings. Such a child will often be seen to be "hugging her baby sister to death." In other words, squeezing her so hard, under the guise of "cuddling," that the baby cries, or tickling her so aggressively that the baby is upset. Let her know that it is normal to have angry feelings, but not permissible to hurt the baby. Introduce her instead to ways she can let off such aggressive "steam" harmlessly. For example, she might act it out with her dolls or kick a cushion around. Always reassure her of your continuing love.

The more secure each child feels in the love of her parents and in her special place in the family, the easier she will find it to resolve the conflicts of siblinghood. If she is confident in herself as a person and in her parents' interest in and love for her, she will feel less threatened by the competition, that is, her sibling. If she feels inferior, neglected, or unloved, she will find it much harder to tolerate the constant comparisons she must make between her lot and her brother's or sister's. She may fight even harder to retain what scrap she sees herself as possessing of parental attention, or she may give up the fight and retreat into depression, resentfulness, or self-deprecation.

Children need to know they are loved and valued as individuals. They do not need to be treated in exactly the same way— they are not exactly the same people. What is right for one will be wrong for the other. They do need to feel, however, that they are each being treated fairly. One of the catch-cries of childhood is, "But that's not fair..." Nothing you do will ever stop these cries of protest. They're almost mandatory, like catcalls to an umpire at a baseball game, and tend to be fairly equally distributed among siblings. What I am talking about is the deeper sense of "unfairness" revolving around the "Cinderella" position in family life. If one child truly feels she is the black sheep and scapegoat, to mix metaphors, of the family, life is going to be neither happy nor harmonious for her or her family.

The concern with a balance and a fair share is illustrated in the drawing my daughter produced in response to this story. She spontaneously drew what she described as a "weighing machine" on the desk, even though it isn't mentioned in the story and there are no scales on any of our real-life desks that she might have used as models.

Sibling rivalry also tends to be more or less intense depending on such factors as the gender and age gap of the siblings. Siblings of the same sex who are close together in age tend to be more rivalrous.

"She's pretty," said Mom. "She's great," said Dad.

With a large age gap, the older sibling has already had a satisfying share of her parents' sole attention and is branching out to a life of greater independence, with friends and school playing an important part in her life. If her new sibling is much younger, the ages and stages they go through are too far apart to offer as much chance for comparison as that in a relationship where both are very close in age and are striving after the same developmental goals. Psychologists usually suggest that a minimum age gap of three years between children provides the best environment.

Siblings of the same sex tend to be more competitive than opposite sex siblings who can see themselves, by virtue of their difference, as each occupying a separate section of the turf.

Although sibling relationshps do contain the seeds of destructive emotions, they can also provide the challenge that enables children to resolve their conflicts and rise above them in the creation of loving and lasting bonds. They can teach them how to cope with the various hurdles that life will set in their way, such as losing, fighting, and envying, and become stronger through coping with them.

Some of the ways in which parents can help are by giving each child a firm and loving sense of her special place in the family and in their affections. They can encourage each child's particular strengths and abilities without comparing her to the other. Comparisons invite rivalry and competition.

They can respect the need that each child has for her private space and possessions. Personal possessions are important to children—they are part of their sense of identity, and it can be very upsetting to them if siblings are constantly making off with or damaging their special things. You wouldn't like it if your neighbor kept taking your car out and forgetting to bring it home or leaving the headlights on all night. Insist that children ask permission before borrowing or playing with each other's possessions. This saves the owner from feeling in constant danger of being invaded and robbed.

It is generally more helpful for parents to avoid the role of judge and jury in the resolution of children's fights. Many fights are staged at some level to gain your attention. If you buy into that, you complete a triangle, and triangles are notoriously difficult to resolve. It is usually preferable to leave the children to sort it out themselves. If violence or constant verbal jeering and abuse is involved, you should make it clear that these behaviors are not tolerated in your household.

Finally, particularly where small children are concerned, love is often thought of as something akin to an apple pie. If one slice is given to someone else, then that leaves less for them. If everyone can feel secure with her share of the love pie and understand that it is infinite, everything else is much easier to overcome.

The story that follows is aimed at the child who is already suffering from feelings of resentment and jealousy about the new baby. Annie's feelings mirror her anger and unhappiness prior to coming to terms with the new situation. If your child is not experiencing such feelings or if you are telling her a story prior to the new baby's birth, tone down Annie's negative feelings. You don't want to make your child feel that she *has* to be resentful or enraged about the new baby. But don't sugarcoat the situation in the manner discussed earlier.

nnie was a little girl who lived in a brown brick house with her mommy and daddy and a big black dog.[1]

She had a little cousin, Peter, who was only two years old. He wasn't even old enough to be going to nursery school. Annie could tell when she was with him that he thought she was very big and grown-up. And very smart, too, because she could do so many more things than he could. She could count properly, she could do up her shoelaces, she could dress herself, and she could draw and paint better than he could. Annie liked feeling clever and grown-up—it made her feel that she was special and important. Annie's mom told her that Peter was always telling his little friends about his clever cousin Annie and that he thought she could do anything better than anyone else in the whole wide world.

One day when Annie and her mom and dad were having dinner, her mom said to her, "I've got some news for you, Annie. We're going to be having a new baby in the family in a few months' time."

"Oh," said Annie. She didn't know quite what to say.

"Where's it coming from?" she asked. She thought maybe Mom meant she was going to borrow it from somewhere, or perhaps she had been asked by a friend to look after it for a while.

Her dad laughed. "It's in your mommy's tummy,

---

1. For this section, change the details to suit your own environment.

Annie—it's going to be our family's baby. A little brother or sister for you."

Annie looked at her mommy's tummy. It looked pretty normal, a bit fatter than usual perhaps, but it certainly didn't look as if it had a whole baby in it. She didn't think she liked this.

"Why do I have to have a brother or sister?" she asked. "I like things just the way they are now."[2]

"Your mom and I think it's nice for a family to have brothers and sisters in it. Sometimes it can get a bit lonely being the only child."

Annie thought for a minute. That was true. "But Eliza's got a sister, and they're always fighting. She takes all Eliza's things and she's always hanging around trying to get in on our games. Eliza gets really mad at her."

"That's true," said Annie's mom.[3] "Lot's of brothers and sisters do fight and squabble about things, and sometimes they feel they hate each other. But you know what? In between the fighting they often play with each other and care for each other and are good friends.[4] Do you remember how you told me yesterday that a bunch of little kids were picking on Eliza's sister and she went up and scared them off?"

Annie remembered Eliza had been very upset when she saw the kids teasing her sister. She had gone up to them and yelled, "Get away from my little sister, you creeps! Don't you dare pick on her like that!" Eliza's sister had looked at her with eyes that plainly said that she was the most wonderful person on earth.

Annie didn't want to talk about it anymore.[5] "Anyway," she said, "You promised me that after dinner we

2. Many children don't welcome the news of the new baby with quite the enthusiasm that their parents feel. Allow them to proceed at their own pace. Find out what they are feeling. Don't force false enthusiasm upon them.

3. It's best not to gloss things over and give children a rosy, unreal picture of sibling relationships. Many of them will have seen their friends' interactions with siblings already and are likely to have seen the squabbles and fights that can arise.

4. You can also fill in the other, more positive, side of the picture.

5. Children often need to take news like this in small doses. They'll leave it and come back to it time and time again. Often they'll ask the same questions over a period of time.

a new baby in the family

could play a game of Monopoly. Can I go and get it now?"

"Yes, darling," said her mom, and Annie ran off to get the Monopoly set. It was more fun to play Monopoly than to talk about babies.

The next day Annie was talking to her friend Alice at school. "My mom's going to have a baby," she said.

"Our baby's one month old now," said Alice.

Annie nodded. She knew that Alice's mom had just had a baby girl.

"They told me they were going to get me a baby brother or sister who would play with me," said Alice.[6] "I was really looking forward to it. I even made her a present. When Mom came home from the hospital with the baby, I didn't even get a chance to give it to her. Everyone was so busy looking at her, I couldn't even get near her. And in any case, every time I went to touch her, my mom got all nervous—like she thought I was going to break her or something. Anyway, by that time I was so mad I didn't want to give the stinky old baby a present. I was mad at my mom too. Babies don't play with you," she said glumly, "they just cry a lot and make messes in their pants."

Annie felt worried. When she got home that day she said, "I thought babies were supposed to be able to play with you. Alice says they don't. She says they're horrible. I don't want a baby in the house."

"You're feeling a bit upset by this, aren't you, Annie?" said her mom. "Come here and sit on my lap and tell me all about what Alice said to you."

When Annie and finished, her mom sat thoughtfully for a minute. "It sounds like Alice was very angry at her baby and at her mom and dad."

"She sure was," said Annie.

"You know, a lot of kids feel like that when a new baby comes into the house.[7] Sometimes they feel as if the

---

6. Many parents use this enticing description to announce the arrival of a new baby brother or sister. It is misleading, as the child then expects a fully grown playmate to arrive back from the hospital with Mom. Babies by no means fit this bill.

7. Let your child know that many children feel angry or rejected after the new baby comes home. It stops your child from thinking she is the only one in the world with such mean and nasty feelings.

baby's taken their place and their parents don't care about them anymore. They can get jealous because sometimes people pay a lot of attention to the baby and not enough attention to them anymore. They think their mom and dad have taken away some of the love they gave to them and given it to the baby instead. That makes them feel very unhappy."

"But isn't it true?" said Annie. She had a horrible feeling in her tummy. She didn't want her mom and dad taking any of their love away from her, not even if it was only the tiniest, weeniest bit that they took away. She wanted it all.

"It's not really true," said her mom. "You see, children tend to think that love is like a big juicy apple pie."

Annie nodded. She loved apple pie. Especially with ice cream on it.

Her mom continued, "They think that if two people share the pie then they each get less than the whole pie.[8] They sometimes get very jealous watching to see who gets a bigger slice of the pie because they think it means that if someone gets the bigger half, then they must have the smaller half."

"Halves aren't meant to be smaller or bigger," said Annie importantly. "Halves are supposed to be exactly the same. Our teacher told us so last week."

"You're right, Annie," said her mother, "I should have said piece instead of half. Kids think that if someone else gets the bigger piece then it means that they're left with the smaller piece. But they're wrong."

"They're wrong?" said Annie. She was surprised. What her mom had said had sounded quite sensible to her.

"Yes," said Annie's mom, "they're wrong because love isn't like a piece of pie. It's quite different. Love is a very magical thing. Do you remember that fairy story I read to you a while ago—the one where there is a sack full of gold coins and when you take the gold out of the sack to spend or give away, the sack just makes more gold coins for you?[9] The more you take out, the more the sack

---

8. Children do think of love in very finite and concrete terms. You should explain to them that love doesn't work this way.

9. Fairy stories offer wonderful metaphors when teaching children about life.

makes. It never stops and it can never be emptied or run out because it just keeps on filling itself up again whenever you take anything out."

"I remember that story," said Annie. She had thought that a sack like that would be very handy. It would certainly help her to buy her toy shop. That was one of the things Annie wanted to do when she grew up—she wanted to own her very own toy shop.

"Well," said her mother, "love is like that magic sack— the more you love people, the more love you have left to give them. Think of the way you love Daddy and me. You don't love me less because you also love Daddy, and you don't love Daddy less because you also love me."

"No," said Annie, "you're right. I love both you and Dad just as much as I can." She wondered why she hadn't thought of it that way before.

"And," said her mom, "when the new baby comes, we'll still love you just as much as before, even though we'll love the baby as well."

"That's good," said Annie. She felt a bit better to hear her mom say that.

"Where do you think would be a good place for the baby to sleep?" asked her mom.

"Not in my room," said Annie quickly. Her room was very special to her. It was her own private place, and she didn't want anyone else intruding.

"No," said her mom.[10] "Your room belongs to you. The baby can have one of the other rooms in the house."

"What about the laundry?" suggested Annie. The laundry was a little room way down at the back of the house.

"The laundry might be a bit small," said Annie's mom. "Also, it's pretty noisy. It would be hard to sleep comfortably in the laundry."

"That's true," said Annie.

"We were thinking of moving some of the things out

---

10. If the baby will be sharing your child's room, this part of the story will need to be modified. Try to put forward the positive side of room sharing, for example—you'll never have to worry about being alone in the dark again at night. Make sure that your child is able to stamp one side of the room as her "territory." Let her have pieces of furniture, such as a chest of drawers, that are hers alone, and so on.

of the spare room so that the baby can have that. We might have to paint it and buy some things to put in it."

"What sort of things?" asked Annie.

"A bassinet where the baby can sleep, and perhaps some colorful posters, and maybe a mobile to hang up so that the baby can look at it."

"That sounds like a lot of things," said Annie. She wanted to get a lot of things too. It wasn't fair that the baby got them all. "Can I get some things for my room too?"

"It is a lot of things," said Annie's mom. "Babies need a bit of equipment like bassinets and carriages and so on. When you were born we bought lots of stuff just for you. When you got older, you didn't need it though, so we gave it away or sold it."

"Oh," said Annie. She didn't know that she had so many things as a baby.

"Also," said her mom, "although it sounds like we'll be buying a lot of things for the baby, you would still have many more things than she or he will because you've had more years to collect them in. I was thinking, though," continued her mom, "that you and I could make some mobiles together. I thought, if you liked, we could make two mobiles, one for you and one for the baby. You could pick which one you wanted."[11]

Annie nodded. She loved making things with her mom. "That sounds great," she said. "When can we start?"

"Well," said her mom, "the baby won't be here for a long time yet, but we could start making mobiles this weekend, if you like."

"Oh good," said Annie. She was looking forward to this.

"We have to decide what colors to paint the baby's room," said Annie's mom. "Would you like to come with us to the paint shop and help us choose the colors?"

"I'd like that," said Annie. It sounded like fun. "I'm

---

11. Involving your child in making something for the unborn baby is very helpful. It gives your child some enjoyable time with you and also allows her to feel like an older benefactor to the baby—a role in which she can feel some comfortable and generous superiority.

a new baby in the family

very good at choosing colors for my dolls when I make houses for them." Annie used to make houses for her dolls out of old shoe boxes. She would decorate each box like a room and stick them on top of each other and next to each other so that they looked like a proper house.

When Annie came home from school the next day, she said to her mom, "One of the kids at school said that babies are brought by storks."[12]

"What do you think, Annie?" her mom asked.

"Well, I don't think so, because you told me how babies are made when the man puts a seed inside the woman and then the baby grows in the woman's tummy."[13]

"That's right," said her mom. "Some kids have all sorts of funny ideas about where babies come from. They think they're true, but they're not. What I told you is true."

"Charlie said you found them in cabbage patches, like Cabbage Patch Kids," said Annie.

"That would be funny," said her mom. "What if you got confused and brought back a doll instead of a baby?"

Annie laughed. "Sarah says that you buy babies in a hospital."

"No," said her mom, "you don't buy them in a hospital. Usually when it's time for the baby to come out, the mother goes to a hospital, and the doctors and nurses look after her there until the baby has come out and is ready to go home. You might pay the hospital some money for looking after you, but the baby is yours, you don't have to buy it."

"Oh," said Annie. "Will you have to go to a hospital?"

"Yes," said her mom, "only for a few days."

"Can I come too?" asked Annie. She didn't want her mom to go away without her.[14]

---

12. Children, even modern day ones, still have a fascinating variety of explanations as to where babies really come from. It's as well to clear these up with your child.

13. Explanations don't have to be complex. If your child wants to know more details, she will ask you. Often the simplest of explanations is sufficient.

14. Often, a mother's trip to the hospital is the first time she has been parted from her child overnight. Separation from the mother is usually an upsetting and disturbing event for a young child.

a new baby in the family

"I'd love to have you with me," said Annie's mom, "because I'll miss you, but the hospital wouldn't have enough room for you, or for Dad. So you'll be staying at home. Dad will be here to look after you, though, and he'll take extra special care of you."[15]

"You won't go away without telling me?" said Annie.[16]

"Of course not," said her mom. "I'll make sure I tell you before I go."[17]

"Oh good," said Annie. "When will you go into the hospital?"

"Not for a few months yet," said her mom. "I'll tell you when the time is getting close, so don't worry."

"Okay," said Annie. She felt a bit better to know that her mom wouldn't suddenly disappear without telling her. "Can we start to do the mobiles before the weekend?"

"Okay," said her mom. "Why don't you do some drawings of what you'd like the mobiles to look like?"

Annie sat down with a pencil and papers. At first she thought she might make a monster mobile for the baby's room. Then, after a while, she thought that might be too frightening for the baby. So she made funny, smiley monsters that looked as if they would laugh with you instead of big, fierce monsters that looked as if they would eat you up.

As time went by, Annie saw that her mommy's tummy was getting bigger and bigger. Her mom showed her pictures in a book about how babies grew. Annie thought they looked pretty weird. She couldn't believe that she had looked like that once.

One day when Annie's mom was reading her a story, she suddenly took Annie's hand and put it on top of her tummy.

---

15. It's important to let the child know that she will be well cared for. It is preferable if she can remain in her own house and be looked after by someone she knows and trusts.

16. Many mothers slip away to the hospital without saying goodbye to the child. This can be very distressing for the child.

17. If your child is at school or unreachable by phone when labor has progressed enough for you to go to the hospital, leave her a note or drawing before you go to let her know you remembered to say goodbye.

"Feel this," she said. "The baby's kicking."

Annie was amazed. It felt very funny, like someone pushing or kicking underneath an eiderdown quilt. "Golly," she said. For the first time she was really getting the idea that there was a real, live baby in there.

"How does the baby breathe?" she asked. "Doesn't it get squashed? And is it afraid of the dark? It must be very dark in your tummy."

"The baby doesn't breathe the way you and I do, Annie," explained her mom. "It has just enough room so that it's cozy for it. When it gets too big for my tummy, it will come out. I suppose it's dark inside tummies, but babies don't mind the dark."

"What would it feel like in there?" asked Annie.

"I don't know," said her mom. "Probably pretty nice, I would think."

Annie crawled under her bed.[18] "I'm a baby in my mommy's tummy," she announced. Then she started to crawl towards her mom—it felt a bit cramped under the bed. "I'm coming out to be born," she said, and hopped up and gave her mom a kiss.

"What a beautiful baby," said her mom. "I'm glad you were born to me."

One of Annie's dolls was having a baby.[19] She put cotton balls under its dress so that it would look big and round like her mom. Her mom was getting rather tired these days, so Annie made her doll get tired too. Sometimes she fussed over it, making it lie down in the doll's house while she tucked it in. Sometimes she got cross at it because it was too busy being tired to play enough games with its daughter doll. Sometimes she took the cotton balls out so that she could make it not pregnant.

When spring came, Annie's mom told her that she was going to have the baby in the next few weeks. Annie told her teacher. She felt very important when she announced that she was going to have a new baby very soon.

Annie's mom said to her, "When the baby's ready to

---

18. Many children will play pregnancy/birth games as they work through the emotional issues that the news of an impending baby brings. Often children will announce that they too are pregnant.

19. Dolls often play a part in these games and play-acting.

come out, I will have to go to the hospital. Usually mothers don't know exactly when the baby will be ready to be born. If it happens in the middle of the night, for instance, would you like me to wake you up to say goodbye before I go?"

"Yes," said Annie. "Please wake me up. I don't want you to go without saying goodbye."

"All right," said her mom. "If you're too sleepy to wake properly, I'll leave you a special note on the kitchen table. I'll be able to talk to you on the phone from the hospital anyway."

"Okay," said Annie. She felt a bit better to hear that.

"If it happens in the middle of the night," Annie's mom said, "Grandma will come over here to look after you so that Dad can drive me to the hospital. She will stay with you till he gets back.[20] And look, I've got a special present for you." She held out a little box.

"What is it?" Annie asked. She loved presents.

"It's a tape recording I made for you of me reading your favorite stories.[21] You can play it on the cassette recorder here. While I'm away at the hospital, whenever you want to hear me read you a story, all you have to do is play this tape."[22]

"Oh wow!" said Annie. She thought that sounded great.

Days and days went by. It seemed like a long, long time to Annie since her mom had told her that the baby would be coming soon.[23] She got tired of waiting. She decided that maybe her mom had been wrong and the baby wouldn't be coming after all.

So it came as a big surprise to her when her mom came up to her room just as she was about to go to sleep and

---

20. Make sure your child knows that there will be someone to look after her at all times.

21. A tape recording of your voice reading your child's favorite stories can provide a helpful emotional buffer in your absence.

22. If you don't have a cassette recorder, a series of notes, drawings, or tiny gifts to be unwrapped one a day while you're away will also give your child a sense of your loving presence.

23. Children have a different sense of time than adults. To them a week seems like a month and a month seems like a year. It's helpful to keep this in mind when you make announcements of impending events.

said, "Darling, I think the baby is ready to come out. Grandma is coming over, and then Dad will take me to the hospital."

"What will I do while you're in the hospital?" said Annie, feeling suddenly upset.

"Grandma and Dad will take good care of you," said her mom, "and I'll be back soon." She gave Annie a hug and a kiss. "Sweet dreams, darling. I'll see you in a few days and I'll talk to you on the phone each day." And she gave Annie another big hug and kiss.

The next morning when Annie got up and went to the kitchen, Grandma was there in her bathrobe, making a cup of tea. It felt strange to see Grandma there instead of her mom. At first Annie couldn't remember where her mom was.

"Where's Mommy?" she said, worried.

"Your mother's at the hospital, darling," said her Grandma, "and she's just had a lovely baby girl. You've got a sister."

"Oh," said Annie. She didn't know quite what to feel. It was hard to imagine her mom coming home with a sister for her. "When is she coming home?"

"Probably tomorrow, darling," said Grandma. "Now what would you like for breakfast?"

Annie missed her mom. Her mom didn't have to ask her what she wanted. She knew.

The next day, Daddy came home from visiting Mommy at the hospital. He had a photo with him. "Look," he said to Annie. "Do you want to see a photo of your new sister?"

Annie looked. The photo showed a bundle of white with a little red face poking out. Mommy was in the photo too. She was smiling at the baby as if the baby were the most beautiful thing on earth. Annie felt very left out.

The next day Daddy announced at breakfast, "Mommy's coming home today." Annie was very excited. Now everything can get back to normal, she thought.[24] She

---

24. Children find it hard to conceptualize beforehand what difference a new baby will really make to the household. They often hold the fantasy that once Mommy comes home, everything will magically settle back to being just the way it was before.

gave Grandma an extra hug just to show that it wasn't her Annie had been sad about. It was just Mommy being away that had upset her.

Annie started to make Mommy an extra special drawing. Mommy loved her drawings. She would hang them on the walls and sometimes people who came to visit would say how nice they were and what a clever girl Annie must be.

Annie thought that if she did an extra special drawing for her mom, she would see how special Annie was and look at her the way she and Dad had looked at the baby. The people who came to the house would also see what a special and clever girl Annie was.

Annie waited with excitement to hear the sound of Daddy's car driving up. He had gone to pick up Mom an hour ago, and Grandma said he should be back any minute. She knew her mom would just love her drawing. She would pin it up in the kitchen the way she always did and when friends came she would show it to them and be very proud of her daughter.

Suddenly there was the sound of a car. Mommy was home! Annie looked out of the window. Mommy and Daddy were walking up the path. Mommy was carrying the baby. Annie rushed to the door.

"Hi Mommy!" she said. "Look what I did for you!" and she pushed her drawing at her mom.

"Annie!" said her mom, "I missed you, darling! It's so nice to be home again." And she bent and gave Annie a big kiss. She couldn't give her a hug because her arms were full of baby. She couldn't take the drawing either because her hands were busy holding the baby. Daddy took the drawing instead.

"Look at your baby sister, darling," she said. "Say hello to her."

Annie bent down and looked at her. She looked wrinkled and ugly, Annie thought. Why would anyone want one of those?

Inside the house, Daddy put Annie's drawing down on the table. Her mother didn't even look at it again. "Let's put Cindy to bed," she said. "Would you like to help, Annie?"

Annie brightened up. She loved helping her mom.

a new baby in the family

"Why don't you straighten out that blanket in the bassinet," her mom said, "and then you can help me change Cindy's diaper."[25]

Annie's mom laid Cindy down on her changing table. "Now, I'll do the wiping," she said, "and you can help me by wetting balls of cotton and handing them to me. That will be a great help."

It felt very good to be such an important helper to her mom.

Cindy had her eyes open and was looking around her. She had very big eyes and she particularly seemed to like looking at Annie. She waved her little hands around while she looked.

They were the tiniest hands Annie had ever seen. Annie touched one. It was amazingly soft and silky. Annie had never felt hands like that. Cindy curled her fingers over Annie's as if she had been waiting to hold them for a long, long time. She kicked and babbled. She looked happy.

Afterwards, Annie's mom said, "Thank you Annie, that was a big help." Then she clapped her hands together and said, "Oh! I nearly forgot. I've got a present for you!"

"Oh wow!" said Annie. She was really excited. "What is it?"

"Here it is," said her mom, handing her a big box.

Annie tore the wrapping off. It was a big baby doll.[26] It came with diapers and a bottle, a little bar of soap, a bib, and a baby blanket.

"That's great!" said Annie. "I'm going to call her Veronica." That was the name Annie had thought her parents should call Cindy. "I'm going to change her diaper," she said, and dashed off to the bathroom with Veronica.

Annie had thought that when her mom came home, everything would go back to normal. But it didn't.

The reason was—Cindy. If Cindy didn't need her dia-

---

25. Allowing the child to help you with the new baby is a very positive move. Your child feels useful and important instead of being on the outside looking in. It also helps her in developing a relationship with the baby.

26. A baby doll is an excellent present at a time like this. It provides a medium for the child to act out and work through her feelings and fantasies about the new baby.

per changed, she needed to be fed; if she didn't need to be
fed, she needed to be put to sleep; if she didn't need to be
put to sleep, she needed to be played with, and so on, and
so on. In the rare times when her mom wasn't doing
anything with Cindy, she was so tired that she didn't have
the energy to play with Annie the way she used to. Annie
hated Cindy.[27]

"Why don't you take her back to the hospital?"[28] she
said. "She's ruining everything. No one ever has time to
do anything anymore." What she really meant was: "No
one ever has the time to notice me anymore—I feel really
miserable. If Cindy weren't here, people would go back to
loving me the way they used to."

"Come here, Annie," said her mom. She held out her
arms and sat Annie on her knee. "I know you feel really
angry at Cindy some of the time.[29] I know you sometimes
feel as if you really hate her. Lots of boys and girls feel like
that when they first get a baby brother or sister. They
think that because of the new baby, their mom and dad
don't love them anymore."

Annie nodded her head.

"Do you remember what I told you about love?" said
her mom, "about its not being like a piece of pie and that
there's more than enough love for *everyone* in the family?"

Annie nodded again.

"Well, Dad and I still love you just as much as before.[30]
Lately I haven't been spending as much time with you as I
used to, but it doesn't mean that I love you less. It's just
that babies are very helpless, and looking after them
takes time. But if you ever feel you need some extra loving
and attention, all you have to do is just come to us and tell
us, and we'll give it to you."[31]

---

27. Put this in only if your child is already feeling this way.

28. This is a very common reaction to a new baby.

29. Let children know that you understand and accept their feelings.

30. Children need reassurance about this.

31. Tell your children that when they feel neglected or deprived, they can
simply ask for more of your loving attention—they should not need to "play up"
to get it.

Annie felt a bit better to hear that.

"You know," her mom went on, "some children think that the only way they can get that extra attention is by being bad or silly or being like a little baby themselves. But you don't need to do that. All you have to do is tell us that you want a little more loving and attention."

That afternoon, when Mom was feeding Cindy, Annie felt a bit left out. "You told me to tell you when I wanted some extra attention, Mom," she said, and she tried to climb up on her mom's lap.

Her mom gave her a kiss. "Are you feeling a bit left out?" she said. "Well, as soon as I've finished feeding Cindy, you could help me change her diaper and then we'll play a game together, okay?"

Annie nodded. She felt better.

"Why don't you feed Veronica now?" Mom said, "and then when we've finished feeding, it'll be time to change the diaper."

"Okay," said Annie, and she ran off to get Veronica.

Sometimes Annie got very cross with Cindy. Once she was so cross that she smacked her.[32] Her mother stopped her immediately. "I know that you're angry at Cindy," she said, "but you mustn't hit her. If you feel so angry that you need to let off some steam, you can bat the cushion or Punchinello, your rollover punching doll. Just as Daddy and I would not let anyone hurt you, we won't let anyone hurt Cindy. So you are not allowed to pinch her or shake her or smack her or do anything to hurt her. I know that there'll be times when you feel so angry at her that you want to hurt her, but you must stop yourself from doing that and do other things instead."

"What other things could I do?" asked Annie.[33] She was interested.

"You could come and tell Dad or me about being angry," said her mom. "Sometimes that can help you feel better. You could stomp up and down in the backyard or kick your beach ball around—sometimes stomping or

---

32. Make sure your child understands that while you can accept that she may be angry at the baby, she is not allowed to hurt her.

33. You can teach your child that there are other allowable methods of giving vent to aggressive feelings.

kicking balls helps get rid of the angry feelings. It's okay to kick balls or cushions or leaves on the sidewalk. It's not okay to kick pets or babies or other people."

"What else could I do?" asked Annie.

"You could throw tennis balls at the fence or make water bombs in paper bags and watch them go splat in the garden as you hurl them at things."[34]

"I like that one," said Annie

"I thought you would," said her mom and gave her a hug.

"Another thing you could do," said her mom, "is make drawings or paintings about being angry. Or you could make clay families and be angry with them."

"I'm good at making clay models," said Annie. She loved to paint and draw and model.

Cindy started crying. Her mother picked her up. "I think it's time to feed her," she said.

Annie went to her room and picked up Veronica. She yelled at her. "Naughty baby!" she said. "You're always crying and taking up people's time. Naughty baby!" and she put her in a corner so that she would know what it was like to feel left out.

Later that day she gave Veronica a big hug. "I'll take care of you now," she said. And she gave Veronica a bath and put her to bed. She felt like a very kind mother.

One day Annie's mom was doing something in the kitchen when Cindy started crying. "Will you play with her, Annie?" she asked. "See if you can stop her crying."

Annie went up to Cindy. She was lying in her baby bouncer looking very upset. Her arms and legs were kicking around and she was very red in the face.

Annie came close and smiled at her the way she had seen her mother do. She held out the rattle she had picked up. Cindy instantly stopped crying and gave Annie a big smile. Annie smiled back even harder. Cindy looked at her as if she was the most wonderful thing in the world. Annie gave the rattle a jingle and Cindy chuckled with joy.

---

34. Think of some ways of doing this that would be appropriate to your particular household.

"You know, Mom," said Annie.[35] She had just realized something. "I think Cindy likes me."

"Didn't you know that?" said her mom. "Cindy thinks you're absolutely terrific. You're her big sister. She's fascinated by you. You're not an adult, but you can do everything better than she can and you can do so many more things than she can. She would love to be able to do things just as well as you."

"Really?" said Annie. "You mean just like my cousin Peter?"

"Yes," said her mom. "Just like Peter."

"Gosh," said Annie. "I never knew that." She felt pleased. She felt a little bit sorry for Cindy too, because she knew that Cindy would always be younger than she, so she would always know more and be able to do more than Cindy. Poor Cindy. Perhaps she might even teach her some things, the way she sometimes taught Peter things. She liked teaching people. Maybe she would even be a teacher when she grew up.

"Maybe I'll teach you some things," said Annie to Cindy and waved the rattle again.[36] Cindy gurgled with delight and smiled. Annie smiled back. Cindy could be a pest, she thought, but she sometimes could also be fun. Maybe having a sister wasn't going to be so bad after all.

35. This is a very positive realization for older siblings. Babies usually do think their older siblings are absolutely the greatest.

36. This is the positive ending, suggesting that even though the situation has some drawbacks, there are also good aspects to be found that can make it all worthwhile.

first days at nursery school

tarting school is a momentous occasion for most children, an entry into a whole new world. As with anything else, children will react to this in their own different ways, depending on their personalities and particular circumstances. A lot has been written on how to minimize your child's distress on her first days of school or nursery school. Within such pieces of advice there is often the implicit assumption that starting school is an inevitably distressing event that should be approached by the parent with trepidation and the assumption that they could scar their child for life should they slip up on this job. Such predictions of doom are, of course, totally invalid.

For many children, starting school is a longed for and exciting event. It is stressful, to be sure, but only in the sense that going to the circus is stressful. It's very exciting and demands a lot of emotional energy, but is not particularly anxiety producing. These children are likely to be the ones who react to new situations with enthusiasm and curiosity and are confident and outgoing. Sometimes if you prepare this sort of child for school in a very protective way, stressing, for instance, that you'll stay with them awhile, they may start to wonder what the hidden catch is and why they need to be so protected. With this sort of child, taking them into the classroom, introducing them to their new teacher and waving a cheery good-bye may be all you need to do .

On the other hand, if you have a child who is slow to warm up to new situations, a different strategy might be more appropriate. The slow-to-warm-up child takes time to feel confident in new situations and will usually respond best if eased into them gradually. Thus a program of staying with them a certain amount of time the first day, less the second, less again on the third, and so on may be the most helpful strategy to adopt. This allows your child to get her bearings slowly with the security of your presence, so that by the time you leave her completely alone, the environment will already be somewhat familiar to her, and she'll be able to cope much better with your absence.

Some nursery or kindergarten teachers encourage the parents to stay with the child on the first few days. There are some children, however, for whom this may be problematic. These are the ones who pick up new routines the way wet concrete picks up paw prints. Once they're imprinted, it takes a lot of extra work to change them. Such a child may feel quite comfortable about going to nursery school alone but if accompanied by a mother who stays on for the first few days, may quickly define nursery school, as a mother-child experience, and refuse to accept anything less! It's usually best to start these children off in the manner to which they are going to have to become accustomed. This may apply even to the child who is shy about starting. If this child is the type who latches on to habits with the tenacity of an obsessional crab, staying with her over a period of days may simply be prolonging and increasing the eventual agony of parting.

If you are working, for instance, and are unable to stay with your child on the first day, prepare her for this beforehand, both within the story and as you tell her the nursery school routine.

Practice by leaving your child with friends, relatives, or babysitters for periods of a couple of hours well before her first leave-taking of you at school. The first day at the nursery is much more traumatic for your child if she has never been parted from you before. This does not mean that you have to go off and leave her for a week in order to get her used to it, but rather that you let her get accustomed to being away from you for small intervals of time.

Children will also vary as to how they settle into the new

routine. Just because your child spends a lot of time watching the others instead of joining in doesn't mean she has to be rushed off to a psychologist. She may be a slow warmer-up who is perfectly happy and well-adjusted. She simply likes to take time to size up new situations. Just because you wouldn't be happy sitting on the sidelines for days doesn't mean she isn't. There is a tendency to equate gregariousness and energetic play with "good adjustment," and we should be wary of this. A quieter child who is more in tune with solitary activities can be just as well-adjusted as the outgoing socializer.

For many children nursery school is the first big arena where they are continually exposed to a large group of their peers. They may have spent time with other children before, in play groups and so on, but here they are with the same, relatively large number of children of their own age for extended periods of time, day in and day out. Put any group of animals in this situation and you start to see the social structures and strata of groups forming. Children are no exception.

For some children it is easy to find a favored or prestigious position in the group. For others it is more difficult. Perhaps the most important aspect though is that the child be comfortable with her position in the peer group culture. This does not necessarily involve being the most popular child at school or the brightest or the natural leader. Many children, whose parents are urging them on to become Chiefs while bewailing their lack of progress, are perfectly happy being Indians.

Some children will enjoy having lots of friends; others will be content with very few. This does not sentence them to a life as an unhappy misfit. It simply means that they enjoy more solitary pursuits and are less dependent on the company of others. If they are happy as they are, allow them to continue with the path they have chosen.

Many children, however, are unhappy with the position they find themselves in with regard to their peers. Such children often feel themselves to be disliked by all or most of the group. My daughter's illustration here conveys the feeling of just how stressful this can be. Sometimes these children are in fact disliked, but sometimes the dislike is imaginary. Whichever it is, it should be examined. Talk to your child's teacher to see if your child is indeed disliked. Find out how your child approaches other children. Is she too aggressive? Is she too shy? Plan to invite schoolmates home to play. Tell your child Annie Stories which are appropriate. For instance, if your child is losing friends because she always wants her own way, let Annie discover new and more positive ways of relating to classmates. Act these Annie Stories out with you as Annie and your daugh-

"I hate you," said the little boy.
"You're dumb," said the little girl.

ter as the classmate. Then reverse roles. All this will give her positive role models to follow and helpful practice in the skills of socialization.

When you talk about school to your child, try to speak of it in a positive way so that it becomes exciting and interesting rather than something to be dreaded.

Let your child know what to expect by describing to her the sort of things she is likely to do there. If possible, visit the school beforehand to familiarize her with the layout. Be sure to point out where the toilets are. If you're packing her lunch in a lunch box, make sure it's one she can open and shut by herself. Dress her appropriately so that she'll blend in comfortably with the other children. Kids can be very cruel to someone who is "different," and you want these initial days to be as easy as possible.

Be aware too of your own feelings about separating from your child. School is a big milestone for mothers as well as children. Sometimes children who dislike school are actually reacting to their sense that Mother needs them to stay close to her.

Once upon a time there was a little girl called Annie who lived in a big brick house with a mommy and a daddy and a big black dog.[1] Annie was five years old, and sometimes she felt like a very big, important, grown-up girl who could do all sorts of things by herself, like tie her shoelaces and pick her own clothes to wear. But sometimes she felt like a tiny little girl who got scared at things and wanted to snuggle up safe and sound in her mommy's lap and never, never leave her just like a baby kangaroo in his mommy's pouch.[2]

Some of the things that made her feel big and strong and grown up were when she got dressed all by herself in the morning and picked out just the right clothes that she wanted to wear all by herself.[3] And when she played with friends who had baby sisters who couldn't even stand or walk properly, she felt very big and grown up then too.

But sometimes, when she went to a strange place or met a whole lot of new children at once, she felt very small and scared, and she would get shy and afraid that they wouldn't like her or not want to play with her or that they would laugh at her or even hurt her, and she would be all alone with no one to protect her.

So you can imagine that when she was eating breakfast one day (she liked to have corn flakes with milk and a boiled egg in a funny Humpty Dumpty egg cup with legs that always looked as if it was going to walk off the table), and her daddy said to her, "Well Annie, it's nursery school time next week," she got very, very worried.

When Annie got worried all the parts of Annie's body used to worry too, and sometimes Annie's head worried itself into a headache that went thump, thump, thump, as if there were a rabbit jumping around in it, or felt like someone was trying to put a rubber band around it. Sometimes Annie's tummy felt that it was all twisted up

---

1. When beginning your story, place it in a setting as similar to your own child's as possible.

2. Try to let the heroine mirror your child's feelings. If your child is initially nervous about the upcoming event, let the heroine also feel like this, although gaining confidence as the story progresses.

3. Although the heroine is feeling scared and nervous, take care to also highlight some of her strong points. When people feel unsure of themselves they often forget they have any strengths at all.

with worrying. Annie's daddy saw that she was looking worried, and he said to her that school would really be fun and that the kids would play with her and she would have a great time. But Annie knew that her daddy was so big and strong and could do so many things that he would never have been scared by little kids, and so of course nursery school would have been fun for him. Annie was different. She was little and shy, and she got scared by lots of things, and she thought sadly that Daddy just didn't understand how frightening nursery school could really be.

While Annie's tummy was aching and worrying she went to tell her mommy about it. Annie's mommy gave her tummy a little rub and said, "I think maybe your tummy is worried about going to school." Annie thought that that might be true, and her mommy said, "Why don't we sit down and make a storybook about a little girl who goes to nursery school?" And so they sat down and did some drawings about school.[4] Annie drew children and teachers and toys. And she got quite interested in the toys because she just adored toys, and when she grew up she wanted to own a whole toy shop bigger than the biggest shop you ever saw. So Annie and her mommy talked about the sort of toys that might live in a nursery school, and they drew pictures of jigsaw puzzles, blocks, and picture books.

Annie drew a picture of a little girl at nursery school sad and alone with a big tear rolling down her nose. But she also drew a picture of a girl playing with a jigsaw puzzle with a big smile on her face. Annie's mommy explained to her that on the first day of school she would stay with her for a long time so that Annie didn't need to be scared of being by herself, and that made Annie feel a bit better.[5] Her mom told her about all the things that would happen at nursery school—the sort of things they would do, the way the children would have fruit and milk

---

4. Drawing, sculpting, and modeling are all very helpful ways of allowing a child to express, and work through, fears.

5. Adapt this in accordance with how long you plan to stay with your child. If you can't stay with your child, focus on the fact that after Annie's mom leaves her, Annie enjoys doing other things at school.

in the morning, and all sorts of other things.[6]

When the big day came, Annie got herself dressed and did up her shoelaces, but she still felt very small inside because she was worrying about nursery school and what might happen to her there.

Annie's mommy held her hand and took her in to meet the teacher. There were so many new faces—Annie hid her head in her mommy's skirts and pretended she was making them vanish.

"Look, a jigsaw puzzle," said Annie's mommy, and Annie poked her head out because she liked jigsaw puzzles and was very good at them. Annie wished there were jigsaw-puzzle-doing competitions with toys as prizes because then she could win them all and have lots of toys to start her toy shop with.

While they sat doing the jigsaw, Annie's mommy said, "Look at that little girl over there; she looks a bit shy and lonely.[7] Do you think we should ask her to help us finish this puzzle?" So they asked the little girl to play with them. Her name was Lisa, and Lisa and Annie got very busy working on the jigsaw together. After a while Annie's mommy said, "Would you mind if I popped down to the shop for fifteen minutes?—I'd be back by twelve o'clock," and she pointed at the clock because Annie was a big girl and knew how to tell time.[8] Annie was quite busy enjoying her jigsaw with Lisa, and so she thought that might be all right. After a while she looked up at the clock and it was nearly twelve o'clock. "Mommy should be back soon," she thought, and sure enough there was Mommy at the door.[9] Annie felt very pleased that she had been grown up enough to stay all by herself, at least without her mommy, at nursery school.

---

6. The more your child knows what to expect, the less frightening it will be.

7. Picking out someone who also looks a bit shy will enable your child to feel that she is not alone in her predicament, an experience which is a comfort for us all.

8. If your child can't tell the time, cue your return to the activities the class will be pursuing at that time. For example, "I'll get back just after story time." Check with the teacher to find out what the class schedule is.

9. It is very important to return when you say you will. Lateness in this situation can cause unnecessary panic and fears of abandonment.

"I'm very proud of you," said Annie's mommy, and gave her a big kiss and a hug.

Annie couldn't wait for her daddy to come home that night.

"I was at nursery school all by myself!" She jumped up and down and tried to swing on his arm as if it were a monkey bar. Daddy must have been very proud because he didn't even get cross when she swung too hard on his arm and hurt it. "I'm so pleased," he said and lifted her right up and gave her a big kiss and hug.

Even Blackie the dog got excited and wagged her tail so hard that Annie thought she might go straight up in the air like a big black helicopter. "Then she could fly Mommy and me to school," she thought.[10] She had seen pictures of people flying up in the air in a big wicker basket with a huge balloon on top. A flying dog would be better than a balloon, she thought, because you could tell it where to go. Daddy spent hours at obedience school on Sundays telling Blackie where to go, so she thought Blackie should be pretty good at it by now. She imagined how all the kids would stare, and even the teachers too, as she and Mommy landed in their big basket on the school lawn. All the kids would be thinking that they wished they had a flying dog and a big traveling basket too. Annie would feel very important. She would climb out of the basket, kiss Mommy good-bye, and wave to her as they flew off into the sky until it was time to fly back and collect her. Annie smiled when she thought about it.

The next morning though, when Annie woke up, she was not feeling quite so smiley. In fact, she felt a little bit worried again. Like yesterday, but not quite so much. She remembered how awful she felt sometimes when she was alone without her mommy, and she could feel her tummy begin to worry again.

Daddy was just finishing his breakfast when Annie came into the room. She gave him a big kiss but didn't say anything about being scared again. She felt a bit embarassed to do that because she had already told him how

---

10. Humor enables us to see things from a different and less worrisome perspective.

brave she had been yesterday, and he had been so proud of her.

Annie felt even more miserable when she thought of this. She squished her corn flakes around and wished she were a corn flake. At least they didn't have to go to school. Then she remembered that they got swallowed. She wondered what would be worse, getting swallowed or going to nursery school. Then she remembered what her daddy had told her about food. He said it starts off in your mouth and, after you swallow it, goes into your tummy and ends up going out into the toilet. Yuck, Annie thought, maybe school was better after all.

Annie's mother noticed that Annie was a bit quiet. "Are you still worried about school?" she asked.

Annie nodded and drooped over her corn flakes.

"I was scared of going to nursery school when I was little," said Annie's daddy.[11]

Annie was so surprised, she sat up straight and almost squeaked. Fancy her big, strong daddy scared of going to nursery school. She was very interested. "What did you do?" she asked.

"I just kept going, and after a while it started to feel better and I liked it."

"Lots of children are scared of going to school," said Annie's mom.[12]

"Even on the second day?" Annie was beginning to feel better already. It felt good to know that she wasn't the only one who was scared.

"Even on the second day. It sometimes takes a few days to get used to it. And you know I'll still be staying with you for a while today too."[13]

That cheered Annie up a bit. She began to remember that parts of yesterday really had been fun. Such as when she had played with Lisa.

When they actually came to the school playground

---

11. Letting children know that you, the epitome of strength and success in their world, were once scared, will help them to realize that there is life after school, and that even though they may be scared, they can still go on to be strong and brave.

12. Children are reassured to know that this sort of fear is shared by many other children.

13. Include this only if you are able to stay the second day.

again, Annie started to feel a bit nervous. There were
such a lot of children there. She could feel her tummy
start to worry again. They had just walked into the yard
when all of a sudden she remembered Blackie the flying
dog putting Mommy and her down for a landing. The
thought was so funny that she started to smile. Then she
started to laugh. "What are you laughing at?" asked her
mommy.

Annie told her, and they both thought the joke was so
funny that they laughed and laughed.

Annie felt much better.

Inside the school she saw Lisa playing with a toy. Lisa
looked up and waved at her. Annie waved back. Annie
and her mom walked over to where Lisa was playing. She
had a Lego set and was making Lego towers. "Can I play
too?" asked Annie.

Lisa and Annie sat playing happily. They decided to
make very high towers, which were exciting because they
got wobblier and wobblier, and you never knew when
they were going to fall down. When they fell they made a
loud "splat" sound and crashed all over the place.

Annie's mother tapped her on the shoulder. "I'll leave
you now," she said. "The class is just about to do some
painting, and I think you'll like that. I'll come back at
twelve o'clock as I did yesterday."

"Okay," said Annie, and then she said to Lisa, "Let's
see if we can make one more tower before the painting
starts."

Annie loved the painting. In fact she was so busy
painting that she didn't even notice her mom coming
back.

"I had a great time today," she announced as they
walked back to the car. "We did singing and drawing and
played counting games. I have a peg of my own to hang
my coat on!"

"That sounds great," said her mom.

"It is," said Annie. She felt very happy.

The next morning when she woke, Annie felt a lot
better about going to school. She noticed that a lot of kids
didn't have their moms staying with them that day.

Her mom said to her, "What if I stay till singing time
today?" That was before painting time.

"All right," said Annie, "and then you can pick me up at twelve o'clock."

"Right," said her mom. "I think you're being a very big, grown-up girl. I'm very proud of you."

Annie felt great when her mom said that.

The next day, Annie's mom said to her. "When I take you in today, I might only stay for ten minutes."

"Okay," said Annie. She was really liking school. It was funny how she didn't feel scared anymore. There was so much to do and so much fun to have that she didn't miss her mommy at all. Hardly anyone's mom stayed with them that day.

Annie liked being part of the class. She felt quite big and grown-up when she went to school, and she knew too that if anything worried her, the teacher would take care of her.

So when Annie's mom said to her the next morning, "I think you might be ready to stay at school without me today," Annie nodded and said, "I think so too."

So after Annie's mom took her in, she gave her a big kiss and waved good-bye.

Just for a moment Annie was a bit unsure and she was just starting to feel worried about missing her mom when the teacher came up and said, "Would you help me set up the blocks, Annie?"[14] Annie was pleased, as she loved helping the teacher. She was so busy helping the teacher and playing with the children that she quite forgot to worry. In fact she had fun.

At the end of the day, Annie felt terrific.

"I'm so proud of you," said Mom.

"I'm so proud of you," said Dad.

"I'm so proud of you," wagged Blackie.

And Annie felt very proud of herself.

Nursery school was fun, she thought as she snuggled into bed that night.[15] She was really looking forward to tomorrow.

---

14. Let the teacher know that your child is shy or nervous so that she can keep an extra watchful eye out for signs of distress.

15. The ending offers hope, a positive resolution, and the enjoyable promise of tomorrow.

divorce

divorce is an enormously complicated subject. Everyone's situation is different, and yet if you gathered a roomful of people to compare notes on how divorce affected them you would find that the room was filled with nods of recognition—"Yes, I felt like that too!"

It would be impossible to write an Annie Story that encompassed all the variations upon the divorce theme. So instead, I have devoted some extra space to sketching out information about divorce and children's reactions to it for you to draw on when making up your own Annie Story.

Divorce of course is becoming increasingly common in our society. Although it has lost some of its old shock value, it nevertheless generally manages to bring in its wake a bundle of assorted sorrows.

A divorce places enormous stress on everyone concerned. People react with a multitude of emotions—rage, guilt, sadness, fear, relief, yearning. Although a divorce is highly traumatic for most children, research suggests that in the long term it need not necessarily inflict lasting emotional damage. It is the "background" of the divorce that affects the way a child recovers from this painful event. I'll be talking about the factors that make up this background as we go along.

Children's reactions to divorce

Most children show signs of stress in the first year or so following a separation or divorce. Anger, sadness, and confusion are chief among the emotions they may experience.

Children may be angry at either or both parents for not keeping the family together. They may be angry at themselves, feeling that it was their naughtiness that drove Mom and Dad apart or that they failed to do something that would have kept them together. These angry feelings may be difficult for the child to handle and express. She may fear, for instance, that if she shows her anger to the noncustodial parent, she may be rejected entirely and lose even her visiting times. Similarly, she may imagine that if she gets too angry at the parent she is living with, this parent may reject her as well. She may be scared by the intensity of her anger, fearing that if she lets even a little of it out, it will become uncontrollable.

Anger at one parent may be redirected to the parent with whom it is "safer" to feel angry. This is something we all do. Think back to the times we've displayed outbursts of anger at old friends we know won't desert us. With new friends we might have held the anger back, scared that if we made a wrong move, they'd be off and running. It's a sort of compliment to that person, really, to feel that he or she is "safe" enough to get angry with—although that rarely helps while you're on the receiving end.

Sometimes the child's anger may spill out onto school friends and teachers or be displayed in destructive acting-out behavior. This is the "kick the cat" phenomenon. Typical of this is the businesswoman who comes home furious after being told off by her boss. She can't kick the boss so she lets out her anger on the nearest moving object—the hapless cat.

Sadness is an almost universal accompaniment to divorce. It is natural to feel sad about such a painful loss, and children as well as adults have to go through the process of mourning the breakup of their family.

Coupled with the sadness may be feelings of inadequacy and low self-esteem. The child may feel she is worthless, bad, or unlovable. She may feel that she can't do anything right.

Sometimes a child's sadness may take the form of a passive

withdrawal from life. She may mope around, uninterested in school, her friends, or any of the other things she used to enjoy. Sometimes there can be a frenzy of agitated overactivity, as if the child is trying to run away from the sad feelings.

The child may be weepy, crying at things that never used to upset her. She may redevelop fears, such as a fear of the dark, that she had previously mastered, or she may regress in other ways. If she has been toilet trained, for instance, she may slip back into wetting herself. She may become extra demanding of attention and find normal everyday separations, such as going to school, hard to tolerate. She may develop physical symptoms such as tummy aches or have problems concentrating in school.

In the chaos of a divorce it is also common for the child to feel lost and forgotten. Often the parents are finding it difficult to deal with their own feelings and have little emotional energy to spare for their child. This is very frightening for her, and she may frantically redouble her attempts to get attention—only to end up being perceived as whining or naughty.

She will often feel confused as well, prey to conflicting feelings. Sometimes she will feel relieved that the fighting will end when Daddy moves out, and at the same time she may painfully wish that he would stay. It is hard for her to look into the future and grasp the finality of divorce. Young children have trouble comprehending next week, let alone next month or next year. She may be confused about what caused the divorce and what her new relationship with her parents will be. She may feel torn between her parents, alternately angry and pleading, not sure who, if anyone, is to blame. She may wonder how or whether to tell her friends, her teachers, and the other people in her life. Overall, she is also likely to feel painfully and frighteningly helpless. This may be the most excruciating and overwhelming event of her life so far, and there is not a thing she can do about it.

Childrens' fears and fantasies

Perhaps the most pronounced fear that the child going through a divorce experiences is the fear of abandonment. If we think back to our own childhood, most of us can remember the dread we felt on some occasion—for instance, when we lost sight of Mommy in the supermarket. We stood there, filled with the sheer cold terror, the sickening emptiness, of being little, lost, and horribly alone. This fear of abandonment is common even in children of intact families. It has to do with the child's innate helplessness and dependence on her parents. Fairy tales from all over the world feature this theme of abandonment—"Hansel and Gretel" is one example. With divorce, all of the child's fantasies about being abandoned may seem to be coming true. It is very important to reassure your child that she will not be abandoned. This reassurance will most likely have to be repeated frequently. Everyday situations such as being left with a baby-sitter may rekindle the fear that you are never coming back. Telling your child where you are going and leaving a contact number where she can phone you can be reassuring.

Children often carry the fantasy that they were to blame for the divorce. A child may feel that it was her naughtiness that drove Daddy away from the house. Or she may feel that her naughtiness made Mommy and Daddy argue so much that it caused them to split. This belief that they have caused certain events stems from children's sense of omnipotence. When we're little we believe the world revolves around us and that all the things that happen in it are affected by us. As we grow up, most of us are forced to discard this regal outlook and come to terms with our real relative place in the scheme of things.

When a parent actually blames the child or children for the divorce, the child's fear of being the cause is, of course, tremendously exaggerated. To tell your child that she was responsible for your divorce is to put an intolerable burden on her. This should never happen.

Young children also exhibit what psychologists call "magical thinking," believing that thoughts or feelings can actually cause things to happen in the physical world. For instance, the child who has felt angry at a parent after being punished may believe that her angry thoughts caused the parent to trip on the staircase or to become ill or to separate from the family.

"How silly!" you may exclaim, secure in your adult wisdom. But think about it the next time you avoid walking under a ladder or knock wood for luck. Magical thinking isn't that foreign to most of us.

Parallel to the child's feeling that it was something she did that drove her parents apart is the equally common fantasy that there is something she can do to bring them back together again. A great many children try all sorts of tactics to have their family reunited. A child may think that if she is very good, Daddy will come home again. Or that if she is very bad, her parents will need to get together to consult with each other about her behavior. She may sometimes feel that if she were sick, Daddy would need to come home again. For a long time after the divorce has become final, children almost invariably hold on to the fantasy that their mother and father will get back together again.

Children fear, too, not only for their own welfare but for that of their parents. They may worry about "poor Daddy" alone in his apartment and having to look after himself. Or they may worry about Mommy, who is looking so sad and tired with her extra burden. They may worry about financial matters— worries which can be fueled by parents' comments such as "She's taken every last cent from me" and "We're never going to be able to live on the money he's giving us."

Children are also prone to fantasize about an absent parent. With a parent whom they only see infrequently, for instance, they may build up such an idealized image that the real thing is bound to be a disappointment.

Sometimes the weaker and more inadequate a parent is, the more the child idealizes him or her. This is because it would be too painful to the child to truly acknowledge how pitiful or inadequate her father, for instance, really is, so she builds up a fantasy picture instead. With a competent parent, it is easy to acknowledge his or her faults because the child knows that even with a few faults the parent is still a good enough and solid enough person to love, look up to, and rely on.

These fears and fantasies are common to many children, but it is also a good idea to ask your own child what her fears are about the divorce. If she can't readily verbalize them, perhaps she can draw them or paint them.

How to tell children

Whenever possible, break the news about the upcoming separation before you or your spouse has actually moved out. This will give your child time to think about the news, get over some of the initial shock, and talk to you both about what it all means for her. Children need to have repeated opportunities with both parents to ask questions and talk about their feelings. They need time to digest the new situation and come back to it. Don't expect that a single heart-to-heart talk will take care of everything.

Sometimes it may be difficult for children to express their feelings verbally. It's always a good idea to provide crayons or paints and to encourage them to let their thoughts and feelings out through artwork, puppet play, or storytelling. Children's artwork gives a wonderful glimpse into their inner thoughts and feelings. The drawing produced by my daughter, for instance, illustrates the sense of misery and helplessness a child can feel. Notice the upright flaps around the bed that seem to act as protective buffers from the parents' arguing voices. And totally

"I hate you," said her parents to each other.

spontaneously, she has drawn an old-fashioned pair of scales on the desk—a symbol of the continual weighing-up and balancing that the child caught in the middle must do.

When you're explaining the divorce, make sure, too, that your explanation is phrased in terms your child can understand. Research has shown that a surprising number of children were either not given an explanation of the divorce or were given one that was over their heads. Children who were given an explanation they could understand fared much better emotionally than those who were not. Children who were left in the dark were forced into a desperate search for clues and meanings in their effort to make sense of the world they now found themselves in.

It is important, too, that the explanations you give your children are appropriate to their age group. It is not appropriate, for instance, to flood an eight-year-old girl with details of Daddy's affairs.

Be aware that children will need different levels of information as they get older. As the ten-year-old becomes a twelve-year-old, for instance, she will have more awareness of how adult relationships function and may want to know, and will be able to understand, more about the complexities of your divorce. It's important to remember that divorce is a process in a family's life, not a single discrete event.

When talking to your child about divorce, it is important to emphasize that while marriage partners can divorce each other, parents cannot divorce children. Make it clear that you will always be her parent and will be there to take care of her. For the noncustodial parent who has visitation rights and expectations, it is important to stress to your child that even though you won't be living with her, you still love her, you are still her mother (or father), and she will always be a part of your life. Don't make these promises, however, if you don't fully intend to keep them. Broken promises of this kind are truly heartbreaking for children.

When a parent has deserted or does not want contact with a child, it is important to let your child know that the problem lies within that parent. Children often think that their "badness" or worthlessness is the reason why a parent deserted them. Explain to your child that the deserting parent was simply not grown-up enough to be a parent or had too many problems to be able to parent properly. Bolster your child's self-esteem, and reassure her about her worth and value.

In general, when telling a child about your impending separation or divorce, let her know that it is not her fault—she did nothing to cause it, could have done nothing to prevent it, and cannot bring you back together again. Divorce is a decision made by adults, not by children. Also stress the finality of the divorce. For a very long time after the divorce, children often maintain the fantasy that parents will reunite. It is best not to encourage that fantasy.

When you talk to your child about divorce, it is worth acknowledging that it is a difficult process to get through, but reassure her that you will make it. Too often parents make remarks such as "Things will be better after the divorce," when in fact it usually takes some time for the expected improvement to take place. Children then become confused and mistrustful when they see that things are in fact worse immediately after the divorce.

Finally, make sure your child understands your explanations. Just because your daughter can parrot you by saying "Mommy and Daddy are getting a divorce" does not mean that she understands the meaning of a divorce. Make yourself available for repeated questions. Children need to come back time and time again to this subject. They may ask different questions or they may ask the same question many times. They are not trying to be a nuisance; they are trying to grapple with an enormous upheaval in their lives, and they need time, thought, information, and repeated reassurances to help them through.

Problems and pitfalls

One of the major pitfalls about divorce is that it is such an overwhelming and painful time for the parents that they may have little emotional energy left over for their child. Thus the child may feel abandoned by both parents, not just the one who is leaving. Often, too, the mother has to take on extra work for financial reasons and is then left with even less time and energy for her child.

During this period parents often find themselves falling into the compelling, but killing, trap of competing for the child's affection and loyalty. They may engage in a battle to try to make the child choose between them. Sometimes the parents do this as a way of bolstering their own self-esteem, out of a desire for revenge on the spouse, or out of a need for the divorce to be validated by the child's recoil from the ex-partner. There are many reasons why parents compete against each other in this arena, but only one inevitable conclusion: the child will be severely disturbed and traumatized by this excruciating battle.

Sometimes in an effort to win his child's approval, the noncustodial parent showers her with presents and attempts to make every moment of her visit an exciting, fun-filled extravaganza. Often underneath this orgy of fun is the fear that without it the parent would be rejected. Sometimes it masks the fact that the parent feels unable to communicate comfortably with the child and so enters into a frenzy of doing rather than simply being. Although most children love presents and circuses, in the end what they usually crave most is simple, ordinary time with you—a time when they can tell you what happened at school, for instance, as you companionably put away the dinner dishes.

During the divorce and post-divorce period, children are often forced to act as spies and/or message carriers. They may be subjected to intense questioning on returning from a visit to one parent. They may be asked to keep secrets from one parent, or to relay messages that should more appropriately be conveyed by the parents to each other. All of these roles are distressing for children. In the beginning, the heightened intimacy of the "secret-keeper" or the power of the "messenger" may be enticing, but finally the continual rending of loyalties can lead to an unbearably painful situation. It is too heavy a load for a healthy adult to carry, let alone a vulnerable child.

Children also may try to manipulate their parents, perhaps by playing one off against the other, sometimes with a constant nudging and prodding to see how far they can go with one or the other parent. This generally reflects the child's attempt to test the limits of her new situation. How much can she get away with before she is brought back into line? Although children can enjoy the power they feel as successful manipulators, it can also leave them feeling very insecure. If their parents aren't strong enough to control them, how can they be strong enough to be looked up to as guides, models, and protectors in a tough adult world? Children feel much more secure with firm, reasonable limit-setting. They aren't adults yet—they need parents to lay down appropriate rules and to see that they are adhered to. So despite the fact that it may look as if their hearts' desire is total anarchy as they attempt to break rule after rule, most children are simply seeking the relief of a solid adult force that will contain and protect them. Discipline is a common problem in the post-divorce period, and I'll be talking about it more in a later section.

Children may also have difficulty in expressing some of their emotions during this period. Sometimes, for instance, their anger at one parent can spill out onto the other or onto some unrelated person or event. Visiting times often bring conflicting emotions, and the transition from one parent to the other is usually a particularly delicate period for the child. She may have been looking forward to the visit for days with mounting and even painful excitement. Then when the day comes, she may suddenly fear leaving the custodial parent. What if Mommy isn't there when she comes back? What if Mommy gets sick while she is away or is sad and lonely without her? What if she gets scared in the unfamiliar surroundings of Daddy's new apartment? Parents too are often feeling mixed emotions. The custodial parent may be glad of the respite from child-caring and yet be sad or worried to see her child go. The noncustodial parent may be confused or hurt at seeing the child holding back and, to his eyes, obviously hedging about the visit.

Sometimes in the aftermath of a divorce, children are turned into little parents. The child may become her parent's prime confidant and source of emotional support, for instance. This is an inappropriate and burdensome role for a child. Sometimes the child takes too much responsibility for household tasks, and she may also take on the role of parent to her younger siblings. While there is obviously a great deal more work and responsibility to be shared in a single-parent household, it is important to give children the time to be children.

One of the traps of the divorce period seems to be loaded against little boys. All children will have increased emotional needs during this period—they may need extra cuddling and reassurance, be weepy or clingy. Researchers have shown that little girls tend to have their dependency needs met more satisfactorily than boys. Parents tend not to cuddle boys as much and are less tolerant of such signs of dependency as clinging or weepiness. You won't spoil your children by fussing over them and meeting their needs for extra attention during this period. You'll simply enable them to feel more secure and therefore more able to work through this difficult phase.

What you can do to make it easier

Perhaps the most important thing you can do for your child during this most difficult time is to give her permission to be close to both of her parents. Don't try to force her to choose between you or make her feel that she is being disloyal to you when she responds positively to her other parent. Most children want a continued, close relationship with both parents. Most children love both parents despite their faults. The most loving thing you can do for your child is to recognize that she has her own feelings about your ex-spouse and that they do not have to coincide with yours.

Fathers often feel like outsiders during this time if they are the noncustodial parent. They may feel that their weekly visits, for instance, are of not much importance compared to the number of hours the child spends with her mother. Researchers have shown, however, that these visits, and the continued contact with the father that they represent, are extremely valuable to most children and play an important part in their healthy emotional adjustment. Unfortunately, it is a common pattern for the frequency and predictability of visits to taper off after a few years. Children generally react to this loss with feelings of intense pain and sadness, which are often marked by a pose of indifference or anger.

The transition periods before and after visits are often times of extra stress for the child. You can help by letting her know that she is free to enjoy her time with Daddy without your being hurt or upset by it. Don't ask her to spy on Daddy or to keep secrets from him. Don't re-create the Spanish Inquisition each time she comes home from a visit. Reassure her that you will be fine while she's away and that you will be there to welcome her home again. Plan a quiet day for her first day back at your home—she may need time and space to settle down and cope with the transition.

Ordinary everyday partings—going to school, staying with a baby-sitter—may also become difficult for your child at this time. This reflects her increased insecurity and her fear of abandonment. Lots of reassurance is in order; you would never abandon her, will always come back to pick her up, and so on. Giving her a special object of yours to keep while you're away can sometimes be helpful. It provides a link with you and also an extra, concrete reassurance that you will be coming back.

During a divorce, children are likely to exhibit signs of stress. They may have difficulty in concentrating at school, for instance; they may become clumsy on the sports field and lose their place on the team; they may be grouchy with their friends or develop fears or phobias. If this happens, it is helpful to talk to your child about the way stress affects our ability to concentrate or our energy and confidence. Reassure her that her fading concentration doesn't mean that she's stupid, that her clumsiness doesn't mean she's a klutz, and that her fears don't mean that she's a baby. Let her know that lots of children feel and do these things in times of stress. Most of us can remember times when we behaved in such out-of-character ways that we thought we were going mad. What a relief it was to find that we were simply exhibiting signs of stress and not lunacy or some peculiar degenerative disease!

If your child is tense, it can be helpful to teach her how to relax. For more information on this, see the story on relaxation.

It is also a good idea to let your child's teachers know about the divorce so that they can understand if her behavior at school changes. They may be able to give her some extra support during this time.

During and following a divorce the custodial parent often finds herself spinning frantically in a whirlpool of extra work. If it is the mother, she may have to take on new or extra work to make up for the drop in her financial status. Added to her extra working hours is the worry, strain, and general emotional drain experienced by those going through a divorce. This means that at a time when the child needs more of you, she is actually getting less of you. It can often seem that each time you draw breath your child is asking or wanting something of you. As you try to do several dozen things at once as well as field your child's requests for attention, it is easy to degenerate into something resembling the Wicked Witch of the West. One way of helping to alleviate this situation is to set aside some special time for just you and your child, say a half-hour every evening. This is a time when you can simply sit with your child, read stories, play games, talk about the day, and most important of all, nourish your child's self-esteem. Hug her, kiss her, talk about her special talents, how proud you are of her and so on. Let this be a time for making sure your child feels loved and appreciated.

This sort of time really makes a difference to children— imagine how good you'd feel if someone did that for you every day! And because they are getting this special gift of your undivided, loving attention, they will feel much more nourished and secure and less needful of your constant attention at other times of the day.

At this emotionally chaotic time in their lives, children particularly appreciate a secure, predictable home routine. Try to change as few things in their life as possible—if you can, keep them at the same school, in the same neighborhood and the same house. Let them know well ahead of time when they'll be visiting Dad and for how long. A structured, familiar routine will give them an extra sense of security at a time when they are likely to be feeling very insecure.

If you are moving to another house or apartment, bring along familiar items of your own to put in the new home. Also, if possible, allow your child to help pick out something for the new home—perhaps a piece of furniture, an ornament, or the color of her bedroom curtains. (This advice holds true for the noncustodial parent, too. Your new home will seem very strange to your child at first. If you let her help decorate her room or her corner, it will help her feel more at home.)

Discipline is one of the things that often goes haywire after a divorce. But discipline, in its fair, consistent, and stable form, is one of the things that children, and particularly children in chaos, need most. There are many reasons why discipline tends to dissolve in divorced families. Sometimes it's because the father has been the disciplinarian in the family and in his absence, the mother may be struggling with a new and unfamiliar role. Sometimes the father, in his new role as noncustodial parent, stops disciplining the child for fear the child will reject him or because he wants to win extra favor with the child. Often both parents are so preoccupied with their own problems that discipline becomes an on-again, off-again affair. Sometimes they let the child do things that normally wouldn't be allowed as a sort of compensation for the divorce or because they cannot tolerate their child's disapproval or tears.

Children at this stage often seem to be opposing discipline in any way they can—breaking the rules, being naughty or defiant. Sometimes this is their way of letting out the anger they feel about the divorce. Often it is their way of testing the limits—seeing how far they can go before a parent really rejects them, or finding out how securely in control their parent really is. The best thing you can do is reassure your child that you are committed to loving and looking after her no matter how naughty she may be at times.

Often children are secretly convinced that just one more fight will make you serve the divorce papers on them, just as happened with you and Daddy. They may feel compelled to check this out by taking it to the limit. This motivation, though common, is not necessarily something that they can verbalize to you or understand at a conscious level. It is imperative that at the same time as you reassure them of your commitment and love for them, you also let them know that you will not let them run wild and that rules must be abided by. Consistent, reasonable, and caring discipline is a wonderful gift to a child. It gives her a great sense of security as well as enabling her to learn skills, such as self-control, which will aid her in the path to maturity. Either extreme of disciplinary style—the harsh authoritarian style or the permissive style—has been shown not to work as well as the middle ground: the authoritative style, a style that is affectionate, and has reasonable and consistent rules. With an authoritative style of discipline, the parent can explain the reasons behind family rules as well as allowing the child to express her thoughts on their appropriateness or fairness. Once rules are made, they are adhered to firmly and consistently.

If the style of discipline at your house is different from the style at your spouse's or your parents', don't worry too much. Children will simply adjust to whatever household they're in, though obviously the household where they spend the most time will have the most impact on them.

Sometimes in the round of weekday-mother and weekend-father, the parents' roles seem to get crystallized into goodies and baddies. Mom gets cast as the nagging no-sayer, while Dad gets to be the fun-fair father. If you find yourself in this trap, with weekdays a continual round of nagging, screaming, and saying no, it's worth re-evaluating things. First, make sure that there is space left for some loving and fun time in your weekly routine. Look at the way you've been handling discipline. If it's not effective, seek some help. There are excellent books on the market now, or if you feel you need more, talk to a counsellor or family therapist. Talk to the kids about what's going on. Tell them how you're feeling. Find out how they're feeling. See if together you can work out ways of living more cooperatively and supportively with one another. Focus on praising them when they're doing the right thing. Too often we just focus on the negative behavior of our children and neglect the positive. Think about your own and your children's emotional state—is one or more of you really depressed, for instance? If so, seek professional help—you don't have to tough it out on your own. There are many people trained to help with these sorts of emotional problems. It's a big burden to carry on your own.

Finally, realize that recovery from a divorce takes time. It is foolish to expect that everyone will be perfectly adjusted to the new situation from day one. Each member of the family is bound to go through emotional ups and downs for some time as he or she works through the traumas, pain, and confusion to its eventual resolution.

nnie was a little girl who lived in a brown brick house wth her mommy and daddy and a big black dog.[1] Annie loved her mommy and daddy very much. Her daddy worked in a bank and went off to work every morning at 8:30 and came back home at 6:00. Annie would always be the first to hear his car stop outside the house and then his footsteps coming up to the door. She would run to greet him, and Blackie the dog would run to greet him too. Sometimes they would get all tangled up in each other so that when Daddy opened the door it looked like he was being greeted by a large, furry little girl.

Annie's mommy was a nurse. She only worked at the hospital for part of the day so that she could be home when Annie was home and at work when Annie was at school. She would make Annie's breakfast each morning and take her to school and then she would be there to pick her up at 3:00 when school was over.

She would take Annie home and they would chat together while her mom did things around the house. Sometimes they would go for a walk or Annie would have friends over to play.

When Annie had friends over, they would drink orange juice and eat toast with peanut butter and jelly; Annie liked to squish the peanut butter and jelly on all by herself. Then they would play games. Sometimes they would play dress-up or hide-and-seek. Sometimes they would play tag with the dog.

Annie's friends would usually leave at about 5:30, and then she would wait eagerly for her dad to come home so she could tell him about the things that had happened to her that day.

---

1. For this section, add your own details.

Usually they would all have dinner at 6:30. Annie used to like having dinner with her mom and dad, but lately she was liking it less and less. Recently it seemed that her mom and dad just couldn't agree on anything. If her mother liked one thing, her dad didn't. If her dad liked something, her mother didn't. Sometimes it was nice all being together, but most often now her mom and dad would be arguing or disagreeing or just sitting silently at the table.[2] Annie didn't like it at all. She would try to tell them about all the good things she had done at school, hoping they would be proud of her and forget about disagreeing with each other. Sometimes she worried that they got cross at each other because of things she had done. Once when she had left her toys on the floor, her dad had come home and yelled at her mom about the mess in the house. And her mom had yelled back at him. Annie had felt very bad that time.

What she hated most was when her mom and dad started having arguments over her.[3] Sometimes Mom thought that Annie ought to be able to do one thing and Dad thought she shouldn't. Sometimes Dad complained that Mom spoiled her and Mom complained that Dad was too strict. They would always start the same way, in low hard voices as if they didn't want her to hear, and then their voices would get louder and louder and more and more angry and Annie would want to run upstairs to the bedroom and hide under the bed and cover her ears so that she wouldn't have to listen.

Sometimes, at night, she would hear them arguing.[4] At first she would try to pretend that it was the TV because she hated to hear them argue. Then when she couldn't pretend it was the TV anymore, she would wriggle under the blankets and press her hands to her ears and try to think of something else so that she wouldn't have to hear their voices.

---

2. Again, add your own details. In some pre-divorce families there are many loud, fiery arguments; in others it's all held in, with prolonged silences.

3. Children can feel like the meat in the sandwich in such situations. It adds to their sense of guilt over the divorce.

4. Parents who argue only at night when the children are in bed may imagine that their arguments and hostility go unnoticed. This is usually not the case.

She hated the sound of their voices when they were arguing. They sounded ugly and hateful. It was hard to think of those voices as her loving mommy and daddy. She felt very sad and lonely as she lay in her room with the sound of those angry voices floating up the stairs and through the door.

When she woke in the morning it would be as if nothing had happened. Her mom would give her breakfast in her special cereal bowl. Her dad would smile at her from behind his paper and say, "How's my darling daughter this morning?" And Annie would hope that all the anger and fighting had gone away for good.

Usually, though, things were nice for a few days and then the arguments would come back again. Annie hated them, but she figured that all moms and dads must be like that. She had never had any other mom and dad, after all, so how could she know? Sometimes she would look at her friends' moms and dads, who looked so happy together, and think about them fighting each other at night in the downstairs room after dark.

Lately it seemed that Annie's mom and dad had been arguing more. Her mom seemed quieter than usual when she was with her, and her dad didn't seem to be home as much. He would come home later and later from work, so that some days Annie hardly saw him at all.

Sometimes when her mom was quiet and sad, Annie would ask if something was wrong. Her mom would smile and say something like "Nothing darling, it's just that I'm thinking about things."

Sometimes Annie was worried that it was something she had done that had made her mother sad and her father stay away so much, but mostly she tried not to think about it and to pretend that it wasn't happening and would be better soon.[5]

One day after dinner, Annie's mom said, "Your dad and I have to talk to you about something."[6] Annie felt a nasty shivering feeling creeping all the way through her.

---

5. Children often worry that somehow it may be their fault. It is important to reassure them on this point.

She didn't know what it was, but she felt awful.

Her mom and dad sat down next to her, and her mom began to speak.

"Darling," she said, "your dad and I have decided that we're too unhappy living with each other and we've decided to get a divorce."

"That means we won't be married anymore," said her dad, "and we'll live in different houses."

Annie's mouth opened. She felt as if all her insides had suddenly dropped out though her feet. "But you can't," she said. "You can't get a divorce, you're my mommy and daddy." And she began to cry.

"Annie darling," her mom said, and she looked as if she was almost crying too, "we tried to stay together, but it makes us too unhappy."

"But why?" asked Annie. "Why can't you stay together?"

"Sweetheart," her father said, "when we met each other, long before you were born, we loved each other and that's why we got married. Then a lot of time went by and we started to change. We each started to like and dislike different things. We started not getting along with each other, and we were making each other miserable. We can't live together happily anymore, so it's best if we live separately and get a divorce."[7]

Annie's daddy went on, "A divorce means that we won't be married to each other anymore, but I'll still be your daddy and Mom will still be your mommy. That won't change."[8]

---

6. It is best if the parents break the news together. This prevents it from being one-sided and allows the child to address questions to both or either parent. If there is more than one child in the family, it is generally preferable that they all be told at the same time. This allows the siblings to draw support from each other and prevents one sibling breaking it to another before the parents have had a chance to do so themselves.

7. Your explanations don't need to be complex. They can be as simple as this one.

8. It's important to stress to your child that even though you are divorcing each other, you are not divorcing her. Of course, if one parent wants to have no further contact with the child, then a different explanation is necessary. See the introduction to this chapter for more details.

divorce

"But if you loved each other before," said Annie, "why can't you just start loving each other again?"

"Love is very hard even for grown-ups to understand," said her mom. "We tried to keep loving each other but it just didn't work."

"What will happen to me when you don't live together?" said Annie.[9] She was suddenly very scared. What if they didn't want to live with her either? What if they wanted to divorce her?

"You'll stay here with Mommy, darling," said her dad. "I'm going to be moving out of the house soon."[10]

"But how will I see you?" asked Annie. She couldn't bear to think of not hearing her dad come home each evening.

"You can come and visit me," said her dad, "whenever you like. You can come and stay on weekends."

"Why can't you stay here?" asked Annie. She didn't want to go visiting her dad. She wanted him to go on living with her.

"I can't stay here, Annie, because when parents divorce, they live in different houses from each other," said her dad, "but you can come and stay with me. Mom and I will work out regular times for you to visit."[11]

"But I don't want to visit," Annie said, and she began to cry again. Why couldn't her dad understand that she just wanted him to stay here and be with her? How could he love her if he wanted to live away from her?[12]

Her father shrugged his shoulders and looked at her mom. Her mom put her arms around Annie and said, "Come up to bed, darling. It's late. I'll sit with you awhile and read you a story to help you fall asleep. We'll talk some more in the morning."

When Annie woke the next morning she knew that something terrible had happened. Her body felt horrible

9. This question is of dire importance to children. They may need continual reassurance on this subject.

10. It is helpful to give children some notice of the divorce so that they have time to work things through.

11. It is important for children to feel they can have good, consistent contact with the parent who is moving out.

12. Children often find this hard to understand.

and heavy as if it didn't want to wake up and she felt miserable inside. It took her brain a few minutes to remember exactly what it was that had happened.

When she remembered, she rushed downstairs, terrified that Daddy had already left without her.

He was still there, though, looking a bit tired but eating his breakfast as usual. For a moment Annie thought, Maybe it didn't really happen, but then Mom came in and Annie saw that she had been crying and she knew that it really had happened.

"Please don't go," she said to her daddy.

Her daddy looked up very sadly. "I have to, Annie," he said.

Maybe, Annie thought, if she was very, very good, her parents would realize what a nice family they really had and not leave each other after all. That day, and the next, and the next, she did every single good thing she could think of. It was a strain doing so many good things and being so very, very good all of the time, but Annie thought that if she could just keep it up, she could keep her parents together. But it didn't work.[13]

On Saturday, her dad moved out to his new house. Annie felt so sad, she couldn't even speak. She went upstairs to her dollhouse and took the father doll out. "I'm going to punish you," she said. "Fathers are supposed to take care of their children." Then she took out the mother doll. "Mothers and fathers are supposed to stay together," she said. "You've been bad, bad, bad."[14]

That afternoon she felt very sick. Her tummy ached and her head ached and her eyes ached. She felt as if she were one big ache. "I think I'd better stay in bed this afternoon," she said to her mom. "Will you phone Dad and tell him I'm very, very sick. If I'm sick, he has to come home to stay."[15]

---

13. This is a common reaction in children. Alternatively, sometimes they can be very bad so as to bring the parents together in the common goal of controlling or helping them.

14. Play helps children work through some of the intense feelings that are aroused. It is common for one of these to be anger.

15. Sometimes children feel that if they are sick and helpless enough, the other parent will come back to stay and look after them.

divorce

Annie's mother gave her a kiss and smoothed her hair back. "Darling, Daddy still loves you, but he can't come back to stay—he's staying somewhere else now."

"Will you phone him anyway?" said Annie. She was sure that if her daddy knew how sick she was, he would come back.

Later that afternoon, her father came upstairs. He gave her a kiss and said, "How are you, darling?"

Annie got so excited. "I knew you'd come back," she said.

"Darling, I haven't come back to stay," her daddy said. "Mommy and I aren't living together anymore. But I still love you and I'll always be your daddy and we'll still keep seeing each other."

"If you loved me you wouldn't go away," said Annie.

"I know it's hard for you to understand," said her daddy, "but I promise I do still love you and I'll never stop loving you. You'll always be my daughter and I'll always be your daddy," and he gave her a big hug.

But Annie shut her eyes and pretended not to hear. She didn't want a daddy who lived away from her. She wanted a daddy who lived here with her. She heard her daddy walk quietly down the stairs and she began to cry.

Sometimes when she thought about the divorce, she worried that it was something she had done that had made her dad want to leave home.[16] She remembered the times she had been naughty and her parents had had a fight over it. She wished she could take back the naughtiness and just have been a super-good girl all the time so they wouldn't have been able to fight over it. Maybe if they hadn't had so many fights they wouldn't have divorced.

Annie was scared to ask her mom about that because it made her feel so bad inside to think that maybe if she had been a better girl it wouldn't have happened. But one day when they were going for a walk, her mom said to her, "You know, Annie, when parents divorce, a lot of kids think it was their fault—that if they had been better kids their parents wouldn't have separated."

---

16. It is common for children to feel this. They need reassurance that the divorce is not their fault.

"Really?" said Annie. She was very surprised to know that lots of kids felt like that.

"I want you to know, darling," her mother went on, "that Daddy and I separating had nothing to do with you. You're a wonderful daughter and you always have been. We both love you very, very much and always will. Our divorce is because of the way we were with each other—it has nothing to do with you."

"Whose fault was it, Mommy?" asked Annie.[17] She had been thinking about this a lot. Sometimes she thought it was Daddy's fault because he had moved out of the house and left them, and sometimes she thought it was Mommy's fault that she had made Daddy so unhappy that he had to move out of the house. She kept thinking about it, but she hated thinking about it. When she got angry at Daddy because she thought it was his fault, she felt sad for Mommy—and then sad for Daddy too because he was alone too after all and she loved him. When she got angry at Mom and thought it was her fault, the same thing happened and she just didn't know whose side she was on. She wished she didn't have to take sides. It made her feel like she was split right in two, and neither side was happy.

"It's no one's fault, darling," said Mommy. "No one's to blame. We both just changed and it wasn't right for us to stay married. Both of us are very unhappy that it ended this way. It's not like a baseball game where you cheer for one side and boo the other. And it's not that one of us did something very wrong to the other—it's not like TV where there are good guys and bad guys. We both said bad, angry things to each other when we were upset, but we did try to make it up. We just found that we couldn't agree anymore and we would be happier apart."[18]

"What about me, though?" said Annie. "If I ever said bad, angry things to you, would you divorce me?" She had

---

17. Children are often told that one parent is to blame in a divorce, but apportioning blame to one or other parent leaves them feeling split, disloyal, and distressed. You don't need to lie about being pleased with all your spouse's actions. They know you are not—that's why you divorced, after all—but try not to get them involved in taking sides.

18. It's important to help children understand that divorce is not a simple black-and-white affair.

been worrying about this a lot. After all, if parents could divorce each other, why couldn't they divorce their kids?[19]

"We would never divorce you, darling," said her mom. "It doesn't work that way for children. I will always be your mother and your dad will always be your dad. It doesn't matter how bad or cross we get with each other, I'll still be your mom and you'll still be my daughter. I'll always love you and look after you and I'll never leave you. I'll always be there for you, darling."[20] And she gave Annie a great big kiss.

That weekend it was Dad's turn to have Annie. She went to stay at his new house every second weekend, and he would call her during the week to say hi. Annie had his phone number, too, so that she could call him whenever she wanted.

At first she had hated coming to his home. Everything was new and strange to her, and it didn't seem right to be seeing her dad here when he really belonged at her house. But now she had become used to it.

Annie remembered the first time she had come to visit Dad in his new house. It had been really weird. It was her first weekend visit with him and she had been looking forward to it for days so that her tummy felt like it was jumping up and down and she had trouble sitting still when she thought about it. She had woken early that morning and kept looking at her watch and trying to make the hands go around faster so that Daddy would be here sooner. And then suddenly there he was and Mommy was giving him her little weekend bag and it was really time to be going.

Annie had suddenly felt very scared. What if she didn't like it at Daddy's house? What if Daddy had changed and wasn't like he used to be? What if he

---

19. It's important to reassure children on this point—that even if they are bad or angry, you won't "divorce" them.

20. This explanation will have to be modified in the case where one parent is refusing to see the child. It is unreal and confusing to continue to tell the child that a parent who has disowned her still loves her and always will. It gives a very distorted idea of parental love.

couldn't take care of her properly? And then she had seen Mommy preparing to wave good-bye. What if something happened to Mommy while she was away? What if Mommy wasn't there when she came back? What if Mommy was lonely while she was away?[21]

Annie's lower lip had begun to tremble and her eyes began to feel hot, the way they did before she cried. She had turned around to her mom.

"Annie," her mom had said, putting her arms around her. "It's really going to be all right. Daddy's new house might seem a bit strange at first, but he'll take good care of you. And I'll be fine here. When you come back tomorrow, I'll be waiting here for you." And she had given Annie a big hug.

The first few times that Annie had gone to visit her dad, he had seemed different from the way he usually was. For a start, he kept buying her things. All sorts of things. Almost anything she looked at he would buy for her. At first it was fun, but then after a while it got to feel sort of strange. It just didn't feel normal. And more than anything else, Annie wanted to feel normal. Also her dad kept taking her out—to the zoo, to the circus, to the amusement park—to almost anyplace where there was noise and crowds and things to do. At first that was fun too, but then Annie would start to get tired—all the excitement and rides and sticky candy. And when she got tired she got grumpy. Often her dad would get grumpy too.[22]

One day she said to her dad, "Maybe we could just hang around the house today. We could play checkers or I could help you wash your car."

"Sure," her dad said. He seemed relieved. "Sure, we could do that. That would be just fine."

At her dad's new house, she had a special room that was her room, and her dad had asked her to come with

---

21. The transition time between visits—that is, leaving or returning home—is often a very anxious period for children. They may need extra reassurance at this time. Let them know you'll be safe and waiting for them, and that it is fine for them to have a good time with the parent they are visiting.

22. This pattern is very common and not very helpful to children. See the introduction to this chapter for extra discussion.

him to pick out some of the things to put in it. Annie had picked out some things she liked and it made her feel like the room really belonged to her.[23]

"What did you tell the kids at school about the divorce?" her dad asked one day.[24] They were drying dishes together, and he knew that Annie had been worried about how to tell her friends at school.[25]

"I just told them what you and Mom suggested," said Annie. "I said that my mom and dad were divorcing and would be living in different houses. It wasn't as bad telling them as I thought it would be. Some of their parents are divorced too, you know."

"Yes, I know," said her dad. "Divorce is very common and thousands of children have parents who are divorced."[26]

"Really?" said Annie. She hadn't known there were that many. "My friend Betty's parents divorced last year," she said. "Betty said her mom's always saying bad things about her dad and trying to get Betty to say them too. She hates that."[27]

"Yes, that's terrible for children when their parents do that," said her dad.

"She said that every time she visits one of them, the other spends hours and hours asking her about every little thing they said and did. She says it just makes her want to scream and not say a word for weeks."[28]

"That does sound horrible," said her dad. "Sometimes it's hard for parents because they get so angry with each

---

23. It helps if the child has the sense that at least some part of the new house, even if it's only a corner, is specially hers.

24. Children are often concerned about how to tell their friends. You might help them think of and practice appropriate phrases and explanations and work out how they will deal with questions.

25. Being able to discuss things comfortably and in a normal domestic situation is more helpful to the child than a constant swirl of amusement parks and presents.

26. It helps to let the child know that divorce is indeed common and that there are many, many children like her.

27. This is very distressing for children. They feel pressured into taking sides and must cope with feelings of disloyalty, guilt, deceitfulness, and so on.

28. This is putting an enormous amount of pressure on children. They often feel like captured spies.

other and feel so bad inside that they don't always do the right thing. You know what it's like when you get upset."[29]

"Yes," said Annie. She knew that when she got upset she sometimes did really silly things.

"Will you and Mom ever get back together again?" asked Annie.[30]

"No," said her dad. "We'll always be your parents but we'll never live together or be married again."[31]

Annie sort of knew that. At first after they had separated, she had kept hoping they would get back together again. Her parents had always told her they wouldn't, but she had kept on hoping. Now she was kind of used to it, though, and somewhere inside her, she really knew that they would never come back to live with each other.

Annie's mother had had to go to work for more hours since the divorce because they needed the extra money. She would take Annie to school in the morning and go off to work herself and she wouldn't get back until 5:00. Mrs. Johnson, who lived down the street, would pick Annie up from school and look after her until her mother came home. Annie missed having her mom there when she got home from school. And her mom was tired after work and didn't have as much time to play with her as she used to.

Once, soon after Daddy had left, Annie had walked into the room to find Mommy just sitting and crying. Annie was frightened. It was scary to see a grown-up cry. Grown-ups were supposed to look after you when you cried, not cry themselves.

"It's all right, Annie," her mom had said. "I know it's scary for you to see me cry. But all people have to cry sometimes when very sad things happen. Even grown-up people. And I'll still be able to look after you even though I might be sad. And after a while, the sadness will get better too."

---

29. It helps to explain to children that parents too are distressed and can behave irrationally.

30. Children take a long time giving up the hope that their parents will get back together. Sometimes even years after the final divorce, children are still entertaining this fantasy.

31. It is important to be clear here and not build up unrealistic hopes, which can only delay the healing process.

At first when Annie's mom had started working all day, Annie had been very miserable. It seemed like she hardly ever got to see her mom. She missed her dad and she missed her mom too. She wished things could go back to the way they used to be.

At school she couldn't concentrate. She kept thinking about other things. When she tried to concentrate on her spelling, the letters would jump out and jumble themselves all over the page. She got 30 on her spelling quiz that week instead of her usual 90 or 100. She felt very miserable.

"I've gotten stupid," she said to her mom. "I used to be able to do things at school and now I can't. I feel so dumb."[32]

"Honey," said her mom, giving her a big hug, "you're not stupid. You've been worried and miserable with all the things going on at home. When people get really worried they can feel as if their brain's fogged up. They do silly things that they wouldn't usually do. They can't work properly or they trip over things and drop things. It happens to most people—it doesn't mean that they're stupid, just that they're worried or upset."

"Really?" said Annie. She felt relieved to think that she wasn't really dumb. And even more relieved to find that it happened to lots of people and not just her.

"Poor old Annie," said her mom, giving her another hug. "You've had a really rough time, haven't you. And I haven't been able to be around as much as I used to, and I've probably been a bit grumpy when I have been around. I get more tired with all this extra work, and you know what it's like when you're tired—it's much easier to get grumpy! Tell you what," she went on, "I've got a good idea. Why don't we set aside a special time for just you and me each day, say a half-hour before bedtime. We can play a game or tell a story or just talk. That way no matter how busy I am during the evening, you'll always know that we'll have that time together."

---

32. Children may fail in all sorts of areas as a result of stress. Reassure them about their worth and ability, and explain to them that many people react like this to stress. You might also want to teach them relaxation, as explained in that chapter.

"That sounds great!" said Annie. She felt better already. "That's a really good idea."[33]

Time went by and Annie started to feel better. There were still a lot of days when she wished Mom and Dad were back together again, but she was getting pretty used to the way things were now. Her mom still worked hard, but they always had their time together before bed and that was nice. She stayed with her dad every other weekend and she liked being there now. Sometimes, after a whole weekend with Dad, she thought she saw even more of him than she did before the divorce. One day when her mom was dropping her off at school she said, "As a special treat today, I'm going to pick up your favorite chocolate cake on my way home from work."

"Oh goodie!" said Annie. "Can my friend Emily have dinner with us tonight?"

"Sure," said Annie's mom. "I'll call her mother and arrange it."

Annie couldn't wait for Emily's visit, but when Emily came, instead of being her usual bouncy self, she looked very, very sad.

"My mom and dad are divorcing," she said to Annie.

"When my mom and dad divorced," Annie said, "it was just awful."

"It's horrible, isn't it," said Emily.

"I felt so sad, I thought I was going to die," said Annie. "I didn't know I could feel so sad."

"What happens?" asked Emily. "What did you do?"

"I didn't really do anything," said Annie. "I just felt really sad. I talked with Mom and Dad a bit, and then after a while I guess I just started to get used to things and it just started to feel better. I still feel sad about it sometimes. But mostly I don't think about it much and I feel happy a lot of the time. Good things still happen, you know. You think they're going to stop happening—that nothing good will ever happen again. But they don't. Like

.

---

33. Finding some special time to be alone with your child in a loving, supportive way is one of the greatest gifts you can give her.

after a bad dream, it sort of fades and then you start to feel better again."[34]

"Oh." Emily looked doubtful. "Do you think that'll happen to me too?" she asked.

Annie gave her hand a squeeze. "For sure it will," she said, and she took her arm and led her out into the kitchen.

"Look," she said, "Mom's bought some cake specially for us."

The cake was sitting on the table, big and plump and special. It had shiny icing all over its top and around the sides. Right in the middle was a big, juicy strawberry with chocolate leaves. It stood out from the brown icing and shone in the light like a little red heart.

"Here," said Annie, getting two plates, "a big piece for me and a big piece for you."

[34]. This is the positive ending, stressing that even though events may be painful and traumatic, one can still come through them to the light on the other side.

when somebody dies

death in our modern society is taboo almost to the extent that sex was in the Victorian age. It is not talked about, although its presence is felt; its name is denied: Grandma's "gone away," we've "lost" Uncle. Our children are "protected" from it: "She's too young to know," or "He's not old enough to go to a funeral." We generally try to pretend that it's not really something that happens to us.

Sex, to a large extent, has now come out into the open. Death in many families is still something that only just dares to poke its nose out of a very dusty closet.

Death is a natural part of life. Children come across death in various ways—a dead insect or bird on the sidewalk, the death of a pet, and so on. Too often, however, we try to protect them from the reality of death. Many a parent has raced to the pet shop in a frantic search to replace, before the child notices, the white mouse which has departed for the Big Cheese in the Sky. The opportunity to observe, learn, and understand about death in a meaningful way is lost. In doing this we are creating an unreal world for the child. Death and loss are always painful, but to pretend that they do not exist does not make them any less painful. Rather, it takes away from us the comfort of familiarity and understanding, the knowledge, for instance, that it does happen—white mice do die, you do feel sad, you recover, and then after a while feel ready to care for a new pet. Recognize too that some children will be more distressed than others over the death of a pet. The length of their mourning periods will vary, as will the time when they feel ready for a new pet. Don't force one on them prematurely.

Children go through various stages in their understanding of death.

Roughly speaking, three- to five-year-olds see death as only temporary. In their eyes it is a reversible absence. So when a three-year-old in a temper yells, "I wish you were dead," what she's really meaning is, "I wish you'd disappear for a while."

From five, children begin to gain the understanding that once dead, you cannot come back to life.

Around nine to twelve, they are coming to an adult understanding of death.

When explaining death to a young child, it is often helpful to describe it in terms of the absence of all familiar functions of life—for example, "When you're dead you can't move, or see or feel or breathe. You can't think or be aware of anything." This is the sort of concept that is meaningful to a young child.

Don't equate death with going to sleep. Young children can become terrified of going to sleep in case it means they are going to slip into death.

If someone your child knows has died in a hospital, stress that most people go to the hospital to get well and that being in a hospital, *per se*, does not kill you. A phrase like, "She's been taken to the hospital to die," can instill fearful fantasies about the meaning and function of hospitals.

Stress that simply getting sick does not lead to death. A phrase like, "She got sick and died," can lead an impressionable child to suppose that any sort of sickness can lead to death. She may become terrified of being sick or of seeing other people sick.

Saying that God took Jane because she was so good or because He loved her can be confusing to a child—does that mean that she, whom God left behind, is neither good nor loved? Equally, if the child does not yet feel ready to leave this world she may try to be bad or unlovable so that God is not tempted to take her.

Many of the euphemisms we use to describe death can be

very confusing for young children who take them literally. Sometimes instead of saying, "Mary died last night," we'll say such things as, "we lost Mary last night." This is very distressing to the child who takes you literally. If you lost Mary, why aren't you looking for her—don't you want to find her again? Such expressions as, "passed away," "not with us," and so on can be equally confusing. It is best to be clear and direct in the language you use to discuss death with children and avoid euphemisms.

When faced with a loss, children need to mourn and grieve just as adults do. It is important that they be allowed to express their feelings and that a sympathetic adult is able to provide them with a sense of security, comfort, and understanding as they work through their loss.

Children's artwork and imaginative play with toys will mirror their inner emotional state. A child trying to come to terms with someone's death may, for instance, become totally distraught over a broken toy and obsessively try to mend it. Children's drawings can poignantly express their grieving feelings. In the drawing my daughter did for this story the empty space that death leaves is clearly expressed in the empty room.

Notice too, the half-read book, the balls that Pirate must have played with on the floor, and the open door. In them, I think, is the expression that it was too soon for these two loved characters to die, as well perhaps, as the hope that they will walk in through the open door to finish their reading and playing.

Sometimes children can feel tremendously guilty about a death. If they had a fight or were angry with the deceased, they can believe that their anger caused him or her to die.

They may be openly sad and weepy or silently withdrawn. Sometimes they find it hard to verbalize the empty feeling of loss and may describe it as boredom. They may express their distress nonverbally with bed-wetting, nightmares, behavior problems and so on.

They can feel very angry at the deceased for deserting them. They may fear further abandonment by the important people in their life and can become very clingy and panic-stricken at the thought of separation. They need to be reassured that their feelings are normal and have their fears and guilt assuaged.

Children can often cope with grief only in fits and starts, so they have periods of intense sadness interspersed with what seems like normal, light-hearted play. This does not mean that they are heartless, but simply that it is difficult for them to cope with such intensely distressing feelings for long periods at a time.

If someone whom the child is close to is dying, it is helpful if the child can see him in order to say good-bye before he dies. If he is on a life-support machine, or looking very ill, prepare the child for his appearance beforehand, and explain the therapeutic purpose of the machines.

Explain how ill the person is and that he is likely to die. Holding hands, cuddling, or offering some sort of nonverbal reassurance as you explain is comforting to the child.

Doing something caring for the dying person can help a child to say a loving good-bye. She can feel that she has been able to give something to the person she loves.

Reminiscing about the dead person is part of the healthy working-through of the mourning process. We usually need to talk about, think about, feel pain about someone before we are ready for a healthy "letting go."

You can share your sadness with your child too. She may be puzzled if you show no open grief over the death of someone close to you. But make sure you let her know that your sadness is due to your loss and is not caused by something your child has done.

It is common at first for children to deny the death of a

loved one. Very young children, of course, have difficulty in understanding the permanence of death, but older children can still harbor the fantasy that the loved one will come back. Funerals and viewing of the body reinforce the concrete reality of the death and provide a closure of the experience.

Many adults don't allow children to attend a funeral under the mistaken belief they are saving the child from pain. However, a funeral can help a child face the reality of death. It can also provide the experience of sharing one's sorrow with others. It is a concrete indication of the finality of death. Children should be allowed to choose if they wish to attend a funeral. If they attend, they should always be accompanied by a loving adult who is able to provide security for them and to be sensitively aware of their needs.

The various procedures likely to take place at a funeral should be described beforehand to the child. Sometimes the uncontrolled display of grief at funerals may be distressing for children. It is usually frightening for them to see grownups out of control. If the child wishes to go to the funeral and there are likely to be such displays of grief, these should be explained to her beforehand.

In this story, I have not described the funeral in detail. As there are so many variations in funeral services, I have left it to you to fill in the details appropriate to the funeral your child might be attending.

I have also avoided religious and spiritual explanations of death, again for the reason that each family has its own particular set of beliefs.

When you are talking to your child about death, it's important that your explanation of what death is, and whether the soul continues on, is an explanation that you believe in. Children will become confused if you tell them that "Uncle Joe has gone to heaven," when your body language and other communications suggest that you don't believe there is such a place.

*a*nnie was a little girl who lived in a brown brick house with her mommy and daddy and a big black dog.[1]

They lived in a very busy street that had lots of traffic all day long. Sometimes Annie used to play

---

1. Change the details here to suit your child's environment.

guessing games about cars with her friends who came to visit. They would sit on the fence that ran around Annie's front garden and swing their legs and try to guess how many, say, green cars would go by in the next five minutes. Whoever was closest got to choose the next color to look for.

Sometimes Annie's Aunt Gerri, who lived across the road, would see them and wave from her front garden. Or else she would cross the road and come and sit with them and join in their game or teach them a new one. She was very good at games—she was the one who had taught Annie the car-color guessing game in the first place.

Annie loved Aunt Gerri. Her real name was Geraldine, but everyone called her Gerri. The first time Annie met a boy called Gerry she got a shock because she thought Gerry was a girl's name!

Gerri was Dad's sister, but she didn't look at all like him. He had dark hair and a round face and wasn't quite as tall as most of the other dads Annie knew. Aunt Gerri had red hair that looked as if it had lights inside it, and a long lively face. She was taller than anyone Annie knew. Or almost anyone.

Dad used to say that Gerri never stood still, and Annie thought that was true. Even when she was sitting, she didn't stay still. Her long hands moved around when she talked to you, and her face crinkled and creased into different expressions. She made you feel that everything was exciting and that you were exciting too.

Gerri didn't have any children. She had been married once, but her husband didn't live with her anymore. Annie's mom used to say that Gerri had worn him out. Annie got very puzzled by that. She had had cardigans that had worn out and holes had appeared in the sleeves. She tried to imagine that happening to Gerri's husband. Did that mean that holes had appeared in him? When she asked her mom, her mom had laughed and said it was just a saying. What she meant, she had explained, was that Gerri had had too much energy for him, and that he had gotten tired trying to keep up with her.

Annie used to love spending time at Gerri's house. Gerri was a bit messy and never threw anything away, so she had boxes and boxes of all sorts of things stacked in a special room in the house. Gerri would let Annie go through the boxes when she came over, and Annie would find all sorts of fascinating objects. Gerri let her play dress-up too in the old clothes which were in a closet in the room that held all the boxes. Annie loved to play in that room. Most of the things were very old, coming from a time before she was born. There were photos of people who were alive then and dead now. Annie would ask Gerri about them and her face would light up as she talked to Annie about them. Annie would say, "I wish they weren't dead; I want to meet them," and Gerri would say, "As long as you remember people, it's as if a part of them stays alive, even though their bodies are dead, so that although you can't touch them and talk to them, it's as if you can still get to meet them in your mind. Through my telling you about them too, you can feel almost as if you knew them as well."

Gerri liked to take Annie places. She would take her to the zoo, to the amusement park, or for walks on the beach. Everywhere she went, even when it was just to the corner store, Annie felt was the funniest, the most interesting, the most exciting place on Earth. When Annie said this once to Gerri, Gerri said, "But it's not just because I'm there. It's because you're there too. If you didn't have the energy to be interested in things, everything would be boring to you. If you weren't curious about things, nothing would be fascinating to you, and if you couldn't see the funny side of things, nothing would make you laugh."

Annie liked to think about that. It was nice to think that she could make things interesting or exciting or funny too.

One day there was a knock on the door. Even before Annie's mom answered it, Annie could hear Gerri's voice calling, "Hurry up! Look what I've got here!" She rushed to the door. Gerri stood there clutching a little wriggly bundle of fur. It was a kitten. It had long, silky fur and a pink nose and was white all over except for a black patch on one eye.

"The man at the shop gave it to me," Gerri explained. "His cat had kittens, and he's trying to find homes for them, so I said I'd take one."

Annie reached out a hand and stroked the kitten. It purred as if there were a little motor inside it.

"What shall I call it?" asked Gerri. "I thought you could help me name it."

Annie looked at the kitten. "I know what we can call it!" she said. "We can call it Pirate, because it's got a patch over one eye."

"I like that," said Gerri. "Pirate it is then."

Annie spent hours playing with Pirate. She would make balls out of crumpled newspaper and scuttle them across the floor. Pirate would pretend they were mice and chase after them to pounce on them. Sometimes she would dangle a ball of string, and Pirate would leap up like a dancer to try to catch it.

Sometimes Pirate would snuggle up in Annie's lap while Annie stroked her and purr and purr and purr.

Gerri had a tiny little door made in her kitchen for Pirate. It was only big enough to let a cat through, and Pirate would butt at the door with her head until it opened. Then she would squeeze in or out. It meant that she could go outside whenever she wanted.

"Cats like to roam around," said Gerri. "It's not fair to keep them shut up inside."

One day when Annie was playing in the kitchen, she heard a terrible sound from outside. It was a screeching sound, like a car swerving or putting its brakes on suddenly. There was no bang though. "They must have missed each other," she thought, and went on playing.

An hour later, there was a knock on the door. It was Gerri, and she looked very sad.

"I've got some bad news, Annie," she said. "Pirate was hit by a car, darling, and I'm afraid she's dead."[2]

Annie caught her breath. "But she can't be dead!" she said. "I was playing with her this morning."

"This happened later on, sweetheart," Gerri said. "It was only about an hour ago. The driver brought her in to me, but she died straight away."

Annie couldn't believe it. "But I was only playing with her this morning," she said again.

---

[2]. The death of a pet can provide a painful but valuable learning experience for children.

"I know," said Gerri, and put her arms around her. "It's very sad, isn't it?"

"How did it happen?" said Annie. She still couldn't believe it.

"Pirate ran out into the road, darling," said Gerri. "There was a car coming and the driver couldn't stop in time. The car hit her and it killed her." And Gerri gave Annie another hug.

"Can I see Pirate?" asked Annie.[3]

"Yes, darling. She's at my house. I'll take you over," said Gerri.

Pirate was lying on her blanket in Gerri's kitchen. Her eyes were closed and there was blood around her head.

"Will she wake up?" asked Annie. She kept thinking that she saw Pirate breathing.[4]

"No, darling, she won't wake up," said Gerri. "She's dead. That means she's not breathing or thinking, and she can't move or feel anything.[5] When someone dies, it's not as if he's sleeping. It's quite different from sleep. When someone's sleeping, he's alive and will wake up again. When you're dead it means you'll never wake up or get up ever again. You can't come back to life after you're dead."

Annie nodded.[6] She really knew that. When she was little she had thought that death meant you just weren't there for a bit and then you'd come back. Now she knew that death meant you could never come back.

She felt very sad. "I hate that driver!" she said. "I hate him!"[7]

"I know you're angry," said Gerri, "but it really wasn't his fault. Pirate ran out without looking, and the driver couldn't stop in time."

"I heard it, you know," said Annie. "I was in the kitchen. Maybe if I'd run out I could have saved her."

---

3. It can be helpful for children and adults to see the body of the person or animal. It helps bring home the reality of the death.

4. Denial is a very common early response to the news of a death.

5. This is an explanation of death that a child can understand.

6. Very young children see death as impermanent.

7. It is common for children to feel intense anger over the death of some person or animal they have loved.

"No, darling," said Gerri.[8] "There was nothing you could have done. It all happened too quickly."

"What will happen to Pirate now?" asked Annie.

"I'm going to bury her in the garden," said Gerri. "Do you want to help me?"

Annie and Gerri found a spot in the garden to bury Pirate.[9] It was in the shade near a rose bush. Gerri dug a hole, and they put Pirate in and covered her body with earth. The winter wind blew around their shoulders. They both felt very sad.

"I feel awful," said Annie, and a tear dripped down her nose.

"I know," said Gerri, giving her a hug. "We both feel sad about Pirate. It feels terrible. But after a while you know, with the passing of time, we'll start to feel better. We'll always remember Pirate, but we won't feel sad anymore."

"Will she mind being underneath all that earth?" asked Annie.[10]

"No," said Gerri, "because now that she's dead, she can't feel or see anything."

"I played with her a lot," said Annie. "She liked that."

"Yes," said Gerri, "she loved to play with you. You gave her lots of fun in her life."

Annie put some pretty pebbles on Pirate's grave, and they both stood silently for a minute. Then they went inside.

Quite a lot of time went by. The winter turned into spring, and spring turned into summer. Annie liked summer because it was a good season for swimming. Often in summer, Gerri would take Annie down to the beach. Annie's mom and dad didn't like the beach—they said it was too hot and sandy and there were too many flies, but Gerri loved it. On a hot day, she and Annie would change into their swimsuits, hop into the car, and head down there. They would splash each other in the waves and go

---

8. Children need reassurance that it wasn't their fault and that there was nothing they could have done.

9. The ritual of burial and mourning can provide a sense of comfort for the bereaved.

10. This is a common question that children want reassurance on.

for long walks, collecting shells or just talking. There was a food stand there, and Annie always had trouble deciding what flavor ice cream to get. Sometimes she thought she liked chocolate best, and sometimes vanilla.

Today was the first really hot day of summer, and Gerri had promised to take Annie to the beach. Annie had been looking forward to it for ages. She got herself all dressed up in her swimsuit, packed her towel, sun hat, and suntan lotion, raced downstairs, thinking that her mom would be proud of her for having remembered to pack everything. Instead, her mom just looked rather worried.

"Darling," she said, when she saw Annie, "I was just coming up to tell you something. Gerri called to say that she can't take you to the beach today after all."

"But why?" said Annie. She was very disappointed. She had been looking forward to it so much.

"She has to go to the city instead," said her mom.

"But that's not fair," said Annie. "She promised me she'd take me to the beach. Why does she have to go to the city today?" She felt really upset.

"She has to see a doctor," said Annie's mom.

"Couldn't she see the doctor another time?" said Annie.

"No," her mom said, "she had to see him today."

Annie wandered off to her room. She felt very miserable. She thought it wasn't fair of Gerri to promise things and not to do them. She felt angry at Gerri.

Later that day, the phone rang. Annie's mom came upstairs. "It's Aunt Gerri," she said, "and she wants to speak to you."

"I don't want to speak to her," said Annie. She was still cross with Aunt Gerri.

That evening at dinner, Annie's mom and dad were very quiet. They had been talking about something when Annie came downstairs, but they had stopped talking as soon as they saw her.[11] Annie wondered if they had been talking about her.

---

11. If there is a lot of "secret" talk about illness and death children can develop frightening fantasies as to what terrible things the grownups are trying to hide from them.

The next morning Annie's mom said to her, "Do you want to go over and visit Aunt Gerri?"

"Yes," said Annie. She started to go upstairs to get her new doll to show to Aunt Gerri.

"She's been rather sick, you know," said Annie's mom. "That's why she had to see the doctor."

"Oh," said Annie. "Is she better now?"

"We don't know," said her mom. "The doctors are doing their best to treat her."

Gerri was sitting out in the garden when they came. She looked tired and a bit pale. Annie's mom looked sad when she saw her. "Can I do anything for you, Gerri?" she asked, giving her a hug. "I'm going down the street. Is there any shopping I can do for you?"

Annie thought it was strange that her mom should be asking Gerri, who had so much energy, whether she could do the shopping for her. Usually it was the other way around.

"Why can't Gerri do it herself?" she asked.

"I'm feeling a bit sick," said Gerri. "The doctor said I should rest a lot."

Annie and Gerri played quieter games that day. They played cards—Gerri taught Annie how to play Old Maid— and Annie taught Gerri how to play Go Fish. Her father had just taught her that.

The first half of summer went by and Annie was still waiting for Gerri to get better. She knew that when Gerri got better, she would take her down to the beach, and they would go for all their old walks again. Each day Annie ran in hoping to see that Gerri was getting stronger and healthier again, but each day Gerri seemed to get paler, thinner, and weaker.

One day Annie said to Gerri, "How long will it be before you're better?"

Gerri sighed and took off her coat—she had just come back from the doctor's. "Darling, the doctor says I may not get better."[12]

---

12. As far as possible, be honest with children. They will usually pick up that something's wrong somewhere, and it is usually more frightening for them to be left to fantasize about what it is than to have a sensitive and comforting adult tell them in terms they can understand.

"You mean you'll always be sick?" asked Annie.

"Yes, darling," said Gerri. "Mine is the sort of sickness that doesn't get better—it just gets worse and worse. When it gets very bad, you die, because your body can't stay alive any longer when it's so sick."

"Oh," said Annie. She didn't quite know what to say. "But Dr. McDonald's a very good doctor." Her mom was always saying the Dr. McDonald was one of the best doctors around. "He'll fix you up and make you get better. That's what doctors are for, aren't they?"

Gerri looked very sad. "Even Dr. McDonald can't fix me up," she said. "He can fix up a lot of illnesses, but he can't fix up this one."

"They could put you into a hospital then," said Annie. "They could do an operation and fix you up that way."

"No," said Gerri, "Even an operation won't make my sickness go away."

"I don't want you to die," said Annie, and she began to cry.

Gerri put her arms around her. "I know darling. I don't want to die either, but everyone has to die sooner or later."

"Why can't you die later?" said Annie. She was still sobbing. "Why can't you wait till I'm old and grown up before you die?"

"I wish I could, darling," said Gerri, "but we can't choose when to die," and she gave Annie another hug.

Annie felt very sad. She hated feeling sad like that. It was scary. Her mom and dad looked sad like that too, and that was even more scary.

Annie tried to make herself happy so that she wouldn't have to be sad. She raced around the house at top speed, laughing and yelling and trying to make the dog chase her. Her mom caught her in the corridor and gave her a hug.

Annie felt frightened.

"Isn't it all right to be happy?" she asked.

"It's all right to be happy, darling," said her mom. "It's just that we might not all feel happy at the same time. But even if we're sad, it's all right for you to be happy."

"It's hard for me to be happy when you're sad," said Annie.

"I know, darling," said her mom and gave her another hug.

"Will we ever all be happy again?" asked Annie.

"Yes darling, we will," said her mom, "but in between, there'll be times when we'll be sad too."

The next morning Annie felt worried about visiting Gerri. She was scared it would make her too sad.

"I don't think I'll go to Gerri's today," she said to her mom.

"That's all right," said her mom. "You can go whenever you feel like it."

That afternoon, though, Annie's mom said to her, "I'm popping over to Gerri's now. Would you like to come?"

"Okay," said Annie. Somehow it felt safer when her mom was with her.

When they saw Gerri though, it wasn't really frightening. Gerri was still Gerri, and she smiled and talked and played games with Annie. Annie felt better. She wouldn't need her mother to go with her next time.

"I felt scared to visit Gerri this morning," she said to her mom on the way back.

"I know," said her mom. "Sometimes it can feel scary to visit someone when you've been told that they're going to die. It's scary to feel how sad you are. And you think you won't know what to say to them. But you know darling, Gerri's still alive and she's still our Gerri. We don't know exactly how much time she's got left, but we can make the most of it." And she gave Annie a hug.

"The sickness that Gerri has," said Annie, "is it catching?" She had been a bit worried about that.

"No," said her mom, "it's not catching. You couldn't catch it from anyone, no matter how much time you spent with them or no matter how close you got."

"Oh, good," said Annie. She felt better knowing that.[13]

Every day now when Annie went to see Gerri, she watched carefully to see how Gerri was looking. It didn't seem possible that Gerri was going to die. She kept think-

---

13. Children are often reassured to know that a terminal illness, such as cancer, is not infectious.

ing that one day she would start to get better.[14]

Some days Annie thought that if she were very good and did everything right, then maybe God would let Gerri live and grow healthier again.[15]

She went for weeks being very good, but Gerri just got sicker and sicker. Annie was angry with God. "It's not fair," she said to her mom. "Why did Gerri get sick? She never did anything bad."

"Sometimes things happen that aren't fair," said Annie's mom, stroking her hair. "Sometimes good people get sick, and sometimes bad things happen to good people."

"Well, why bother then!" said Annie. "Why bother being good when bad things can still happen to you? It's not fair." She felt very upset.

"We're not good because it means that we won't get sick," said Annie's mom. "We're good because that feels like the best way to behave to us."

Annie felt very sad. She felt very worried too, because she had an awful secret. Sometimes she felt like telling her mom, but then she got worried that it was too awful to tell anyone.

Finally, one day, when she was going home from school with her mom, she looked up and said, rather nervously, "Mom, I did something awful a while ago."

"What was it?" said her mom. "You look as if you've been worrying about it."

"Do you remember," said Annie, "when Aunt Gerri was going to take me to the beach and went to the doctor instead?"

"Yes," said her mom, "I remember that."

"You remember I was really mad at her for breaking her promise?" said Annie.

Her mom nodded.

"Well, I was so mad at her, I wished she'd get really sick.[16] It was only for the day, and I felt sorry afterwards

---

14. It takes time for children to really digest and accept the news of someone's impending death.

15. This sort of "bargaining with God" is often seen.

16. This fear is very common in children. They believe that their anger and bad wishes can be lethal—that they can actually cause someone's death. They need to be told that this isn't so.

and took it back, but it was too late," and Annie started to cry. "I made her get sick, Mom. I wished her into getting sick."

Her mom put an arm around her and patted her head. "You've been worrying about this a lot, haven't you?"

Annie nodded. She felt so awful.

"It doesn't work like that, you know, Annie," her mom said. "You can't wish someone into being sick. Aunt Gerri got sick because her body wasn't working properly. It had nothing at all to do with your wish. I promise you."

Annie looked up through her tears. "Really?" she said. "You promise?"

"Yes," said her mom. "It's true. You can't make someone sick by wishing them sick. But a lot of kids don't know that. They think that if they've been angry at someone, and then that person gets sick or dies, that they've made it happen."

"Really?" said Annie. "A lot of kids feel that?"

"Yes," said her mom. "Lots and lots of kids."

"Gosh," said Annie. It was a relief to know that she wasn't the only one who thought she'd done such a terrible thing.

"And you know," her mom went on, "it's normal to get angry at someone you love.[17] It doesn't mean you don't love him. It just means you got angry at him for a bit. You get angry at me sometimes, but you still love me, don't you? And I get angry at you sometimes, but I still love you."

"Yes," said Annie. She hadn't thought of it like that.

"Getting angry at people doesn't destroy them," said her mom. "People are stronger than that. It can hurt their feelings, but it doesn't destroy them. Imagine if I crumbled into dust every time you got angry with me."

Annie had to laugh. It did sound sort of funny.

"When you get angry at me, I sometimes feel a bit sad or hurt or cross, but it doesn't last long. And all the time, deep inside me, I know that you really love me and that that hasn't changed, and also that I really love you and will go on loving you."

---

17. It's reassuring for children to know that you can be angry at someone and still love him, and also to know that they can be angry and still be loved.

Annie didn't answer. She was thinking.

"And you know, too," her mom went on, "if we get angry, and one of us thinks she did the wrong thing, she'll come up to the other one and apologize."

"That's right," said Annie. "If you've snapped at me for no reason, you'll say sorry afterwards." She paused. "I was thinking maybe that I could tell Aunt Gerri how I was angry with her that day and wouldn't speak to her when she called me and that I've been worrying about it and am sorry because I really do love her."

"I'm sure Aunt Gerri would understand if you told her that," said her mom, "and she does know that you love her. She loves you too, very much."

That day, Annie went over to Aunt Gerri's and told her everything. Aunt Gerri gave her a hug and said, "That's okay, darling. There are probably days when I've been a bit snappy or quiet with you too. That's because I've been worrying about being sick."[18]

"I worry too," said Annie.

"I know," said Gerri, and gave her a hug.

"Are you really, really going to die, Aunt Gerri?" asked Annie. She still didn't believe that Gerri could really die.

Gerri looked sad. "Yes darling," she said. "The doctors say there isn't anything they can do anymore."

"When?" asked Annie. She felt terrible.

"I don't know," said Gerri. "But the doctors have told me that my sickness is getting worse."

Then they both held each other and cried a bit.[19]

Annie tried to visit Gerri every day. She would do special drawings for her in bright colors. Gerri hung them up in her room.

"Thank you for the drawings," she said. "They make me feel better just to look at them. And I love your visits."

Annie felt good when she said that. It was nice to

---

18. Sometimes children can construe the dying person's weakness or depression as a rejection of them. As well, the surviving caretakers can be so immersed in their sorrow that they may also seem rejecting.

19. Sharing the sad feelings can be very helpful.

know she was helping in some way even if she couldn't make Gerri well.[20]

Every day Gerri seemed to look more and more pale. These days she stayed in bed all the time. Annie used to sit on her bed and play cards with her. Annie didn't stay very long because Gerri got tired easily, but she knew that Gerri liked her visits because her eyes always lit up when she saw Annie, and she would always give her a hug and a kiss.

Gerri felt different to hug lately. She was much skinnier and bonier, and sometimes she had a funny smell about her.[21] Annie didn't like it at first, but Gerri explained that it was all to do with being sick.

Sometimes Gerri would ask her to do special things for her like put a letter in the mailbox. Annie felt proud when she did that. It was good to know that she could do something for Gerri.

One day, just before Annie was setting off for school, the phone rang. Annie's mother answered it and Annie knew from her terrible "Oh" that something awful had happened. Her mom came out of the kitchen. Her eyes were red. "It's your Aunt Gerri," she said. "The nurse who visited her this morning said she was much sicker and they had to take her to the hospital." She walked back to the phone. "I'll just call Dad," she said, "and we'll all go in to see her. You don't have to go to school today."[22]

The hospital was very big and busy. They walked down a long corridor. Annie was frightened. She didn't want Aunt Gerri to be in the hospital.

"When will she come out of the hospital?" she asked her mom.

Her mom looked sad. "Mostly when people go to the

20. Children, and adults, feel better able to cope if they experience themselves as being able to help or give to the dying person in some way. Generally our experience of being with someone who is dying is one of terrifying helplessness and powerlessness.

21. Children can often be frightened by the appearance, smell, and other aspects of the severely ill person.

22. If your hospital doesn't allow children to visit, change this part of the story. However, do explain about what goes on in hospitals and what is happening to the patient. Without clear explanations, children construct fantasies that are usually far more terrifying than the reality.

hospital, it makes them well, so they can leave it and go back home.[23] But Aunt Gerri has got the sort of sickness that doesn't get well, it only gets worse. This morning she had trouble breathing, and that's why they had to take her to the hospital. In hospitals they have machines that help you breathe. But the doctors said she's so sick that she may not be able to come home."

"Is she going to die, Mom?" Annie asked. Her voice felt all weak and trembly.

"Yes darling, she's going to die. The doctors and the hospital are doing all they can to help her, but they think she's going to die soon."

They walked along the corridor holding hands.[24] Annie felt very sad.

Her dad said, "When you see Gerri, she will have funny machines around her and tubes going into her.[25] They might look a bit scary, but they're there to help her as much as possible."

Dad was right. There were funny machines around Gerri, some of them making strange sounds. She was very white and looked very small in the big hospital bed surrounded by machines and bottles and tubes. She had her eyes closed, but she opened them when Annie came in, and she smiled faintly as if she were very, very weak.

Annie felt awful. It was scary to see her Aunt Gerri like this. She wanted her to be as she was before, strong and full of energy.

Gerri beckoned to her to come closer. "It's all right," she said. "I know I look funny, but I'm still Gerri."

Annie gave her a kiss. "I love you, Gerri" she said. She felt like crying.

"I know, darling," said Gerri. She looked sad too. "I love you too, and you've made me very happy. You're a wonderful little girl, and I'm so glad I was lucky enough to be your aunt."

---

23. Stress that a hospital is not just a place to go to die, otherwise children may become unduly terrified of hospitals.

24. Nonverbal comforting, such as hand-holding, is a source of security at a time like this.

25. Children can become frightened by the tubes, bottles, and machinery ranged around the patient. Explain to them beforehand, stressing that the machines are good machines and are there to help.

"I was lucky too," said Annie, although she felt very, very unlucky now.[26]

They stayed holding hands until the nurse came in to say it was time for the visitors to go.[27]

Annie drove home with her mom and dad. They all felt very, very sad. No one said very much.

Later that night the phone rang again. Her father got up to answer it. After a few minutes he came back into the room. He had tears in his eyes. "Gerri died," he said. "It was the hospital calling."

Everyone was very, very sad. Annie stayed near her mom a lot. She didn't feel like doing anything much. All the things she used to like doing didn't seem like much fun now.

The funeral was a few days after Gerri's death. Her mom told her that if she wanted to, she could come to the funeral, but if she didn't want to, that would be all right.

"Funerals are when people get together to bury some-one they love," she said.[28] "They don't actually dig a hole in the ground where the body will stay, but they all meet together to lay the coffin in the ground and to talk about the person who died. It's a way of saying good-bye to him. Some people like to say good-bye in a group like this, or others like to do it by themselves. You can do either. At a funeral there are usually a lot of people crying. Some people cry a great deal and sound as if they are in terrible pain. It's natural to cry when you're sad, and it helps to get over the sadness. Sometimes, though, it can be a bit scary for kids to see grownups crying so very hard. On the other hand, it can feel comforting to say good-bye in a group of people who are all feeling sad about the same thing and who have all come there for the same reason."

Annie decided she would go to the funeral. Her mom

---

26. The opportunity to say good-bye is a very valuable one which can help immensely with the grieving process.

27. If your child isn't allowed to visit in the hospital, she might want to write a loving note to the patient or make a little drawing or gift as her way of expressing her feelings, and to say good-bye.

28. This is an explanation of funerals that children can understand. You can fill in the details according to the particular type of funeral you are likely to be attending. It is helpful if children are allowed to choose without pressure whether they wish to attend or not.

and dad told her what would happen beforehand, and they sat with her and held her hand the whole time.[29]

Afterwards she said to her mom and dad, "What would happen to me if you died? Who would look after me?"[30]

"Well," said her mom, "first of all, we're both healthy and strong and are going to live for a long, long time."

"And," said her father, "if Mommy died, then I would look after you, and if I died, Mommy would look after you."

"What if you both died?" asked Annie.

"If we both died," said her mom, "then Grandma and Grandpa would look after you."

"Oh," said Annie. It felt better to know that she would always be looked after.

A lot of the time after Gerri's death, Annie felt sad.[31] Sometimes she felt angry at Gerri for dying and leaving her. Sometimes she felt that maybe it hadn't really happened, and Gerri was still alive in her house across the road. But sometimes, in between feeling sad, Annie would find that she was having quite a good time, watching TV or playing with a friend.[32] Every now and then when she realized she was feeling happy, she would feel bad about being happy, as though feeling happy meant that she had forgotten about Gerri.[33]

When she said this to her mom, her mom said, "I understand how you feel. Even grownups sometimes feel like that too. But it's not wrong to feel happy. It doesn't mean that we've forgotten Gerri, it just means that life is beginning to get back to normal."

---

29. If the child goes to the funeral, it is important that she be given a lot of support.

30. This is a question that children are commonly concerned with in the aftermath of a death. They need reassurance.

31. These are all common emotional reactions after a death. It's helpful if you can reassure your child that what she is feeling is painful but normal.

32. Children can usually only tolerate intense sadness for limited spans of time. Their grieving may seem to be an on-and-off affair—periods of depression alternating with periods of play. This is normal mourning behavior for them.

33. Children, and adults, can believe that feeling happy is being disloyal to the memory of their loved one.

Annie said, "When Gerri died, I thought I would never be happy again."

"I know," said her mom. "Lots of people feel like that when someone they love dies. It's like being in the middle of winter and thinking that the sun will never shine again or that it will never be warm again. But in time, if you just keep going, winter passes and spring comes. Things start to grow again, and the birds sing. The sun comes out, and the weather starts to get warmer and warmer. Sometimes while you're in the middle of winter though, it's hard to believe that spring will come even though it always does."

Annie and her mom and dad talked a lot about Gerri.[34] They remembered her jokes and the things that she had done and said. Annie liked to talk about Gerri.

One day she was talking to her friend, Jill. Jill's grandmother had died last year.

"After she died," Jill said, "no one ever talked about her.[35] It was as if she had disappeared or had never ever been. I hated it."

Annie was glad she could talk about Gerri with her mom and dad.

One day, in the summer again, Annie was sitting on the fence with her new friend, Susan.

"I know a great game to play," said Annie. "You have to guess how many of the same color cars are going to pass by in a certain number of minutes."

"That sounds like a good game," said Susan.

"My Aunt Gerri taught it to me," said Annie proudly, and she began to tell Susan all about Gerri.

It felt good to sit in the sun and play the game that Gerri had taught her and remember all the good things they had done together.[36] Annie still felt sad when she thought of Gerri's death and still wished she were here to play with her, but it was good to sit in the sun with a friend and remember Gerri like this.

---

34. Reminiscing is an important part of the normal, healthy grieving process.

35. It can be very distressing for children if people refuse to talk about the dead person.

36. This is the positive ending, showing that even after great loss and sorrow, life goes on and in time becomes enjoyable again.

relaxation

We all need to relax. Some of us are good at it while others find it hard to do. Children are the same. Relaxation makes almost everything feel better and run more smoothly. We feel less pain when we are relaxed; we work better, play more happily, feel healthier, sleep more easily, and in general function at a significantly more enjoyable level.

Children can benefit from relaxation when they're stressed, over-tired, frustrated, worried, over-excited, or when they simply feel like it. And just as with adults, many of them have to be taught how to relax or reminded when to do it.

Teaching relaxation through the medium of storytelling is a particularly pleasant way of doing it, both for the child and the storyteller. Some children like an active fantasy in which a lot happens. Others like a more passive one where they may just be sitting quietly in a peaceful scene with nothing much going on. Children's wants and needs will differ from time to time as well as from child to child.

Some of the relaxation scenes you might like to try out include, for example, the fantasy of turning into a rag doll, or of a trip to the beach or the countryside. There are a myriad of other relaxing fantasies that you could share with your child and weave in and out of your stories.

When you're describing these scenes, make them as rich in detail as possible so that the imagery is very vivid and alive. Wherever possible, describe the feel, sound, smell, and taste of the scene, as well as the sight. These extra descriptive dimensions add to the vitality and intensity of the experience.

As you read this story, which involves a magic carpet, your child may spontaneously start to comment on her own fantasy scenes with the carpet. It's helpful to listen encouragingly to these and perhaps weave them into the story or into future stories. Don't be dismayed by her talking—she can still be relaxed as she speaks, and it shows that she is entering wholeheartedly into the story. The more involved your child is, the more she will gain from it. It is helpful to suggest to your child that she will enjoy listening to the story even more with her eyes closed.

In this story, Annie's mother tells her a story about a little girl called Andrea. The technique of telling a story within a story and confusing the boundaries between the two can serve to increase the child's involvement and help with the relaxation process.

annie was a little girl who lived in a brown brick house with her mommy and daddy and a big black dog.[1]

Usually she woke up each morning feeling happy and sunny, but this day when she woke up, it was with a cross, grumpy feeling.[2]

She stomped into the kitchen. "Where's my breakfast?" she demanded of her mother.

"My goodness," said her mother, "you look as if you got up on the wrong side of bed this morning."

"A big nasty motorcycle roared by in the street before I was ready to wake up. I didn't want to wake, but it made me wake up," said Annie. She was very cross about it. She thought all motorcycles ought to be scrunched up and fed to a big motorcycle-eating monster.[3]

"Well, here are your corn flakes darling," said her mom. "I've got them all ready for you."

"I don't want corn flakes—I want Wheaties," snapped Annie.

"Well darling, I'm sorry about that but I've already poured the milk, so you really should have them. You can have Wheaties tomorrow."

"I don't want Wheaties tomorrow, I want them today. It's not fair!" said Annie, and she marched into the TV room. "You should have asked me before you poured them."

In the TV room she looked at the TV Guide and then she looked at the clock. Darn it! She had missed her favorite TV show. It was just not fair.

"I've missed my TV show," she wailed to her mother. "You should have reminded me. It's not fair!"

"I'm sorry, darling," said her mom, giving her shoulders a pat, "but I didn't know you wanted to watch it. Why don't you play with your new jigsaw puzzle instead?"

Annie looked around. Her new puzzle was lying on the

---

1. Tailor these details to fit in with your child's environment.

2. This provides the motivation for Annie's wish to learn relaxation—it will help her feel better and enjoy the day more.

3. Tailor these upsetting events to fit your child's situation so that she can identify with them.

coffee table. It was a big, shiny puzzle with pictures of hamsters on it.[4] Annie loved hamsters and wanted one, but her parents had said, "No more pets!" It wasn't fair, thought Annie. All she wanted was one little hamster.

"Why don't you get dressed first," said her mom. "It's a bit cold in here with just your nightie on."

Annie went to her room. She knew just what she wanted to wear today—her favorite red jogging suit. She looked in her closet.

"My jogging suit's not here!" she said to her mother.

"It's in the laundry," said her mother. "Why don't you pick out something else?"

"I don't want to wear something else. I want to wear my jogging suit," said Annie. "It's not fair." And she stomped back into the TV room.

She had just organized the jigsaw puzzle into a pile of straight-edged pieces which went on the sides, and the others, when Blackie, the dog, walked in. Now Blackie loved three things in life—she loved playing fetch, going for walks, and eating tissues and jigsaw puzzle pieces.

She came in very quietly so that Annie didn't hear her. Slowly her black muzzle began to sniff, sniff, sniff at the table where the jigsaw pieces were. She really loved tissues best, but jigsaw pieces would do, and so, suddenly, with a quick snatch, she grabbed three pieces and ran off down the hall.

Annie ran after her yelling, "Bad dog! Bad dog! Give me back my jigsaw!"

Annie's mom came around the corner, grabbed Blackie, and took the pieces from her mouth. "Here you are," she said to Annie. "Here are your jigsaw pieces."

"They're all wet!" said Annie. "Yuck! It's not fair!" And she felt like crying.

"You're really having a rotten morning, aren't you?" said her mom. "And you feel just terrible."[5]

"Yes," said Annie. "I feel rotten. It's a rotten day."

"Would you like me to show you a way of feeling

---

4. My daughter currently has a hankering for hamsters, so I've made use of this in the story. You can make similar use of your own child's fads and fancies.

5. This sort of response enables your child to feel listened to and understood. She is then likely to feel more ready to listen to your suggestions.

better?" asked her mom. "That way you might at least be able to enjoy the rest of the day and it wouldn't be such a waste for you."[6]

"Okay," said Annie. "How would I do it?"

"Well, sit down and let me tell you a special story," said her mom, "and as you listen to the story, you might begin to feel better and better."

"Okay," said Annie. This sounded good.

Annie got settled down comfortably and her mom began.

"Once upon a time, there was a little girl named Andrea. Normally she was a happy little girl, but today she had been having a horrible, horrible day. Everything she did went wrong. Her lunch was a yucky lunch, her drawings didn't work out right, and her favorite story-book was missing.[7]

" 'I feel yucky,' she said to her mom. 'I'm having a horrible day.'

" 'Would you like to know how to feel better?' said her mom.

" 'I certainly would,' said Andrea, because she didn't like feeling yucky like this. 'How do I do it?'

" 'Well,' said Andrea's mom, 'why don't you sit down comfortably, and I'll show you how to do some very special breathing that will help you feel better. We can just sit here and take some very quiet, deep breaths. They're very special breaths because it's a very special, magical way of breathing. I'll explain to you why that is in a minute.' "[8]

And then Annie's mom said to Annie.[9] "You can breath along with me, and Andrea and her mom too if you

---

6. This provides some motivation for your child—at least the rest of the day won't be such a waste.

7. Andrea's upsetting situations are similar to Annie's. This enables the child to identify easily with Andrea as well as with Annie. Again, suit these situations to your own child's experience.

8. Children love things that are special or magical—their interest is immediately captured.

9. The Annie and Andrea stories are becoming interwoven here as they will continue to be for the rest of the story. This double interweaving can allow your child to become more fully absorbed by the story.

like, and then you can be part of the special, magical breathing."

"Oh, great," said Annie. She had been going to do that anyway, even if her mom hadn't said it.

"Then," Annie's mom went on, "Andrea's mom said, 'Now we can just sit here and breathe quietly for a few minutes, and feel the breath coming in and going all through our bodies, filling us up with air and then coming out again.'

" 'Yes, I can feel that,' said Andrea."

"I can feel that too," said Annie. She was enjoying breathing and listening to the story. She was waiting to hear too what the special, magical part of this breathing was. She liked things that were special and magical.

" 'Now the special, magical part of this breathing,' went on Andrea's mom, 'is that if you close your eyes and look very closely, you can actually see the special breaths as they go through your body. When the breath comes in, it's clear and sparkling, like light or glass. Everyone's breath is a different color. As it goes through your body, it changes color. It gets gray or muddy, and by the time it goes out of your body, it's very gray or muddy.'[10]

" 'Ooh, I can see it now,' said Andrea. She had her eyes closed and she could really see the breath coming in and going out of her body, very slowly, because she was breathing very slowly and quietly.

" 'What color is it?' asked her mom.

" 'When it comes in, it's a lovely sparkling white, like a diamond. When it goes out, it's yucky brown.' "

"I can see mine too," said Annie. She also had her eyes closed and was breathing quietly. "It's white when it comes in and it's a yucky, muddy color when it goes out."

" 'Why does it change color?' asked Andrea.

" 'It changes color,' said her mom, 'because as it travels through your body, it's picking up all the bad feelings and all the rotten things that have happened to you during the day and it's taking them away with it, outside your body.'

---

10. Your child might volunteer what the color of her breath is here, or you might like to ask her what she imagines it would be like.

" 'You mean the way a sponge does when you wipe up spills on the table?' said Andrea.

" 'That's exactly right,' said her mom. 'And just like a sponge, the more we wipe up, the less yucky stuff there is left. If you look at your breath coming out now, for instance, you would probably see that it's not quite as brown as it was before.'

" 'That's right,' said Andrea."

"It's happening to me too," said Annie. "This is great."

" 'And as you keep watching your breath,' Andrea's mom said, 'you can see that it keeps on getting lighter and clearer as it goes out. That's because there's less and less yucky stuff left in you. All the bad feelings and rotten things that happened to you today are being cleared away by the magic breaths.'

" 'This is great,' said Andrea. 'My breath's nearly completely clear now.' "

"Mine's clear already," said Annie. "It cleared up even faster than Andrea's. It's white all the way through. This is terrific. It feels really good. I like this."

"That's great," said Annie's mom, and then she went on. "And Andrea's mom said, 'Tell me when your breath is completely clear, and then we can do something more that you'll really enjoy.'

" 'It's clear now,' said Andrea.

"Andrea's mother continued. 'That's great. Now we can go on a very special magic trip in our imagination. And it's something that you can really enjoy.'

" 'What is it?' asked Andrea. She was really looking forward to this. She loved magic trips.

" 'It's a trip on your very own magic carpet,' said her mom.

" 'Oh wow!' said Andrea."

"Oh goodie," said Annie. She had always wanted to take a trip on a magic carpet, but she just hadn't known that you could do that in your mind.

" 'You can do anything in your mind,' said Andrea's mom. 'And because it's your mind and your imagination, you can control it. You can make anything happen that you like. You can change anything that you like. And everything that happens can feel just right for you.' "

relaxation

" 'Oh wow,' said Andrea."

"This is going to be great," said Annie. She was really looking forward to this.

" 'First of all,' said Andrea's mom, 'you have to choose what color your magic carpet will be. Will it be pink or red or yellow or blue? Will it be green or purple or black or white? Will it be just one color or a few different colors?'[11]

"Andrea thought for a few moments."

Annie thought too. It was funny how it was easier to think of these things when you had your eyes closed. She began to see lovely colors floating across her mind. Which of them would she choose?[12]

" 'I'll have purple and white,' announced Andrea, and she imagined a beautiful purple and white carpet to herself. 'Purple is for princes and princesses, and I like that.' "

"My carpet will be white and purple," said Annie, and she imagined a wonderful white and purple carpet to herself. "White is for unicorns, and I like that."

" 'What sort of patterns does your carpet have?' asked Andrea's mom. 'Are they swirly, circle patterns or are they straight, square patterns? Are they simple, separate patterns or are they all tangled-up patterns? Or are they not patterns at all? . . .'

"Andrea looked closely at her carpet. It had a lovely pattern of white moons on a purple background.

" 'I've got moons on my carpet,' she said. 'They're beautiful.' "

Annie looked closely at her carpet too. It was lovely. It had a beautiful pattern of purple stars on a white background.

"I love my carpet," she said. "It has purple stars on it."

" 'That sounds beautiful,' said Andrea's mom.

"That sounds beautiful," said Annie's mom, and she

---

11. This imaginative exercise involves the visual sense—what do you see, what does it look like, for example. The more senses you can bring into play, the more vivid the imagery becomes. Other senses are called up as the story continues.

12. A pause here allows your child the time to meditate on what color her carpet will be. Whenever you see a series of dots (. . .) in this story, pause for a moment or two before going on with the story.

continued on. "And Andrea's mom said, 'What does your carpet feel like, I wonder. Is it smooth and silky or is it soft and furry? Is it cool like sheets, or warm like blankets?[13] I wonder what nice feelings your carpet has for you? . . .'

" 'Mine's warm and woolly,' said Andrea. 'I can snuggle up in it.' "

"Mine's comfortable and cozy," said Annie. "I can cuddle up in it."

" 'That sounds nice,' said Andrea's mom. 'Now where do you think you'd like to fly in it? Would you like to fly somewhere special, or would you just like to fly around in the sky over the rooftops for a while?'

"Andrea thought for a moment. 'I think I just feel like floating around in the sky for a while,' she said.

" 'That sounds nice,' said her mom."

"I might just enjoy flying around and seeing what I can see," said Annie.

"I think you'll enjoy that," said her mom.

" 'I wonder how fast your magic carpet can fly?' said Andrea's mom. 'Will it whoosh along like a jet plane, or will it just ease along gently, drifting here and there? Will it fly in a straight line or will it curve around in circles?'

" 'I'm not sure,' said Andrea. 'I might just fly around wherever I feel like.' "

"Me too," said Annie. She was enjoying this. It was nice flying around on a magic carpet.

" 'What might you hear, I wonder, on your magic carpet?' said Andrea's mom.[14] 'Some magic carpets sing songs, you know. Some sing music without words and some sing words without music. Some talk to you when you want to, as you whoosh through the sky, and some are peacefully quiet. . . .'

" 'Mine's singing nursery rhymes,' said Andrea. She was surprised."

"Mine's singing my favorite music," said Annie. "I don't know what its name is, but I like it."

---

13. This involves the tactile sense—how does it feel, how do you feel, for example.

14. This involves the auditory sense—what do you hear, what does it sound like, for example.

" 'It's nice to fly on a magic carpet,' said Andrea's mom. 'You can fly over beaches and cities and fields. You can fly over mountains and meadows and trees. You can fly over deserts and lakes and snowfields. Where will you fly, I wonder. . . .'

"Andrea didn't bother answering right away. She was too busy seeing all there was to see. 'I'm flying over meadows and grass and trees,' she said. 'There are rabbits and squirrels. I can see them frolicking in the leaves.' "

"I'm flying over everything," said Annie. She wanted to see it all.

" 'It's feels nice, doesn't it, on your magic carpet,' said Andrea's mom. 'Magic carpets are happy carpets, and anyone who sits on them feels happy. It's part of their magic.'

" 'I feel happy,' said Andrea."

"I feel very happy," said Annie. She was enjoying this. It was a bit like being on a ship at sea. The wind was like the waves, and there was a happy breeze.

"After a while, Andrea's mom said, 'Now you might like to look around and find a lovely place to land and rest for a while. You can find a place that looks just right for you. A place that's smiling and peaceful and just what you like. . . .'

"Andrea looked around her, and then she found just the right spot. 'I've found it,' she said. 'It's wonderful.' "

"I've found my place too," said Annie. "It's lovely. It's green and peaceful, and there are flowers in the meadow. And," and she gave a gasp of surprise, "there are hamsters in the meadow too. They're running up to me now. They want to play, and then they want to sleep, at my feet or in my lap. Oh wow, this is great!"[15]

"That's terrific," said her mom. "You can play with them as much as you like, and then you can all rest. You and the hamsters, at your feet or in your lap."

"It's lovely," said Annie, after a while. "I'm resting now."

"You can have a lovely rest," said her mom. "You

---

15. The hamsters, or something else your child loves, are a special little treat here to make the experience even more enjoyable.

don't have to sleep, but you can sit there and look around you. There are such lovely things to see, and you can feel that everything's just right. It's such a lovely feeling, to know that everything's just right. It's fine and just the way you'd like it to be . . . .[16]

" 'Now,' said Andrea's mom, 'soon you can get ready to say good-bye for now to your carpet. You're not saying good-bye forever because you can come back for another trip whenever you like.[17] Now, though, you are getting ready to be back here with me. But you can take with you that happy, peaceful feeling the carpet gave you. It can stay with you whatever you're doing and whatever you're doing can feel extra nice.[18] You might imagine yourself now, getting up and doing whatever it is you're going to be doing after this.[19] And whatever it is that you're going to be doing you can imagine yourself feeling really good doing it. It feels really nice. And it feels nice to know that it will feel so nice. . . .'

" 'I'm going to be doing some drawing after this,' said Andrea dreamily. 'It will feel really good.' "

"I'm going to be doing my jigsaw puzzle," said Annie. "I'm going to feel really good. I can see myself doing it now. I feel really good."

" 'Good,' said Andrea's mom. 'Now you can see your-self opening your eyes with a happy smile and feeling just so nice . . . .'

"Andrea opened her eyes. 'Gee, that was nice,' she said."

Annie opened her eyes. "Boy, that was nice," she said, and she gave her mom a hug. "I feel really good. I think I'm going to have a great, great day."[20]

---

16. You can extend this resting time for as long as you like.

17. Let your child know that she is able to recapture this experience at another time when it might be helpful for her to relax.

18. Emphasize that this relaxed feeling can stay with her even after she is no longer in the daydream.

19. This is particularly useful when your child's next activity is likely to be something stressful, difficult, or frustrating. The positive visualization of her-self completing this task with equanimity helps promote this attitude in real life.

20. This is the positive ending.

dealing with pain

for most of us, pain is a transient event. We cut our fingers or have a vaccination, feel the pain, cope with it in our own characteristic way, and think no more of it. Nothing could be simpler, we think.

In fact, pain is far from simple. It is a complex phenomenon which everyone experiences slightly differently and reacts to individually. Not only does it feel different from person to person, but for each person, the same pain can be experienced differently depending on its context.

For instance, imagine you were sewing as you watched a gripping TV drama. Just as the true villain was about to be unveiled, you pricked your finger with a needle. The prick would probably go relatively unnoticed due to your absorption in the drama on the screen.

To take an opposite instance, let's suppose you were tired, had had a rotten day, and had just picked up your pile of mending when you pricked your finger. You would experience that prick as more painful and more upsetting than in the previous instance. A relaxed or absorbed person is less bothered by pain than a tense or depressed person.

We can describe the experience of pain in terms not only of how much pain we are experiencing, but also of how much that pain is bothering us or how much suffering it is causing us. A small pain that distresses us greatly is usually a more difficult experience to cope with than a more severe pain that for some reason does not distress us much. The meaning of the pain can affect the degree of suffering.

As an example, a small twinge which we believe indicates cancer is far more distressing than a bad case of sunburn, even though the level of pain caused by the sunburn is more severe than the twinge thought to be cancer.

The way you experience pain in the present is dependent not only on the current pain but also on your memory of what the pain felt like in the past and the anticipation of how much pain there will be in the future.

Let's take a painful medical procedure for an example. Call it X. Let's assume you had never had X before. So you approach X in the present with no anticipation of pain. X is administered and it does indeed hurt, a lot. The doctor tells you that you have to have only one more X and then all your troubles will be over. So, you undoubtedly approach your second X with some trepidation, because you know now that it hurts. However, you can comfort yourself by saying that this is the last time you will have X and that the Xs are making you well. In other words, without the pain of the Xs, you would remain sick.

Think of a different scenario. Your doctor tells you that you have to have an X a day for the next four weeks. He is not optimistic about the chances of a cure. He does not know how much the Xs will help. They may help very little or they may not help at all.

How do you experience your Xs now? You already know they are painful because you have your memory of that past pain. As you approach the time when your current X is due, you cannot even comfort yourself by telling yourself it is the last you will have to endure. Nor can you say that the pain is worth it because it means you'll get well.

Let us look at how you will perceive these two sets of supposedly identical pains associated with treatment X.

Undoubtedly, the second scenario will be the one in which you experience more pain. In scenario one, although the treatment is painful, it is associated with hope and also the knowledge that it is beneficial, worthwhile, and will not continue for long. In scenario two, the pain has an almost opposite psychological meaning. You know that it is not necessarily beneficial,

dealing with pain

that it may not offer much hope, and that it will go on and on.

Another component in our response to pain is our sense of how powerless we feel to do anything about it. My daughter's illustration points out how her anticipation of pain makes her feel small and defenseless when visiting the doctor, who is drawn to look very large and powerful. If we feel that there is nothing we can do to change or ease the pain or to make ourselves more comfortable, we will often experience the pain as more "painful" and distressing.

The experience of pain is amenable to change through the medium of our mind. Most of us just haven't been taught how to do it. We think that pain, because it arises from a physical cause, is a set factor that can't be changed. In fact, although the pain arises from a physical cause, we experience it in a psychological way, that is, through our minds. This is what makes the experience of pain malleable.

Children often have a particular talent for using the power of their minds to deal with pain. This can be done through several methods, some of which are described here. Essentially, the methods involve relaxation and imagery.

Story 1
Anticipated pain

The techniques used in the following story involve imagining such things as coldness, numbness, and that our mind's switchboard for pain has been disconnected. There are many, many useful images which can be effective in controlling pain. The most valuable of these are likely to come from your child. While she is relaxed and listening to the story, feel free to ask her what other methods she might like to employ to ensure that she will not be bothered by pain. Once they have got the general drift of the exercise, children generally come up with wonderful ideas and find it a lot of fun. Don't be dismayed if some of these ideas seem zany or strange to you. Imagery is very individual, and all that counts is that it works for your child. You may also need to try out a number of images and see which works best.

It's important, too, to maintain a confident attitude and communicate that to your child. If the first method you try doesn't work, don't be fazed, just try another method. If none of the methods you try work, simply state calmly and confidently that these methods require some time and practice to start working, and now that she has begun, your daughter's brain can learn to get better and better at turning off pain and may even find its own special method that you haven't even mentioned yet. Don't forget, too, to take your time in helping your child control pain. It's important not to rush your child, and time and repetition help deepen the imaginative experience and its effectiveness.

a nnie was a little girl who lived in a brown brick house with her mom and dad and a big black dog.[1] One day she came home from school feeling a bit upset.

"What's wrong, Annie?" said her mom. "You look miserable."

"Well," said Annie, "today the school doctor came and told us it was the time of the year to get our flu shots."

1. Change the details here to suit your own environment.

dealing with pain

"Well, we can go to the doctor tomorrow after school," said her mom.

"But I hate shots," said Annie. "They hurt."

"I know," said her mom, "but did you know that there are lots of ways to make them hurt less?"[2]

"Really?" said Annie.

"Yes, really," said her mom. "Why don't we sit down on your bed, and I'll tell you some of the things that kids can do to make things hurt less."

"Is it really true that you can do that?" said Annie. "Is it really true that you can make things hurt less?"

"Yes, it's true," said Annie's mom. "You see, in order for something to hurt you, there has to be a message sent from the skin, or wherever it is, to the brain saying, 'Ooh! That hurt!' When the brain gets the message and says, 'Yes, that hurt,' that's when you feel the pain.[3] So, if the brain doesn't get the message, or doesn't take any notice of it, then it doesn't matter what's happening, you just won't think it hurts."

"Gosh," said Annie, "how do I get my brain to do that?"

"Well," said her mom, "you already know how to do that."

"I do?" said Annie. She was surprised.[4]

"Yes," said her mom. "Remember the times when you've been very busy playing an exciting game with your friends and you've fallen over and scrambled to your feet because you didn't want to miss the fun? And it's only later that you've realized that you've hurt your knee?"

"Yes," said Annie, "that's happened to me."

"Well," said her mom. "the reason you didn't feel how sore your knee was at the time you hurt it was that your brain was too busy with the game to take any notice of the hurt messages coming from your knee. That's why you didn't feel any pain. It was only later when your brain

2. An impending injection is the motivating force here in Annie's wish to learn pain control. The more motivated your child is, the better she is likely to learn.

3. This is a simplified explanation of how we experience pain. Children can usually understand such concepts quite easily.

4. It is helpful to remind children that they already do know how to do these things. It makes the task in front of them seem much more manageable.

wasn't busy that it noticed it."

"Gosh," said Annie. She was impressed. "I never knew that."

"It happens a lot," said Annie's mom. "Remember when you had the flu and you were all headachey and sore in the throat, and Daddy brought you home a present?"

"Yes," said Annie. "I remember that."

"Well," her mom said, "when you got the present, you were so excited and so busy playing with it that for a while you didn't even notice your aching head or throat. That was another time when your brain was too busy or too happy to notice the pain. It just didn't listen to the pain messages coming from your head and throat, or it just switched them off. Brains can do that."

"Gosh," said Annie. "That sounds really great."

"Another thing," her mom continued, "that helps make things hurt less is if you're relaxed.[5] When you're all tight and tense, things hurt much more than they do when you're relaxed."

"Really?" said Annie. "I never knew that there were so many things you could do to stop things hurting. Will you teach me how to relax and do all those things?"

"Of course," said Annie's mom, "and then you can feel much more comfortable whenever you have to have shots or anything like that."

First, Annie's mom told her all about relaxation. Annie really liked that. It felt so good to be nice and relaxed. She thought it was great fun.[6]

When Annie was all floppy and relaxed, her mom said, "Perhaps you might like to have a sort of daydream now, where you can imagine that you're outside playing in winter. You've got your friends with you, and you're having a great time. It's been snowing, and you're building a snowman. You've got gloves on, but even through

---

5. The more relaxed you are, the less likely the pain is to bother you. Many children, like adults, need to be taught or reminded to relax.

6. This is a good spot to insert the relaxation techniques used in the story on page 167, if you haven't used it before.

your gloves, your hands can feel the cold.[7] It's a nice sort of cold. It's just the sort of cold that you feel when you put your hand inside a freezer or the fridge—very, very cold."

"Ooh," said Annie, "I can really imagine that. It's freezing, freezing cold. But it's fun."

"You're busy making the snowman now," said her mom, "so one part of your mind is very busy thinking about what part to put on next and whether his body needs more snow or less snow, and whether his smile is straight or crooked, and the other part of your mind can be noticing just how comfortably cold your hands are getting. What does the part of your mind that's thinking about the snowman think about your snowman?[8] Is he a big one or a small one? Is he nearly ready or is there a lot left to go?"

"Mine's big," said Annie. "Really huge. And he's nearly finished. This is great."

"You can pick some more snow up," her mother went on, "and you can roll it in your hands. You can pat it onto the snowman. You can smooth the snowman up and down and round about, and all the time your hands are getting colder. Can you feel how cold your hands are now? . . ."

Annie nodded—her hands felt very cold. They felt so cold she could hardly feel them.

"They're very cold now," said her mother, "and have you ever noticed how when you're very, very cold your hands get sort of numb? Numb just means they don't feel very much. Remember the last time your hands got cold. It would have been in winter when you didn't have any gloves on, and your fingers started to go just freezing, freezing cold."

"I remember," said Annie. "They were so cold I couldn't feel anything with them."

"That's right," said her mom, "because the colder your hands get, the less you can feel anything at all. Just imagine if you'd taken your already freezing cold hand

---

7. A focus on the feeling of coldness is often a useful way of producing numbness in the desired area. If your child seems receptive, encourage her to imagine the cold feeling along with Annie as you tell the story.

8. Encourage your child's participation here. Ask her about her snowman and get her to describe it.

and put it in a bowl of ice-cold water. Just imagine how freezing and cold your hand would be. Just imagine how your hand could be so cold that you wouldn't feel anything at all. That's an interesting feeling, isn't it?"

"Boy, my hands really do feel cold," said Annie. They were so cold she could hardly feel them at all. It was a funny feeling.

"Well you know what?" her mother said. "When you've got a hand that's cold like that, cold in that special way, you can make the cold go anywhere, anywhere at all, by just touching it. So you could touch your arm, for instance, so that it would get all cold and freezing just where the shot would go and it could be so, so cold there that when the needle went in you might hardly feel a thing.[9] You could be so comfortably cold there you might not feel anything much at all."

"Wow," said Annie, and she touched her arm. Her mom was right.[10] As she touched her arm with her cold hand, she could feel the cold start to go into her arm too. It was like magic. Her arm got colder and colder. Soon she could hardly feel it at all. "Wow," she said again.

"You know too," her mom went on, "that one of the things children can also do to stop things hurting is to imagine their skin growing thicker.[11] Right on their arm or wherever they are getting the shot, they can make their brain imagine that the skin is getting as thick as a thick baseball glove. Like layers and layers and layers of leather piled on top of one another. Layers and layers and layers of material that can't feel a thing. So that when the needle goes in, the skin on your arm would feel as thick as the thickest baseball glove. As thick as the thickest thing you've ever seen, so thick and made of such special stuff that it doesn't feel a thing. You might not even notice the needle going in. Because if you stuck a needle in a

---

9. Don't say. "You won't feel anything at all." You may be setting yourself and your child up for failure with such a direct statement. Say instead: "You might not feel much at all," or "You might not even need to notice it."

10. If the cold imagery is working well with your child, you could practice this, either during or after the story.

11. The imagined sensation of wearing very thick gloves or having thick skin can help to produce a sensation of numbness.

dealing with pain

baseball glove, you wouldn't be able to feel it, there would be too much thickness, and leather doesn't feel things. You know when you touch something and you've got gloves on, you can't really feel it, you can't feel it at all. It could be just like that. Gloves all over your skin, so thick that the needle might hardly be felt at all.[12] As if that thick, thick skin could make it feel so comfortable that you might hardly even need to notice it at all."

"Golly," said Annie. "It really does feel thick. How does it happen? What's making my arm feel so weird?"

"Well," said her mom, "it's your brain that's making your arm feel so funny. Your brain controls what every part of your body feels like. When you imagine that your arm feels cold or thick, your brain makes it feel that way. It's very handy for you to know how to do that because you can use it when you have to have a shot or something else that hurts."

"See," Annie's mom went on, "I'm going to touch the arm that feels funny and the arm that feels normal.[13] You can tell me how different it feels to you." She touched Annie's arms.

"Golly, it really feels different," Annie said. "I couldn't even feel it when you touched my funny arm."

"What about if I pinched it?" asked Annie's mom.

"Okay," said Annie, "you can pinch it."

Her mom did.

"Wow," said Annie. "That's amazing. I knew you were pinching it, but it just didn't hurt. That's amazing. You mean I can really do that when I have a shot or go to the dentist and stuff like that?"

"You sure can," said Annie's mom. "But you should only use it for times like that because sometimes pain can be a way of sending an important message to the brain.[14]

---

12. As before, don't make a flat statement such as, "You won't feel a thing." This means that your child has to feel only a *little* pain in order for this to be classed as a failure. Feeling a little pain is a great improvement if on previous occasions your child felt a lot of pain.

13. If this imagery works well with your child, you can practice doing this either during or after the story.

14. It is important to let your child know that she should use pain control only when it is safe and appropriate to do so.

If you broke your leg, for instance, and it didn't hurt, you'd just keep running around on it, and your leg would break even more and never get a chance to mend. That's why it hurts when we break a leg—the leg is sending a message to the brain saying, 'Help, that hurts! You'd better stay off me until I'm better.'"

"How will I know when it's right to use what you've taught me?" asked Annie.

"Well, you can ask me first, and I'll tell you," said her mom, "or if I'm not there and there's a doctor or nurse or dentist or teacher with you, you can ask them."[15]

"Okay," said Annie. "It's okay to use for shots, isn't it?"

"It's fine to do for shots," said her mom. "And when the shot, or whatever it is, is over, your whole arm and hand can return to being comfortably normal. See, just as it is now."

Annie concentrated on her arm.

"See how it's starting to feel warm and normal and just right again.[16] All the cold, thick feelings are just going away, and your arm is feeling like your normal, comfortable arm again."

"It is," said Annie. She was amazed. "Is my brain doing that too?"

"It sure is," said her mom. "You're imagining it back to normal, and so your brain is making it normal again."

"Wow," said Annie. "I never knew I had such a powerful brain. Does everyone have a brain like that?"

"Usually they do," said her mom, "but not everyone learns to use it the way you have."

"Gosh," said Annie, "I bet they would if they knew how handy it would be. I can't wait for my next shot. Won't the doctor be surprised?" And she laughed when she thought of the expression on his face when she held out her arm and said, "It doesn't hurt at all."

The next day, Annie said to her mom, "You said there were lots of ways to make things that hurt feel better."

---

15. It is best to suggest that she use it only after she has checked with a responsible adult first.

16. Be sure to imagine the arm returning to its normal sensations after the injection has been administered.

dealing with pain

"That's right," said her mom.

"Will you teach me some more?" asked Annie. She was really enjoying this. It was nice to know that she didn't have to feel worried about things hurting.

"Okay," said her mom, "We'll start again by doing some relaxing. So you just get nice and comfortable, and we'll do our relaxation."

"Right," said Annie, and she settled down. . . .[17]

"Now that you're nice and relaxed," said her mom, "you might like to take another trip in your imagination."

Annie nodded.

"Just imagine," said her mom, "that your body is becoming as clear as glass.[18] You can see right into it. You might see bones and muscles and veins, which carry the blood around your body. And you might also see lots and lots of thin lines like fine pieces of string which start at your hands or feet or anywhere on your skin and go winding their way up to your brain. They are the nerves, and they carry messages to your brain. Sometimes the messages they carry are about hurting. The brain can be like a big television screen or a blackboard. Which is yours like?"

"Mine's a television screen," said Annie importantly. She could see it very clearly now. A big television screen.

"On the screen is a drawing of your body," her mom went on. "Messages travel up the nerves to your brain. As each nerve brings its message from a particular part of your body, a light flashes on in the drawing of your body on the television screen. All over the drawing of your body are lights going on and off as the nerves bring their messages in."

"There are a lot of lights," said Annie. She could see them flashing on and off all over her body on the screen in her brain.

"Yes," said her mom, "there are a lot of lights because there are lots and lots of messages coming in all the time."

---

17. At this point you can use the relaxation techniques described in the relaxation story.

18. Children are usually quite fascinated by these explanations of bodily functioning. Their interest adds to the effectiveness of the techniques they are learning.

"Now, if you want to stop the pain messages that the nerves can bring to your brain, all you have to do is turn off the lights. That way the brain doesn't get the pain messages, and so you don't feel pain. It's just a matter of looking around you and finding which switch turns off the lights for that particular part of your body."

"I can see the light switches," said Annie. There were two rows of light switches, one under the other. "I'm going to turn off the one that's to do with my arm."

"Ooh," she said, "When I switched it off, all the lights went off in my arm. Now the nerves can't get their pain messages through."

"That's right," said her mom.

"Does that mean that if I had a flu shot in my arm, I wouldn't feel it?"

"Well you would probably feel it in some way," said her mom, "and you would probably know that you were having a shot, but you just wouldn't feel it in the same way as you've felt other shots.[19] It could feel much more comfortable. More like a pinch than a shot. Why don't you imagine that you're trying it? I'll pinch your arm."[20]

"Gosh," said Annie. "That was weird—it really didn't hurt. This is great! Can I try it next time I have a shot?"

"You certainly can," said her mom. "I think it would really help." And she gave Annie a big hug.

"What are the other ways, Mom?" asked Annie. She was curious about this. It was fun as well as being very, very handy.

"Let me see," said her mom. "One of the things you can do is simply take your brain away on a vacation in your imagination.[21] While your brain's away on its vacation it doesn't really notice much what's going on around your body. So that if you were having a shot, for instance, it just wouldn't really get noticed."

---

19. Again don't use an absolute statement such as, "It will not hurt at all." This leaves you and your child wide open to failure.

20. If this imagery is working well with your child, you could try this out with her either during or after the story.

21. This is a very enjoyable method of pain control. You should make the daydream or pleasant imagery as vivid and involving as possible so that it captures all of your child's attention, leaving none left over for the injection.

dealing with pain

"How do I do that?" asked Annie.

"You know how to do it already," said her mom.[22]

"I do?" said Annie. She was surprised.

"Sure you do," said her mom. "You remember all those times when you've been watching TV, or reading a book, or playing with your toys, and I've called you and called you and you just haven't heard?"

"Yes," said Annie, "that does happen a lot."

"Well," said her mom, "the reason you haven't heard me is that your brain's taken an imagination vacation and is in Disneyland or the land you're reading about in your book or seeing on the TV screen. Your brain is so busy playing around and having adventures that it just doesn't notice what's going on around you. So if you have to have a shot, and your brain's busy somewhere else, you wouldn't notice it as much. In fact you might hardly notice it at all, the way you didn't notice me calling you."

"That sounds great," said Annie. "How do I do it?"

"The first thing to do," said her mom, "is to get nice and relaxed."[23]

When Annie was feeling lovely and relaxed, her mother went on.

"On this magic trip," she said, "you can go anywhere you like.[24] You could go to the mountains in your mind and have sled rides or make snowballs. You could build a tower with snowballs. Or a snowman. You might build a snow family and make them a snow house to live in. Or you could go to the beach and swim. You could find wonderful shells or build sand castles.

"Or you might like to go to another place, a special magic place. A place I know called Playland where it's always your birthday and you're always special and everyone plays the games that you want to play. There are all sorts of rides and games in Playland. There are merry-go-

---

22. Pointing out that your child already knows how to do this, as indeed she does, primes her for success.

23. At this point you can use the relaxation techniques described in the relaxation story.

24. Here I give a sample of three possible scenarios. You can extend whichever of them your child seems to be most interested in. Or make up one of your own, perhaps together with your child.

rounds with magic horses that really neigh and talk to you
as you go around. There are picture shows where you can
actually get inside the screen and be part of the adventure. You could join in a Care Bears movie or meet the
Muppets or make friends with Rocky and Bullwinkle."

"Oh wow!" said Annie. "I want to meet the Muppets.
I want to make friends with Kermit and Miss Piggy."

"There are all kinds of things to see in Playland," said
Annie's mom. "There are spaghetti trees, for instance.
The spaghetti hangs from the tree like leaves in a weeping
willow and the fruit is round and full of spaghetti sauce.
When you want to eat spaghetti, you get a plate and pick
off the spaghetti from the tree. Then you pick one of the
fruits and squeeze its saucy juice over the spaghetti. You
can have cheese sauce or meat sauce; the tree grows both,
you know."

"Yum," said Annie, "I'll pick the meat sauce."[25]

"There are also chocolate trees," said Annie's mom.
"Each of the leaves is made of chocolate, and the tree
grows them specially wrapped in silver foil that crackles
when you unwrap it."

"Oh wow!" said Annie. "I like that."

"And there are lollipop flowers," her mom went on.
"Each of the petals is a lollipop, and each flower has four
petals. The flower is so heavy that the stalk has to be
extra thick to hold it up."

"Golly," said Annie.

"And then there's the Anything Bush," said her mom.
"It grows strange, square fruits, and before you eat them,
you say to yourself, 'I want this to taste like grapes,' and
then you take a bite, and it tastes exactly like grapes or
whatever you want it to taste of."

"My goodness!" said Annie. Playland was exactly
where she wanted to be. She could see herself now. It was
very bright and colorful, and there were so many great
things to see and do.

"I like Playland," she said to her mom. "I'm there
right now. It's great. I'm having a great time. I'm eating
spaghetti and picking chocolates from the tree."

---

25. Get your child involved in this fantasy by asking what she would eat, play,
or do.

dealing with pain

"Did I tell you about the Present Machines in Play-land?" asked her mom.

Annie's face lit up. "Present Machines!" she said. "Oh wow!"

"There are Present Machines on every corner," said her mom. "They're very big and filled to the top with presents. You press a button and a present pops out."

"Can you choose what present you want?" asked Annie.

"Yes, you can ask the machine for a special present, and it will give it to you, or, if you want, you can just press the button and get a surprise present."

"Oh boy!" said Annie.

"Then," her mom went on, "there's the games section of Playland. Every game that you can think of is going on at Playland. You can join in if you like, or you can start your own game with your own friends. Everyone likes you and wants to play with you in Playland. There are card games and quiz games, chasing games and sitting still games, loud games and quiet games, clay games and painting games. Every single game you can think of. What sort of game do you think you'd like to play?"

Annie thought for a moment. "I'm going to play jump rope with my friends," she said. "Wow! This is fun."

After a while she said, "Now that we've jumped rope, we're going to go and have some party food."

"You'll want to visit the Birthday Cake Shop then," said Annie's mom.

"What't that?" asked Annie.

"That's a shop that has all sorts of birthday cakes. You don't have to pay for them; you just pick out the one you want. They have doll cakes and train cakes. They have cakes shaped like Mickey Mouse and cakes shaped like houses. They have chocolate cakes and ice cream cakes. They have every sort of cake it's possible to bake."

"I'm going to have a caterpillar cake," said Annie. "It's green and covered with furry green coconut and cream."

"That sounds great," said her mom.

"It sure is," said Annie. "I love it. I'm going to have another slice." And then she yawned.

"Feeling tired?" asked her mom. "All that playing

must have left you feeling a bit sleepy. If you like, you could go down to the dream room."

"What's that?" asked Annie.

"That's a place in Playland where you go when you're feeling a bit sleepy or tired. You can lie down and rest there on the most wonderful beds, and the room is full of especially nice dreams that come to you while you sleep."

"What sort of beds are there?" asked Annie.

"There are soft beds and hard beds, whatever you prefer," said her mom. "There are beds that rock you and beds that are still. There are beds that sing you gently into sleep. There are talking beds and silent beds. There are beds with twinkling lights inside them and dark cozy beds. There is every sort of bed you can imagine."

"I like that place," said Annie. "I think I'll have a nice soft bed. I'm going to have a little nap now."

"Okay," said her mom. "When you wake up again you can come and say hello to me in my study."

Later on, Annie wandered into the study. Her mom was sitting there reading.

"I really enjoyed Playland," she said, "but I'm not sure how it would help me make things hurt less."

"Well," said her mom, "you were so busy being in Playland that you didn't notice what was going on around you."

"Didn't I?" said Annie. She was surprised.

"No," said her mom, "you didn't. Dad came in and out of the room and said hello to you, and you didn't even hear him."[26]

"No," said Annie, "I didn't know he was there."

"And I touched your arm a few times," her mom said, "and you didn't even feel it."

"No," said Annie, "I didn't even notice it."

Then she thought for a minute. "Do you mean," she said, "that if I went to have my flu shot and imagined myself in Playland, I wouldn't notice so much what the doctor was doing to my arm?"

---

26. Try this out as you tell the story. Pick a time when your daughter is totally absorbed to touch her arm or pat her on the head or have someone walk in and out of the room.

"It works that way for a lot of people," said Annie's mom.

"Oh wow!" said Annie. "That sounds great. I can't wait to do that. Wait till the doctor finds out where I've been while he's been giving me my shot."

"He sure will be surprised," said Annie's mom. And they both laughed.

Story 2
Chronic pain or pain that is already present

When your child is experiencing pain, you should always check that there is nothing physically wrong with her. Pain is a warning signal alerting us to the fact that something needs to be fixed up. A stomachache, for instance, may be a signal that something is wrong with the appendix, in which case medical aid is urgently needed. If you had removed the pain, say with hypnosis, you might not recognize the urgency of the medical situation. Once the message has been decoded, you can use the methods described here to tone down the pain, although it is often best to allow a little pain or discomfort to remain so that the doctor can ascertain how the healing process is going.

On other occasions, you may be aware of the physical cause of the pain—a broken leg, for instance—but once it is set, it may require no further medical intervention. In a case like this you could use the pain control methods outlined in the following story. Obviously, it would be inappropriate to take away all the pain before the leg has been set in plaster. If the child felt no pain, she could move or walk on her leg, causing even more damage to it. Pain here is a warning that says, "Keep that leg still and stay off it."

Pain may also be experienced as a result of stress or other psychological factors. A typical example is a tension headache. If such events are common, try to find out why your child is feeling so stressed. What is going on in her life that is bringing about these headaches? Hopefully, the issue will be something that you can tackle together. You can also help her use relaxation and pain control methods as ways of coping with tension, and of relieving her of the extra stress of the pain she is experiencing. These methods can also help her feel stronger and calmer within herself, which will in turn help her to deal with whatever other stresses she is facing.

The following story deals with a headache through imagining its color changing to one that is lighter, prettier, more enjoyable, more innocuous, and so forth. There are many other such ways of changing the experience of pain. If the pain is a piercing one, it can be progressively blunted until it becomes dull and then fuzzy. It can be encouraged to slide down from the head, along the shoulder, down the arm, and out through the hand. It may be shrunk, or displaced to the big toe, for instance, where it may be easier to cope with. If it is a burning pain, it can be cooled down. If it is a throbbing pain, it can be reduced to a buzz and then an itch or a tickle. If it is thick and opaque, it can become thin and transparent. If it is sharp and strong, it can become smooth and softer. Any change that can be effected in it will add to your child's sense of control over it. It is then simply a matter of guiding the changes in the desired direction. You may also want to try out several techniques and see which one works best for your child. If one doesn't work, don't get flustered, simply move on to another. Take your time and pause between sentences to give the changes time to develop. Be aware, too, that the pain may go away only to come back later—it may take repeated sessions to dispel it for longer and longer periods of time.

As with the previous pain story, it is valuable to ask your child for her ideas about how the pain can be taken away or reduced. You might invent a "pain sponge," for instance, which soaks up the pain and can then be thrown away. Your child might visualize the pain as a wild beast and be able to talk to it, tame it, or render it ineffective in some other way. Perhaps imagining a wonderful room deep inside herself where the pain cannot enter and she can be totally safe and protected from it can give her a welcome sense of relief. Perhaps she might give the pain a numerical value and concentrate on allowing the numbers to change and go down.

A final word on the very specific condition of migraine headaches. Although we tend to think of migraine as an adult affliction, many children suffer from it too. Teaching a child relaxation is very useful here, as many migraines are brought about or exacerbated by tension. You can also use some imagery which has been found to be effective in many cases of migraine. This involves imagining that your head is growing cooler (perhaps you could imagine a cold compress or an ice block melting on it), and that your hands are getting very warm (perhaps you could imagine a heater focused on them). This often relieves the painfully engorged blood vessels of the head through the redirection of blood flow to the hands.

dealing with pain

annie was a little girl who lived in a brown brick house with her mom and dad and a big black dog.[1] One day, Annie came home after a very busy afternoon. She had gone with her mom to do the supermarket shopping. It was very noisy and crowded in the supermarket, and Annie had wished she wasn't there. Then, after the supermarket, Annie's mom had taken her to play at her friend Diane's house. Instead of having a great time, though, they had an awful time. Diane's little sister grabbed their toys and then cried when they tried to take them back. Her big brother yelled at them for making noise and disturbing his studying, and then her mother yelled at them all for yelling at each other. It was a horrid afternoon, and by the time Annie got back home, her head was going thump, thump, thump, as if there were a rabbit inside it, and it felt like someone was squeezing a very tight band around it.

"My head hurts, Mommy," said Annie. "I think I've got a headache."

"What does the rest of you feel like?" asked her mom.[2]

"The rest of me feels okay," said Annie. "It's just my head that hurts. I had a rotten time at Diane's. Everyone was yelling at everyone else. My head feels all tight and squeezed up."

Her mom gave her a hug. "You know there are ways that you can make it feel better," said her mom.

"Really?" said Annie. "Can you teach me?"

"Of course," her mom said. "First, why don't we do some relaxation? Everything feels better when you relax."

"Okay," said Annie. She liked doing relaxation.[3]

When Annie was nice and relaxed, her mom said to her, "Now I want you to really notice your headache. Just

---

1. Change the details here to suit your own environment.

2. Always check whether the headache, or other sort of pain, is indicative of something that needs medical treatment. If you are not sure, see a doctor first. In this story, the headache is simply a tension headache.

3. At this point, you could describe the relaxation techniques in the story on page 167, if you haven't already done so.

study it very carefully so that you know all about it."

Annie nodded.

"Now," said her mom, "what color is it?"[4]

Annie thought for a bit. "It's red," she said, "a very bright red."

"Look at that color very carefully," said her mom. "I'd like you to notice which parts are more red than others. Headaches are never exactly the same color all the way through, you know. And they change colors too."

Annie nodded. This was interesting. She had her eyes closed so that she could see her headache better. It was true; the headache wasn't exactly the same color all the way through.

"I wonder," said her mother, "if you can notice how your headache can change color—to a nice light pink, for instance.[5] I'd be interested to know where it starts to change color first. Is it starting by getting lighter around the edges, and moving inward? Or is the lightening starting from the middle and flowing outward? Is it perhaps getting lighter in patches, with all the light patches growing larger and larger and joining up? Or is it all getting lighter at once? Is the change happening suddenly or is it happening very slowly? Did you notice the change when it first started happening or did you not notice it until after it had happened?"

Annie was absolutely fascinated. Her headache had started to turn a very pretty shade of pink on the outside, like the inside of sea shells, and was flowing inward so that all of her headache was becoming a lovely pale sort of pink.

"Wow," she said to her mom, "my headache's all pale pink now."

"That's great," said her mom. "Would you like it to go any paler?"[6]

---

4. I have used color here as the focus of change. There are many other characteristics that lend themselves to change.

5. Give lots of options for change here. Perhaps it's not getting lighter all at once, but it can still get lighter in patches. Perhaps it's not changing color quickly, but that still means it can change color slowly.

6. Let your child decide how much change she would like to produce. It's what she feels comfortable with that matters.

dealing with pain

"Maybe a little bit," said Annie.

"Okay," said her mom, "why don't you just let it go a little paler?"

So Annie let the pink become an even paler pink, so pale that it was almost white. "I like the color it is now," she said.

"Good," said her mom. "Now, tell me, how does your headache feel?"

"It's gone," said Annie with surprise. "It doesn't hurt anymore."

"That's nice," said Annie's mom. "It's a fun way of helping with headaches, isn't it?"

"It sure is," said Annie. She really liked this way. "Can I do it every time I get a headache?"

"Sure," said her mom, "but you must always tell me before you do it, because sometimes aches and pains are a message from our brain to say we're sick or we need to see a doctor.[7] Sometimes, though, we get headaches or tummyaches because we're unhappy or tired or worried. So if you tell me first, I can decide whether you need to see the doctor, or stay in bed, or whether it's an ache that means you're worried or tired.

"Then, when we've decided what sort of ache it is, so that your brain knows that its message has been received and understood, we can make that ache go away or feel much more comfortable."

"Great," said Annie.[8] It felt good to know that there was something she could do about aches and pains. She felt very pleased with herself.

---

7. Make sure your child knows that she should use this method only when it's appropriate to do so. Explain why this is so, and suggest that she use it only after she has consulted a responsible adult first.

8. This is the positive ending, with Annie feeling strong and in control of her experience.

going to the hospital

a hospital stay is generally a frightening and taxing experience for young children. For many it means not only a separation from their parents and all that is dear and familiar to them, but also a series of intrusive and often painful medical procedures. They are subjected to a regime that they often neither understand nor have any control over. They may be unsure of how to respond and which behaviors are premissible or taboo in this new environment. They often experience themselves as abandoned and at the mercy of strangers.

Anything we can do to lessen these feelings of helplessness and abandonment will help the child cope with the experience in a more positive way.

It is vital to reassure your child that you are not abandoning her. Tell her when you will be visiting and for how long. Don't say you'll be with her all the time if you won't. Explain hospital visiting regulations to her and let her know where you'll be and what you'll be doing during the day. This gives an added sense of security—you haven't simply disappeared into the blue. Make sure, too, that you visit your child at the times you say you will. Missed visits often cause a great deal of anguish for children. It is a good idea to leave little notes, or inexpensive gifts to be unwrapped in your absence. These reassure your child that you are still thinking of her. If you can, make a tape recording of your voice reading her favorite stories so that she can play it back in the hospital. Give her a hanky with your perfume on it so she can sniff at it and be comforted by at least part of your presence. These parts of ourselves can be very comforting. Most of us have had the experience of treasuring letters, gifts, or souvenirs, which bring back powerful and comforting memories of another time, place, or person.

Prepare your child for the hospital by telling her in advance as much as possible about what will happen to her, what her environment will be like, what sorts of people she is likely to meet, and what sort of medical procedures are likely to be carried out. Don't tell her that procedures or tests won't hurt if they are likely to. Stress, instead, that the hurt won't last long, and it is helping to make her better. Teaching her methods of pain control and relaxation is extremely beneficial here. These are explained in separate Annie Stories. Capitalize on your child's natural curiosity by explaining to her how her body works and how doctors have learned to measure its functioning by pulse-taking, temperature-taking, and other common procedures. If you are in doubt as to what will happen in the hospital, ask your doctor for more details. As my daughter's illustration emphasizes, not knowing who or what to expect leaves a mind open to all sorts of fantasies.

All this information helps a child cope better with what can be a bewildering and overwhelming experience. It enables her to make some sense out of the various hospital routines, to know what to expect and also what will be expected of her. We all feel more secure with a road map when driving through unfamiliar country.

Reassure your child that she is not going into the hospital as punishment. Many children have this fantasy. Let her know that she is going there to be helped so that she can feel well again. It is a common fantasy among children that the hospital is a place where you go to die. Reassure her that going into the hospital does not mean that she will die.

Many children feel lonely, homesick, and scared in the hospital. Let your child know that such feelings are normal and that you can understand them, but also reassure her that she will be taken care of by people you trust. Saying, "I know you feel frightened, but you will be taken care of..." is quite different from saying, "You *shouldn't* be frightened; you'll be taken care of...." Telling people they shouldn't feel something rarely stops them feeling it. It usually makes them feel bad or inadequate so that they then have that to contend with as well as the original feeling. After you have talked about her sad feelings, perhaps you can talk about ways of coping with them. Perhaps when she is feeling sad and missing you, she could do a drawing for you of how sad she feels. Perhaps she could listen to a tape recording of you reading to her. Perhaps she could call a nurse, and so on.

"Hospital" games and toys can be very beneficial in allowing your children to work through their feelings about the hospital. These can range from store-bought toy doctor kits to homemade finger puppets or figures made from modeling clay. You can improvise using common household materials—a clear straw can be a thermometer, and an old white shirt can be a doctor's coat. Crayons and drawing materials will help too.

I have also included some positive visualization in this story, where Annie imagines her body fighting off the germs and becoming well. This is a very helpful technique. Our mind can influence the physiological functioning of our body in many ways, but apart from this, the technique helps the child to feel she is playing an active part in her recovery and is not just a helpless victim of illness.

Remember, too, that it may take a few days for your child to readjust to the home environment after coming out of the hospital. Sometimes children can be a bit disoriented with the change, particularly if they have been in the hospital a while.

a nnie was a little girl who lived in a brown brick house with her mommy and daddy and a big black dog.[1]
Annie used to love doing all sorts of things. She loved taking her dog, Blackie, for a walk with her daddy. She loved going to school every day and learning things. She loved being a Brownie. She loved swimming in a pool when the weather was hot. She loved going to the park with her mom and playing on the swings. She loved playing with her friends outside. But when Annie was sick, she couldn't do any of these things.

A few times each winter, Annie would get sick. Her mom would take her to the doctor, and the doctor would look down her throat and say to her mom, "It's tonsillitis again, I'm afraid." Then he would give Annie some medicine, and Annie would have to spend a few days in bed feeling sick and sorry for herself.

So you can guess that she wasn't too happy when one day in winter, she woke up with that familiar scratchy, burning feeling in her throat.

"I think I'm getting tonsillitis again, Mom," she said. "I hate my tonsils! What use are they anyway!" And she stamped off into her bedroom feeling very cross because she had been looking forward to going to the museum with her class that afternoon.

After a while, though, she noticed that Tammy, her teddy bear, was looking sick.[2]

"Oh dear," she said to Tammy, "I think you've got tonsillitis too. I think I'd better take a look at your throat." But this was a bit difficult because Tammy couldn't open her mouth.

"Never mind," said Annie, "I don't really need to have a look. I'm sure it's tonsillitis. I think you'd better go straight to bed."

She tucked Tammy into the bed she had made for her. It was made out of a shoe box, and Annie had cut up some material her mom had given her and made a sheet, a blanket, and a pillow for Tammy. They were all in blue

---

1. You can vary the details here to fit in with your child's environment.

2. Children will often use imaginative play as a way of helping them cope with their frustration and anxieties.

with little yellow daisies scattered on them.

Tammy looked very comfortable in her bed.

"I suppose I'd better tell you what tonsillitis is," said Annie.[3] She knew because her mom had explained it to her.

She stroked her teddy's furry head. "Tonsillitis is what happens when a whole lot of germs get into your tonsils. Your tonsils are like wobbly tubes at the back of your throat. They're supposed to catch germs and help kill them, but sometimes they don't work so well, and the germs come to live in them instead. Mommy told me that when that happens, your tonsils get very red and swollen, and that's why they hurt."

"Poor Tammy," she said, as she tucked her bear in very carefully. "I think you'll need to have a lot of rest. It's a pity you can't drink water. Drinking water is good for you when you have tonsillitis."

"Annie," said her mother, appearing at the door, "get dressed, darling, and we'll go and see the doctor."

So off they went.[4]

On the way home, Annie's mom said to her, "You know, the doctor thinks your tonsils have been bothering you so much lately that they should be taken out."

"Oh," said Annie. "How will he do that?"

"Well," said her mom, "it would mean going to a hospital."

Annie felt a bit worried. She didn't like the thought of going to a hospital.[5] She would rather stay home. "Why would I have to go to a hospital?" she asked.[6]

"Well," said her mom, "to take your tonsils out you need to have a special medicine called a general anesthetic. A general anesthetic makes you sleep while the

---

3. Try to give your child a simple explanation of what's wrong with her. Sometimes their fantasies of what is wrong can be far more terrifying than the reality.

4. At this point you might like to describe the doctor's visit in more detail if your child is unfamiliar with this situation.

5. A stay in the hospital is scary for most children, and they are likely to worry about it.

6. Many children feel they are being sent to the hospital as a punishment, or else to die. It's important to give them a simple but clear explanation which dispels these fantasies.

doctors take your tonsils out, and that way it doesn't hurt you."

"When people have to have something like their tonsils taken out it's called having an operation, and when you have an operation with a general anesthetic it's always done in a hospital. That's because a hospital has the right equipment there and specially trained people who know just how to help you. It's like taking a car to a garage. You know how Daddy can fix some problems at home, but sometimes special equipment is needed to fix the car up, so he takes it to a garage."

"Does that mean that there's something big wrong with me?" asked Annie, feeling worried.

"No," said her mom. "It's really a very simple thing. It's just that to take your tonsils out without hurting you, you need a general anesthetic, and you can only get that done at a hospital. After that's done, you can go home all well again. And your tonsils won't be able to bother you anymore. Thousands of girls and boys all over the country have their tonsils out each year."

"Really?" said Annie. She felt a bit better to hear that.

"I had my tonsils out, you know. When I was eleven," said Annie's mom.[7]

"What was it like?" asked Annie. She was very interested. "Were you scared?"

"I was a bit scared," said Annie's mom. "I didn't like having to stay in a hospital because I missed my mom and dad. But there were some good things about it. I stayed in a children's ward, because that's where children usually stay, and there were a lot of kids there. We used to talk and play together."

"That sounds like it could have been fun," said Annie.

"Yes, that part certainly was fun," her mom said.

"What was the ward like?" asked Annie.

"Well, a ward is a hospital name for a room. Some people have private wards, and that means they have a room to themselves, but children usually all stay in a great big room called the children's ward. Everyone has a bed of

---

7. If you have any first-hand experience of a hospital, it can be helpful to share this with your child in a positive way.

her own and a little chest of drawers to keep her things in. Each bed has curtains you can close to separate it from the others if you want to be private. There are brightly colored paintings hung up, and there are always nurses around to look after the kids."

"Will I be allowed to play with the other kids?" asked Annie. She thought that part sounded good. It would be nice to have people around to play with all of the time.

"Yes," said Annie's mom. "You'll all be able to play and chat to each other."

"Will we be able to get down from our beds to play games?" Annie asked.

"Well, the kids who are feeling well enough to get out of bed will be able to. Some of the children might be feeling a bit too tired or sick to get out of bed. I'm sure you'll be able to wander around the ward, though."

"Will the other kids be my age?" Annie wanted to know. She hoped there would be some, especially if they were girls.

"I'm sure there will be," her mom said. "Anyway, because you're all living in the same room, everyone's pretty friendly even if they're older or younger."

"Will you be able to stay with me in the hospital?" asked Annie.

"I won't be able to stay with you at night," said her mom, "because there won't be any room for me. But I'll be able to be with your during most of the day."[8]

"I'll be lonely at night without you," said Annie.[9] She felt sad at the thought.

"I know, darling," said her mom. "Most children in the hospital feel a bit sad when their moms and dads can't stay with them. But you know that at night, even though I won't be there, there'll be special night nurses to take care of you if you feel sad or sick."[10]

---

8. Be realistic and truthful about how much or little time you will be able to spend with your child in the hospital. Don't tell her you'll be with her all the time if you can be there only for the visiting hours.

9. A hospital can be a lonely and frightening experience for children who are separated from their parents and all that is familiar. This is particularly so at night. Let your child know that you understand her feelings.

10. It's important to let your child know that even though you can't be there, there will be someone trustworthy to look after her.

"Really?" said Annie. She felt a bit better knowing that there would be someone awake to take care of her if she needed it.

"Yes, night nurses stay awake the whole night just to make sure that you're okay and sleeping well. If you need something, all you have to do is press a special button by your bed, and the nurse will come along to see what she can do. The nurses and doctors in the hospital are specially trained to help you and make you feel better, you know."[11]

Annie liked that idea. It was nice to know that there would be a lot of people around who were specially trained to help kids like her.

"When will I be going to the hospital?" she asked.[12]

"We'll be taking you in on Monday morning," said her mom.

"Will I need an ambulance?" asked Annie. She thought an ambulance sounded rather exciting. She knew it was a special car with a bed in it and a loud siren so that all the other cars know to make way for it. She liked the idea of all the other cars having to get out of your way just because you were coming. It would be like riding in a fire engine.

"No, darling," said her mom, "you won't need an ambulance. Some kids who get sick suddenly or who are really ill have to go in by ambulance. I'll be driving you to the hospital in our car. When we get to the hospital I'll take you up to the children's ward, and a nurse will show us where your bed is. I'll help you get into your nightie and take you around to introduce you to the other kids. I'll stay with you until it's time for the operation, and I'll be there for you when you come out."

"What time will the operation be?" asked Annie.

"It will be at 1:30 in the afternoon," said her mom, "and it won't be very long before it's over. It's only a short operation."

---

11. Make sure your child knows how to press the call button when she needs something and that she is not shy or embarrassed about doing so.

12. As much as possible, let your child know in advance what is likely to happen to her in the hospital. Traveling into the unknown is always more frightening than crossing charted waters.

Then she continued, "When we've settled you into your nightie—there might be a special hospital nightie that they give you to wear—a nurse will make you a plastic bracelet for you to wear around your wrist. It will have your name written on it. All the children in your ward will have the same sort of bracelet, each with their name written on it. That's so they don't mix you up with any of the other children. Then the nurse might want to take your temperature or blood pressure, just the way the doctor does.[13]

"A little while before your operation, the nurse will give you an injection.[14] It's a prick with a needle, and it's like the other shots you've had—it stings, but it doesn't last long. An injection helps the medicine get into your body faster than any other way. That's why we need them sometimes."

"Yuck," said Annie. "I don't like shots."

"Nobody likes them, darling," said her mom, "but everyone needs to have them at some time or other, and the good thing is that they're over very quickly. This shot will make you feel a bit sleepy, and your mouth might feel a bit dry. It's really rather a nice feeling. When it's time for your operation, a nurse will pop you onto a special bed with wheels. I'll still be with you, and we'll wheel you along the corridor to the room where you'll have the operation. I'll give you a kiss at the doorway of the operating room, and I'll go to the waiting room until you come out."

"What will happen to me in the operating room?" asked Annie. She wished her mom could go in with her.

"Well, inside the operating room," her mom said, "there'll be a whole bunch of nurses and doctors all there just to take care of you.[15] So even though I can't be there,

---

13. You may want to explain at this point the mechanics and purpose of these procedures.

14. Don't try to say that painful procedures won't hurt. After the first time, it simply makes your child decide that you can't be trusted to tell the truth. Instead, emphasize that the hurt won't last long (if that is true), and that it is serving a useful purpose.

15. Prepare your child for what will happen inside the operating room as well as in the hospital in general.

they'll be taking special care of you. One of the doctors will give you another shot—this one will hurt less than the other one, and then the funniest thing will happen. You'll fall fast asleep, and you won't wake up until the operation is all over. Even if you were to try very hard to stay awake, you would still fall fast asleep because of the special medicine in the shot. And because you're asleep all through the operation, you won't feel a thing."

"Could a child ever wake up in the middle of an operation?" Annie asked.[16] She was a bit worried by that idea.

"No," said her mom, "don't worry, you could never wake up in the middle of an operation. You would always stay asleep until it's completely over."

"What if I didn't wake up then?" asked Annie.

"You would always wake up when it was over because the doctor who gave you the sleep medicine which made you go to sleep would take the sleep medicine away, and that would make you wake up at just the right time. Doctors like that are called anesthetists, and they know exactly how to make people go to sleep and how to wake them up again. When you wake up you'll probably feel a bit confused because you won't remember where you are at first, or else you'll think that they haven't done the operation yet. I'll be with you when you wake, and I bet you anything you'll be really surprised when I tell you that the operation's already over."

"What will you bet me?" said Annie. She liked bets.

"A double hug," said her mom, "and the winner can say—I told you so."

"Okay," said Annie. She decided that she would win this bet.

"When you wake," her mom went on, "you'll probably have a sore throat, like the one you have now, and be quite thirsty.[17] Sometimes they don't like you to drink anything for a little while after the operation, or sometimes they might give you a sip of water. Some people feel a little bit sick, as if they're going to vomit, but that passes

---

16. Many children are concerned by this. It can be helpful to explain to them in simple terms how an anesthetic works and what it feels like.

17. Let your child know what she's likely to feel like when she wakes.

very quickly. When I had an operation, I felt thirsty when I woke up but I didn't feel sick."

"On the day of your operation you won't be able to eat or drink anything.[18] That's because they like your tummy to be empty when they give you the special medicine that makes you go to sleep. So on Sunday, you'll have your dinner as usual, but all of Monday you won't have anything to eat or drink. You'll be a little bit hungry, but you'll know that it's worth it to make you feel well again. After the operation, when you're wide awake again, you'll be able to have something to eat and drink."

"How do I get fed?" said Annie. "Is there a dining room?"

"They'll bring your food to you in bed on a tray," said Annie's mom. "The hospital has a big kitchen, and the staff there cook the meals for everyone in the hospital. It comes around on a cart, and you get to eat it in bed."

"That sounds like fun," said Annie.

"Yes," said Annie's mom, "it is nice to be served your meals in bed. You can enjoy being lazy and looked after."

"What sort of food will they have?" asked Annie.

"Well," said her mom, "all hospitals have different food. Mostly it's pretty ordinary family food. For breakfast, for instance, there are eggs and cereal and fruit juice."

"Will I have to eat everything?" asked Annie.

"No," said her mom, "you just eat what you want to. Because you're having your tonsils out, your throat might be sore and so they'll give you soft food to eat. I'll tell you something that you'll like. One of the things that's good to eat after having your tonsils out is ice cream!"

"Wow!" said Annie. "Does that mean I'll be able to eat lots of ice cream in the hospital?"

"It certainly does," said Annie's mom. "Also, if there's anything special you want to eat, you can just tell me, and I'll bring it to the hospital for you. You'll be staying in the hospital for two days and one night so you might have breakfast and lunch there on the day after your operation."

---

18. Explain to your child about the fasting required before an operation. Some children may think that they are being denied food as a punishment.

"Will they do things that hurt me in the hospital?" asked Annie. She was a bit worried by this. [19]

"Some of the things like shots sting and hurt a little," said Annie's mom, "but they don't usually last long, and the nurses and doctor will help you with them." [20]

Later in the day, Annie came into the kitchen to show her mom some drawings she had done of the hospital. She had drawn herself and her mom walking into the hospital carrying Tammy the teddy bear and Alice the rag doll. Annie had decided that these were the two that she would allow to come to the hospital with her. [21] All the toys wanted to go, she knew, because they wanted to be with her. However, she had decided there was only room for two. She talked to the other toys, explaining that although they would miss her and she would miss them, she would be back soon, safe and sound, and they would all be able to sleep with her again. She had decided that Tammy had to come because Tammy had tonsillitis too. She picked Alice because she was so cuddly and cute.

"I've got a special surprise for you," said Annie's mom. "Look." And she took down a parcel which had been sitting on the dining room table.

"What is it?" asked Annie.

"Open it and see," said her mom.

It was a doctor kit. [22] There was a stethoscope and a plastic thermometer. One of Daddy's old white shirts was there so that Annie could put it on and pretend it was a doctor's white coat. Annie's mom had explained that most of them wore white coats. There was a piece of plastic material to use for taking blood pressure, and there was a pretend plastic syringe for giving shots.

Annie was thrilled. She took it right to her room to

---

19. Children are often worried by the painful procedures that are common in the hospital. Relaxation and pain control techniques can be very useful here. For more details, see the appropriate Annie Stories.

20. It would be a good idea to incorporate portions of the relaxation and pain control stories, in that order, at this point.

21. Encourage your child to bring some of her special possessions with her to the hospital. These may range from a favorite teddy bear to a security blanket.

22. A doctor kit is a very useful present for a child going to the hospital. It helps her to work out some of her anxieties and experiences through the medium of pretend play.

play. She knew that Tammy, the teddy bear with tonsillitis, would really have to be visited by the doctor immediately. She took her bear's temperature and listened to her heart. She wrapped the plastic around Tammy's arm and took her blood pressure. Finally she gave Tammy a shot.

But before she did, she explained to Tammy how to make it feel better.[23] She taught Tammy how to relax and did it herself to show Tammy how easy it was. She taught Tammy how she could make her arm go cold, or thick and numb. How she could switch off the pain in her brain or think herself off somewhere else. She had a great time, and Tammy learned a lot and told her that the shot didn't hurt nearly as much as she had thought it would.

That evening, when Annie's mom came in to read her a good night story, she brought with her the family's little cassette recorder. "We're going to do something special tonight," she said. "When I read you your stories, I'm going to record them on the tape recorder. You can take it into the hospital with you, and then, whenever you want to, you can press a button and you'll hear me telling you a story.[24] It will be as if you've still got part of me with you."

Annie loved that idea. She thought it would be great when she was snuggling into bed in the hospital to be able to have her mom telling her stories on the tape. Annie picked out all her favorite stories, and her mom read them to her and recorded them on the tape at the same time.

That night, when Annie went to bed, she practiced relaxing. She let all her muscles go loose and floppy. It was lovely. It made her feel all nice and sleepy, and she drifted peacefully off to sleep.

In the morning, Annie's mom helped her pack a little bag for the hospital.[25] Annie was going into the hospital

---

23. This paragraph is optional. Include it if you have already read the relaxation and pain control stories to your child.

24. This enables the child to take with her, in part, the comfort of her mother's voice and helps bridge the terrifying chasm of separation from family love and security. If you haven't got a portable cassette player, give your child a series of loving notes and drawings to be opened at different times during her hospital stay. For example, one before going to sleep, one for first thing in the morning, and so on.

25. Let your child help you pack. There may be things that she considers crucial to take with her that you may have overlooked.

the next day. They packed Annie's toothbrush and tooth-paste and a favorite soap that Annie had gotten for a present. It was pink and shaped like a rabbit. Annie picked out some books to read and a big activity book to do. The activity book had pictures to color in, dots to join, and word puzzles to figure out. She took her Monopoly game, too, in case any of the other children wanted to play with her. She packed her favorite nightie and a bathrobe and slippers so that she could keep warm when she was out of bed. Then she packed her favorite blanket. It was only a very little blanket because Annie had had it since she was a little baby, but she really loved it. It had such a nice feel about it, and she had slept with it for so long that when she put it around her and stroked its soft woolly surface, she felt safe and ready for sleep.

Later that day Annie's mom said to her, "You know, I think there's something you might be interested in."

"What's that?" asked Annie.

"I thought you might like to know a way of helping your body fight off germs and get well quickly."[26]

"That sounds good," said Annie. She didn't like being sick—it was much more fun to be up and playing. And besides, she liked the idea of helping her body fight germs. It would be like playing cops and robbers.

"It's all to do with using your imagination," explained Annie's mom. "Your imagination can really help your body to get better as quickly as possible."

"How do I do it?" said Annie. She was really inter-ested.

"Well," said her mom, "first, if you like, you could just relax and get nice and comfortable."

Annie did.[27]

"What happens now?" she asked. She was all loose and floppy and relaxed.

"Now," said her mom, "just imagine that you've put on some special glasses and you can see right inside your body, just as if you're looking in through a window. You

---

26. This sort of healing imagery can be very helpful for the child. It promotes a positive attitude and can speed up recovery as well as boosting morale.

27. The relaxation story can be told here if it has not already been told.

see all the blood cells at work, busy clearing out the germs. They're very strong and very good blood cells, and they can easily take care of you and wipe out all the germs."[28]

"They look funny," said Annie. They were marching up and down like little soldiers dragging away screaming germs.

"Now," said Annie's mom, "after you've had your operation, you can put on your special glasses and look at your strong, strong blood cells again. You can see them making everything better again. You can see them smoothing down the inside of your throat where your tonsils were. You'll be able to see how pink and healthy your throat looks. You might see a few dead germs around—the blood cells will be busy sweeping them up to put in the garbage can. You can see them sweeping and smoothing until there are no germs left at all and your throat looks lovely and pink and healthy. The blood cells like to know that you're thinking about how strong they are, it makes them feel even stronger so that they can clean out even more germs, even more quickly."

"They certainly do look strong," said Annie. "I'm glad they're my blood cells and that they're taking care of me."

Suddenly she had a great idea. "Maybe you could put this all on the tape recorder, Mom," she said. "You could tell me a story all about relaxing and putting on my special glasses so that I can see my body getting all well again. Then I could play it lots of times in the hospital."

"What a good idea," said Annie's mom.[29] And so she told a story into the tape recorder all about relaxing and getting well. Annie loved it.

That night when Annie went to bed, she felt a bit worried because she knew that tomorrow night she would be sleeping in the hospital away from her safe warm room and, most important of all, away from her mommy and

---

28. Pause here and get your child's view of what the blood cells and germs look like. Encourage her in her fantasy and allow her to have a really vivid image of the blood cells winning their battle.

29. The relaxation story can be put on the tape recorder as well as any other favorites your child may have. If she is too young to work the machine, perhaps a nurse could do it for her.

daddy.[30] She felt very sad when she thought of this. She touched her cassette recorder which was next to her bed. It felt a bit better to know that she could hear her mommy's voice whenever she wanted to. She lay awake for a while feeling miserable. Then she rememberd what her mom had told her about letting her mind take her to different places.[31] Maybe, she thought, if she went to Playland, the land her mom had told her about, she would feel better. And so she imagined herelf walking into Playland. As usual, it was her birthday, because every day is your birthday in Playland. The people in Playland had prepared a specially big birthday cake for her. The cake was so big she had to climb on a ladder to cut it. She cut it very neatly. It was a nice cake to cut, and she felt proud that she'd done such a very good job, because cutting a cake was a fairly grown-up sort of thing to do, after all.[32] All her friends were there and they played freeze tag and jump rope, and all of Annie's favorite games. She gave everyone a slice of her wonderful big cake and had a great big piece herself. On the icing was written, "We love you Annie," and the slice that Annie ate had "love" written on it in big red letters on white icing. It tasted wonderful and really filled her up. She felt warm and nice inside. The sun was shining and the birds were singing. The Playland birds are the ones who originally taught our birds to sing, and so to hear a Playland bird sing is to hear something very wonderful indeed. Her friends were all around her listening to the birds sing and playing games, and she had just decided that they would all go for a walk to the Present Machine when she fell asleep with a smile on her face.

The next morning Annie's mom came in to give her a good morning kiss. "Remember," she said, "you're not

---

30. It's important to recognize that your child is likely to have real feelings of sadness and anxiety about her impending trip to the hospital. Dismissing these with a "Don't be silly..." type of remark only makes her feel more fearful and inadequate.

31. Here, Annie is adopting the technique her mother taught her in a very helpful way.

32. This is a particularly nice fantasy for a child going into the hospital for surgery. It involves the image of her mastering the "knife" and coping with a difficult task while feeling nourished and loved.

allowed to eat or drink today because of the operation."

Annie nodded.

"But perhaps tonight," Annie's mom went on, "or definitely tomorrow, you can have ice cream and Jell-O because they're very good to eat after tonsil operations."

They checked over Annie's bag to make sure she had everything in it.

"There's one more thing to put in your bag," said Annie's mom, and she held up a brightly colored parcel. "This is a present from me and Daddy, but you're not allowed to open it until tonight after we've said good-bye to you."

"Ooh," said Annie, "what's in it?"

"It's a surprise," said her mom, "but you'll like it"[33]

Annie said good-bye to the toys in her room and told them that she would be back very soon. She thought that they must feel sad that she was leaving them behind, so she explained to them again that she had to leave but that she still loved them and that she would be back soon. Then she went out to the car with her mother.

The hospital was a big building, much bigger than a house. Bigger even than a school. There were lots and lots of people around, some of them parents with children about Annie's age. Annie and her mom went up in an elevator to the third floor. When they got out there was a sign saying "Children's Ward." There were lots of colorful paintings on the walls. Some of them looked as if they had been done by children. Annie wondered if they would hang one of her paintings up if she did one for them. She liked painting. She was glad she had remembered to pack her crayons so that she could do drawings with them.

At the children's ward, a nice nurse came out to meet them. "This is Annie," said Annie's mom.

"Pleased to meet you," said the nurse. "We're going to take very good care of you here. And there are a couple of little boys and girls who I think you'll enjoy meeting."

Annie smiled. She liked the nurse, and the ward seemed like a nice bright place. She was looking forward to meeting the kids.

---

33. Giving your child notes or tiny, inexpensive presents to unwrap in your absence helps remind her that you are with her in spirit if not in body.

The nurse showed Annie and her mom around the ward. "Here is your bed, Annie," she said. "You might like to unpack your things and get into your nightie."

When Annie was in her nightie the nurse came back. She weighed Annie on some scales to see how heavy she was. Then she took Annie's temperature and measured her pulse. She wrote it all down on some paper and looked up and smiled. "Everything's looking fine," she said. "Come and I'll introduce you to the kids."

For the next couple of hours Annie and her mom played games with the other kids or chatted quietly with each other. A couple of times a nurse passed carrying a funny flat dish with a cover on it.

"What's that?" asked Annie.

"That's a bed pan," said her mom. "That's for kids who are not allowed to get up to go to the toilet. It's like a potty—the nurses bring it to you and close the curtains around your bed and you sit on it in bed."

"That sounds weird," said Annie.

"It does feel a bit funny," said her mom, "but you get used to it. Anyway, I don't think you'll need to use it because you'll be able to get up to go to the toilet." She looked at her watch. "Goodness, time's gone very quickly, hasn't it? Why don't we go back to bed? It'll be time for your shot soon, and you can practice being relaxed and using your imagination."

Annie popped into bed. Her mom sat on the bed beside her and talked about snowmen and thick skins and Playland and all the other things they had talked about the day before. Annie felt very comfortable.

Soon the nurse came up. "Time for your shot, Annie," she said. Annie felt a little bit bothered at first but then she remembered about being relaxed and taking her mind off to somewhere nice. She thought about Playland.

"There, that wasn't so bad," said the nurse. She had already finished giving the shot.

"No," said Annie, "it was over quickly, wasn't it."

"You'll probably feel a bit sleepy after this," said the nurse. "Then, after a while, we'll move you to another room where you'll have the operation, and then, before you know it, you'll be back here with your mom."[34]

After the nurse had gone, Annie and her mom sat and

talked. Annie yawned. She was beginning to feel drowsy. It was a nice sort of feeling, as if she were just about to fall asleep.

Presently, the nurse came back. She had a big bed on wheels that she was pushing in front of her.

"Here honey," she said, "put your arms around me and I'll lift you onto this fancy transportation. It's called a gurney." She held out her arms and the nurse lifted her on and tucked the sheets over her. Annie's mom stood next to her and held her hand.

"I'll come with you up the operating room," she said, "and then I'll be here waiting for you when you wake up."

Annie nodded. The nurse was wheeling the gurney along while her mom walked alongside. Because Annie was lying on her back, when she opened her eyes she was looking straight at the ceiling. It felt funny to be wheeled along in a bed while you looked at the ceiling. It made you feel a bit dizzy.

"Remember," Annie's mom said, "that inside the operating room one of the doctors will give you another shot, and then you'll fall fast asleep."

They reached the door of the operating room. Annie's mom gave her a kiss and said, "See you soon."

Annie felt a bit worried, but the nurse gave her a little pat and said, "Don't worry, we'll take good care of you. And," she said, "you have to promise not to laugh when you see the funny hats the doctors and nurses wear. Are you ready to see them? Look . . . ," and she wheeled Annie in.

Straight away Annie knew what she meant by the funny hats. The doctors and nurses were wearing something that looked like shower caps. They did look funny.

"Why are they wearing those?" she asked.

"That's to stop their hair getting in the way," the nurse said. "They have to wear special clothes in this room so that we can keep things as clean as possible."

"Hello, Annie," said one of the doctors. "I'm just going to give you a little prick now, and then you'll fall asleep." He took Annie's arm. "There we go," he said.

---

34. Letting your child know in advance what will happen as a lead-up to the operation helps her cope with it better.

"Now I'm going to bet you something. I'm going to bet that you can't count up to twenty."

"Of course I can count up to twenty!" said Annie.

"But I'm going to bet that you can't count up to twenty before you fall sleep."

"Okay," said Annie, and she began counting. "One, two, three, four..., five..., six..., seven..., eight..., nine...," and then she was fast asleep.

When she opened her eyes her mom was sitting next to her. At first Annie couldn't think where she was. Then she remembered—she was in the hospital. "When are they going to do the operation?" she asked her mom.

Her mom smiled. "They've already done it, Annie."

"Really!" Annie said. "But I don't remember them doing it."

"Of course you don't," said her mom. "That's because you were fast asleep. I guess I win our bet. Remember, you owe me a double hug." And Annie gave her mom a double hug even though she was still very sleepy.

After a while a nurse came in. "Do you think you'd like some ice cream for a snack tonight?" she asked.

"Yes," said Annie, "I'd love some." Her throat was a bit sore, and she thought some nice cool ice cream would be wonderful.

After a while, it began to get dark outside. One of the nurses came around and said, "It's bedtime in an hour."

"That means I'll have to leave soon, sweetheart," said Annie's mom.

"I don't want you to leave," said Annie. "I want you to stay here."

"I know you do, darling, and so do I, but remember we talked about how I couldn't stay and how the nurses would take care of you." And she gave Annie a big hug. "I know it's frightening for you, but we wouldn't let you stay somewhere that wasn't safe. We know you'll be looked after very well here. And even though we'll miss each other, you'll be back home tomorrow."

Suddenly someone called out, "Annie!" and Annie's dad came up. He had just arrived. He gave Annie a big, big hug. "How are you, darling?" he said.

Annie and her mom and dad chatted by the bed. Annie's mom told her that when they left, Annie would fall asleep very quickly because she was still sleepy from the medicine. She set up the tape recorder and the earphones next to Annie's bed so that she could listen to her stories whenever she liked.

"Will it be completely dark here at night?" Annie asked.[35] She was a bit worried by this.

"No, they always leave a bit of light on, and the nurses stay awake all night just in case you need them. See, here's the button you press if you want a nurse to come to you.[36] You needn't be shy about pressing it either because that's what the nurses are here for. They're here just to help you, and they really like to help kids. So if you need anything at all, whether it's to go to the toilet or whether you're just feeling worried about something, you can just press that button and a nurse will come."

Just then, the nurse came around, "It's bedtime now, Annie," she said. "Mom and Dad will have to leave."

Annie's mom and dad gave her a big kiss. "I'll see you in the morning, darling," Annie's mom said. She took Tammy the teddy bear and Alice the rag doll out of Annie's hospital bag and tucked them into bed with Annie. "Sweet dreams, darling," she said. "I'll see you very soon."

Annie felt very sad. She cuddled Tammy and Alice and drew her special blanket right up close to the three of them.

It felt strange to be in a bed that wasn't her own and in a room that wasn't her own. "At least tomorrow night I'll be back in my own bed," she thought to herself. It made her feel a bit better to remember that.

She snuggled down in the bed and yawned. Her mom was right. She did feel very sleepy. She thought she would try thinking about Playland and maybe that would make her feel better. She had just started thinking about what present she would like from the Present Machine when she fell asleep.

---

35. Children are often worried about this point, particularly children who are used to sleeping with a night light on.

36. Make sure your child knows that it's okay to press the call button if she needs something or is frightened. Some children might feel as if they're being a nuisance or a "baby" by doing this.

going to the hospital

She woke early in the morning. The curtains were drawn back, and the sun was shining in. It took her a few minutes to remember where she was.

"It's breakfast time," said one of the nurses, and set up a tray on Annie's bed. Annie began to eat. She had oatmeal, a boiled egg, and milk. She was very hungry.

"Hello," said the little girl in the bed next to hers. "I'm Mary. Were you operated on yesterday?"

"Yes," said Annie.

"You always feel very sleepy after an operation. I slept for ages after mine."

Mary had bright red hair and looked very friendly. "I've been here a week already," she said.

"What's it like?" asked Annie.

"It's okay," said Mary. "You miss your mom and dad, but it's good to have kids to play with, and the nurses are very nice. I had my appendix out last week and I'll be going home in a couple of days."

One of the nurses came around. "Hello, Annie," she said. "How are you feeling today?"

"My throat's a bit sore," said Annie.

"That's because of the operation," said the nurse. "It'll feel better in a few days, and then you won't have to worry about getting tonsillitis any more, so that'll be good."

She checked Annie's pulse and temperature. "You're doing very well," she said. "Your mom will be here pretty soon."

Suddenly Annie remembered the present her mom had given her. She reached over and unwrapped it. It was a coloring book. On it was written, "With lots and lots of love from Mom and Dad," and there were seven big kisses like X's written next to it.

"Is that from your mom and dad?" asked Mary.

"Yes," said Annie.

"It looks nice," said Mary. "Listen, why don't you put your bathrobe on and I'll take you to meet Eva. She's one of my friends here."

"Why is she in the hospital?" asked Annie.

"She had something called pneumonia and that's why she had to come to the hospital," said Mary. "She's much better. The doctor said she could go home tomorrow."

Annie and Mary and Eva had a good time playing together. They played a card game and then Annie took out her Monopoly board and they all played Monopoly.

Then it was time for lunch. There was ice cream and pudding for dessert and Annie was just scraping up the last bit when her mom appeared in the doorway. "Hello, darling," she said. "It's almost time to go home."

"Can we just play one more game, Mom?" asked Annie. She was enjoying herself.

"All right," said her mom. "I'll just go and pack your things while you play."

When Annie had finished the game she went back to her bed where her mom was packing up. "It'll be nice to be home again," she said. "All my toys must have missed me."

"Yes," said her mom. "They're looking forward to seeing you."

"Me too," said Annie.

"Well," her mom said, zipping up her bag, "time to go now."

So they said good-bye to everyone and walked downstairs to the car.[37] Annie felt like a very big, brave girl. "I can tell all my friends now that I've been to a hospital by myself," she said.

"You certainly can," said her mom, and gave her a great big hug.

---

37. This is the positive ending. Annie has come through a frightening situation and is able to look back with pride at how well she coped and to enjoy the feeling of strength and competence this gives her.

glossary

Behavior therapy: a form of psychotherapy that developed from laboratory experiments on how people and animals learn behavior patterns. It treats symptoms, such as anxiety, as "learned" behaviors and focuses on teaching the person how to "unlearn" these behaviors, and when necessary, substitute new, positive, behaviors such as relaxation or social confidence, rather than succumb to fear and withdrawal.

Desensitization (or **systematic desensitization**): a technique used by behavior therapists for dealing with fears and phobias. It usually involves gradually exposing a person to the object or thing she fears. The exposure is taken in very small steps, starting with something that does not cause anxiety (for example a toy dog in a dog phobia) and ending with full exposure to the feared object (meeting with a real dog). Each step is repeated with alternate periods of relaxation until the person can feel comfortable facing that level of exposure. She then moves on to the next level and deals with it in the same way. Desensitization can be covert (done in the imagination) or it can be overt (using real-life situations or people).

Developmental tasks: tasks that infants and children need to master before they can successfully move on to the next stage of their physical, intellectual, or emotional development. Examples are learning to walk, learning to talk, learning to distinguish right and wrong.

Family therapy: a form of therapy in which the whole family is seen and treated by the therapist. Family therapists have a number of different approaches but generally they focus on the communication within the family, the different roles family members play, and the sorts of conflicts the family is dealing with. They see the child's symptoms as being related to family patterns. In changing these patterns, they therefore change the child's symptoms.

Identification: a technical term used by psychologists and psychiatrists that has now become part of popular speech. Essentially, it describes a process in which we experience a particular sort of bond between ourselves and another person. This bond leads us to behave like that person. For example, a student doctor who greatly admires his senior consultant may identify with him and may take on the habit of pacing through corridors with his hands clasped behind his back just like his superior does.

Nightmare: a dream that is frightening and upsetting. Sometimes the child remains sleeping through a nightmare but sometimes she will awake, feeling frightened. She will be able to tell you that she has had a bad dream. Nightmares are not the same as night terrors.

Night terrors: tend to occur mostly in children under six. They don't have a specific dream content in the way that nightmares do. The child often thrashes around, sits up, or walks around even though she is still asleep. She usually looks very distressed and may scream, cry, or talk to herself. After the night terror the child falls back into a normal sleep and cannot remember the episode in the morning.

Phobia: an intense, irrational fear that is directed at something specific.

Psychoanalysis: a form of psychotherapy that focuses on exploring the unconscious. In contrast to behavior therapists, psychoanalysts believe that symptoms are representations of more deeply rooted conflicts.

Role playing: a therapeutic technique in which you and/or your child act out roles in order to learn what it feels like to behave in a different manner or as someone else. For example, a shy child who acts out the role of a socially confident child can learn how to approach people with a more confident tone of voice, a lift of the head, a smile, and so on. By acting out the role of a confident child yourself, you can show your child how it's done.

Social modeling: involves learning by demonstration. Children learn very readily by watching how someone else does something. This modeling can be covert (when you're imagining someone doing something) or overt (when you're watching a real person in action).

recommended reading

Bruno Bettelheim. *The Uses of Enchantment: The Meaning and Importance of Fairy Tales.* Random House, 1977.

Dr. Bettelheim, a noted psychoanalyst, provides a wonderfully perceptive glimpse into the world of witches, goblins, enchanted princesses, and the part their stories play in our children's inner lives. A fascinating book.

T. Berry Brazelton, M.D. *On Becoming a Family: The Growth of Attachment.* Dell Publishing, 1986.

T. Berry Brazelton, M.D., is Chief of the Child Development Unit at the Boston Children's Hospital Medical Center. His books are wonderfully perceptive and very much in touch with the practical day-to-day concerns of child rearing. He describes real parents and real children in a way that is instantly recognizable and reassuring. All of his books are highly recommended.

Stella Chess, M.D., Alexander Thomas, M.D. *Know Your Child: An Authoritative Guide for Today's Parents.* Basic Books, 1987.

Drs. Chess and Thomas, along with Dr. Herbert G. Birch, conducted the New York study on the development of children's personalities that was mentioned in the chapter Understanding Your Child. In their latest book, Drs. Chess and Thomas discuss the individuality of children in terms of temperament and in relationship to different parenting styles. Their new book contains interesting findings on the capabilities of babies at the earliest stages of life and continues on through adolescence. A very helpful and insightful book.

Dr. Richard Ferber. *Solve Your Child's Sleep Problems.* Simon & Schuster, 1986.

Dr. Ferber is a pediatrician who is recognized as a leading authority in the field of children's sleep problems. For any red-eyed parents whose children fall into this category, this book is a gem. Dr. Ferber explains how these problems originate and offers clear, easy-to-understand, effective ways of solving children's sleep difficulties.

Selma H. Fraiberg, M.D. *The Magic Years: Understanding and Handling the Problems of Early Childhood.* Scribner, 1984.

Noted child psychoanalyst Selma Fraiberg was an enchanting writer, able to share her insights into the world of childhood with freshness, clarity, and humor. First published in 1959, the book is just as timely today as it was then. A classic in its field.

Patricia Garfield, PhD. *Your Child's Dreams.* Ballantine Books, 1984.

Patricia Garfield has done extensive research into children's dreams over many cultures. In this book she explores the fascinating world of children's dreams and how they can be understood and worked with. An absorbing and helpful book.

Dr. Jonathan Kellerman. *Helping the Fearful Child: A Guide to Everyday and Problem Anxieties.* Warner Books, 1986.

This book is an informative, easy-to-read guide to children's fears and phobias for parents. It outlines many common childhood problems and offers practical solutions based mainly on the application of behavior therapy principles. An excellent book.

Eda LeShan. *What's Going to Happen to Me? When Parents Separate or Divorce.* Macmillan Publishing, 1986.

In this book Eda LeShan discusses the emotional turmoil surrounding divorce with warmth, clarity, and a great deal of understanding. It is equally helpful for both parents and older children. Thoroughly recommended for anyone who is dealing with divorce.

Julius Segal and Herbert Yahraes. *A Child's Journey: Forces That Shape the Lives of Our Young.* McGraw Hill, 1979.

This fascinating book provides an overview of the child's psychological development and the many factors that influence it. The authors have covered an enormous amount of material and shaped it into a sensitively written, thought-provoking, and very valuable book.

Montague Ullman and Nan Zimmerman. *Working with Dreams: Expand, Heal, and Transform Your Life Through Your Dreams.* J.P. Tarcher, 1985.

Dr. Ullman founded the Dream Laboratory at the Maimonides Medical Center in New York. In this book, he and his wife, Nan Zimmerman, present a clear and comprehensive outline of how we can understand and work with our dreams.